BETTING
ON BIOTECH

BETTING ON BIOTECH

INNOVATION AND THE LIMITS OF ASIA'S DEVELOPMENTAL STATE

JOSEPH WONG

CORNELL UNIVERSITY PRESS
Ithaca and London

First published 2011 by Cornell University Press

Printed in the United States of America

Library of Congress Cataloging-in-Publication Data

Wong, Joseph, 1973–
    Betting on biotech : innovation and the limits of Asia's developmental state / Joseph Wong.
       p. cm.
    Includes bibliographical references and index.
    ISBN 978-0-8014-5032-7 (cloth: alk. paper)
    1. Biotechnology industries—Korea (South)   2. Bio-technology industries—Taiwan.   3. Biotechnology industries—Singapore.   4. Industrial policy—Korea (South)   5. Industrial policy—Taiwan.   6. Industrial policy—Singapore.   I. Title.
    HD9999.B443W66   2011
    338.4'76606095—dc22   2011013630

Cornell University Press strives to use environmentally responsible suppliers and materials to the fullest extent possible in the publishing of its books. Such materials include vegetable-based, low-VOC inks and acid-free papers that are recycled, totally chlorine-free, or partly composed of nonwood fibers. For further information, visit our website at www.cornellpress.cornell.edu.

Cloth printing   10 9 8 7 6 5 4 3 2 1

For Oliver

Contents

PREFACE

This book is about betting on commercial biotech development in three key Asian economies: South Korea, Taiwan, and Singapore. After more than two hundred interviews with informants in the field, over twenty research trips to the region, and countless hours in the library and in front of my computer, I believe the bets that have been made there on biotech have not worked out in the ways that many had earlier anticipated, myself included. When I began this project in 2002, I aimed simply to revisit the idea of the developmental state and to rejuvenate what had become a relatively stagnant debate about political economy among the former newly industrializing countries. I intended to examine how the developmental state had evolved and adapted in the era of knowledge-intensive, science-based industrialization. I expected that the model would have undergone some refinement and adjustment but that its evolution would reflect the next stage of the developmental state. What I did not anticipate, at least initially, was that the developmental state would have retreated altogether, that what I was researching was in actuality innovation *beyond* the developmental state.

In the course of writing this book, I have learned that sometimes things do not work out as you expect them to. Indeed, from the perspective of the economic planner, scientist, or bio-industrial stakeholder in Asia, what had once been a sense of considerable optimism at the beginning of the first decade of the 2000s about the prospects of commercial biotech has now become a dreaded feeling of impending failure. At a 2010 conference at the University of Oxford, a well-informed colleague from Taiwan put it to me bluntly: "Biotechnology is one of Taiwan's biggest industrial failures." I personally would not state it quite so starkly, yet I write in the concluding chapter that "over the seven years during which I conducted research in Korea, Taiwan, and Singapore for this book, I saw the star that was supposed to be biotechnology dim quite considerably." Indeed, though billions of dollars have been spent, institutions redesigned, universities and labs reoriented, regulatory regimes implemented, and a considerable amount of political capital expended on succeeding in commercial biotech over the past two decades,

Korea, Taiwan, and Singapore still have relatively little, in terms of significant commercial blockbusters, to show for their efforts. Commercial biotech may not be a failure per se, but it has certainly fallen well short of expectations on every measure. And it has severely tested—and as I argue in this book, undermined—the viability of the Asian developmental state model.

The arguments developed in this book draw on the metaphor of betting. The postwar developmental state was quite proficient at betting; that is to say, it mitigated the risks of picking and making commercial winners in industrial upgrading. However, betting on commercial biotech innovation in the current era involves a much more profound kind of uncertainty, one in which technological, economic, and temporal uncertainty frustrates decision makers in both their ability and their willingness to make bets with any confidence. Put simply, this book examines how decision makers in what were once smart developmental states have made strategic and expensive bets in areas about which they know very little. And it is precisely this tremendous uncertainty that has hastened the end of the developmental state. Biotech represents an entirely new set of challenges, an entirely new kind of bet.

One caveat. The challenge of writing a book about a current and dynamic topic such as biotech is that the researcher must somewhat artificially "end" the empirical analysis at some point. The field research for this book was completed in 2008, after which I spent my time writing the manuscript. In line with the broader arguments in the book about uncertainty, circumstances may have changed in Korea, Taiwan, and Singapore since 2008, and indeed, they may have changed quite significantly (though I am doubtful of that). And of course, all errors herein are mine and mine alone.

So many people to thank. At the outset, I extend my sincerest gratitude to the many people in Asia who have helped me over the past seven or eight years, from those who met with me, taught me about life sciences, and explained to me the intricacies of venture capital investing, to those who helped arrange meetings and interviews with informants and who suggested readings, to those who challenged me and debated with me. I am especially indebted to my colleagues and friends in Asia, including Dung-Sheng Chen, Yu-Han Chu, Yvette Flanigan, Michelle Hsieh, Yong-Duck Jung, Byung-Kook Kim, Zong-Rong Lee, Joel Lin, Chin-Tay Shih, David Silver, Joonghae Suh, Jenn-Hwan Wang, and Yu-Shan Wu, among many others. The scholars with whom I worked on Hong Kong's science and technology policies—Suzanne Berger, Douglas Fuller, David Hart, David Mowery, Louis Pauly, Adam Segal, Atsushi Sunami, Eric Thun, Ted Tschang, Poh Kam Wong—were critically important to the formation of the arguments I present in this book; the members of my research crew in Spain—Jorge Niosi, Martin Kenney, Martha Prevezer, and Andreas Pyka—were equally important. The many opportunities to discuss my ideas, my arguments, and my field research over dinners and drinks in Wan Chai and Valencia are very much appreciated.

I also thank all those individuals I met with and interviewed in Korea, Taiwan, Singapore, Hong Kong, Malaysia, China, and the United States. Your candor and innovative visions are qualities I admire deeply. Your insights give this book its depth.

I have benefited enormously from being surrounded by people with sharp minds and good hearts. I am grateful for having such wonderful colleagues at the University of Toronto, including Emanuel Adler, Sylvia Bashevkin, Harald Bathelt, Steven Bernstein, Loren Brandt, Meric Gertler, Matthew Hoffmann, Jeffrey Kopstein, Neil Nevitte, James Orbinski, Louis Pauly, Ito Peng, Janice Stein, and David Wolfe, all of whom graciously lent me their time and expertise to discuss my work and to read over earlier drafts. I am also very fortunate to be part of an exceptional community of scholars and teachers at the University of Toronto, colleagues who have devoted their personal and professional lives to facilitating health technology innovation and transfer in the global south; friends such as Abdallah Daar, Jillian Kohler, Anita McGahan, Peter Singer, and Halla Thorsteinsdottir have had a profound impact on my work and approach to studying and dissecting the impact of health biotechnology in the developing world. Colleagues in the political science field more generally have also been extraordinarily generous with their expertise, including friends and colleagues Dan Breznitz, Tun-Jen Cheng, Greg Chin, Edward Friedman, Douglas Fuller, Peter Gourevitch, William Grimes, Stephan Haggard, William Hurst, Richard Iton, Wei-Chin Lee, Kun-Chin Lin, Gregory Noble, Shelley Rigger, Christine Rothmayr, Victor Shih, Mark Zachary Taylor, Yves Tiberghien, Steve Tsang, Robert Wade, Vincent Wang, and Meredith Jung-En Woo.

I think it is true that one often learns more from one's students than the other way around. I have been very fortunate to work with some outstanding undergraduate and graduate students. PhD students Sarah Eaton, Alanna Krolikowski, Su-Mei Ooi, Marie-eve Reny, and Stephen Trott provided excellent sounding boards against which I tried out (and subsequently discarded) many early ideas. My research assistants—Nina Mansoori, Uyen Quach, and Andi Wilson—worked tirelessly alongside me collecting and analyzing data, searching government documents, editing, reading industry reports, and surfing the Internet for company data. And I learned a great deal from Mi-Ae Jung, my postdoctoral assistant from Seoul National University's engineering faculty.

I also thank my colleagues and friends at the University of Toronto's Asian Institute, whose research inspires me and whose examples are humbling. I have had the good fortune to be a member of the University of Toronto's Department of Political Science and the Munk School of Global Affairs, as well as institutions and programs in other parts of the world. While in the field, I have been attached to such esteemed institutions as the National University of Singapore, Korea's Seoul National University, and Taiwan's Academia Sinica, as well as St. Antony's College, University of Oxford, which I visited in 2008 during my sabbatical and where I finished the first draft of the book. I am very grateful for the research funding I received from the Social Sciences and Humanities Research Council, the Canada Research Chairs Program, the Faculty of Arts and Science at the University of Toronto, the Connaught Foundation, the University of Toronto Centre for Bio-ethics, Bioval in Spain, and the Savantas Policy Institute in Hong Kong.

There are some truly special colleagues who have had a significant impact on my life as a scholar and on this work in particular, and I thank them here. Victor Shih continues to be a major source of professional and scholarly inspiration, though we have not been at the same institution for more than a decade. Dan Breznitz, who has done formidable work on technology innovation in Asia, is an intellectual force whose work I use as a benchmark for the quality of my own. Douglas Fuller, whom I have known since our days as graduate students in Taiwan, possesses, in my opinion, the sharpest analytical mind working on East Asian industrial and economic policy and is someone from whom I have learned a great deal. Edward Friedman continues to be my role model and is never without tremendous insight into Asian politics and our profession more generally. He is simply my best friend in the academy. Louis Pauly, my colleague at the University of Toronto, has been my greatest cheerleader when the writing is rough and my greatest critic, always asking those hard questions, when the writing is apparently too good, and for that I am very grateful. Finally, I have to credit Janice Stein with helping me identify and articulate the core puzzle of this book. It was Janice who introduced me to the theoretical literature on uncertainty and risk, the very concepts that frame this book. She has taught me that when a colleague says to you, "What you really mean to say is this...," you should listen attentively.

It is an honor for me to have again worked with Roger Haydon, of Cornell University Press, on this book. He is, as anyone who has worked with him knows, the best editor in the business. He has a fantastic ear for the writer's voice and a wonderful sense of pacing in prose. He is able to identify what is utterly banal, on the one hand, but is also so good at helping one uncover what is profoundly interesting, on the other. And as I wrote in my first book with Cornell University Press, Roger continues to have the "ability to squeeze the very best writing out of me." Thank you, Roger.

Finally, I want to thank my family, especially my wife, Jen, and our son, Oliver, who make my life the best. This book is dedicated to Oliver.

BETTING
ON BIOTECH

Introduction
Betting on Biotech

Since the 1990s, Korea, Taiwan, and Singapore have poured billions of dollars into the commercial development of biotech. Biotech and life sciences industries more generally have been hailed as the next "star" and "pillar" industries in what are already very advanced economies, and the aspirations of those economies are not modest. Korea aims, in the near term, to be one of the world's top biotech producers. Taiwan looks to develop small but world-class life sciences firms that can generate economic value as integral parts of the global biotech value chain. And Singapore imagines itself one day as a global, and not just regional, biomedical hub for high-value R&D and advanced health technology manufacturing. All three want to become technology creators rather than continue being astute imitators. They aspire to gain first-mover advantages in a cutting-edge, science-based industry.

To realize their ambitions in the knowledge economy, decision makers in Korea, Taiwan, and Singapore have essentially *bet* on biotech. And they have bet large and wide on the uncertain and distant prospects of commercial innovation in the sector, expending extraordinary amounts of energy and money. So far, however, they have little to show for their efforts and investment zeal. Their bets have yet to pay off, and the prospects of failure loom large. Despite this, they have continued to try to succeed in biotech, knowing that success in the sector will require long-term patience, billions upon billions of dollars, deep reserves in human capital, and institutional innovations that can facilitate novel discoveries in life sciences R&D. But most important, they understand that the uncertainties of biotech mean that commercial success is just one blockbuster away, and at the same time a very distant prospect that perpetually teeters on the brink of spectacular failure. This tension—one that is inherent in any high-risk, high-reward gamble—is the key puzzle that I explore.

This book examines how decision makers in industrial Asia make political economic bets, and specifically how they have strategically rationalized their various high-stakes bets in commercializing biotech. As an empirical undertaking, this comparative study reveals how public and private stakeholders in Korea, Taiwan, and Singapore have organized their biotech sectors over the past two decades; what resource allocation decisions have been made in this multibillion-dollar endeavor; and what institutions have been constructed to facilitate innovation in the life sciences. At the core, however, is a more fundamental inquiry into why certain decisions and bets have been made. Examining how decision makers have rationalized their bets on biotech permits a deeper understanding of the strategic logic that underpins state leadership in the development of science-based industries. In this book I evaluate the extent to which the challenges at the cutting edge of the global knowledge economy have transformed the postwar Asian developmental state, a mode of industrial development that relied heavily on coordinated state leadership in the allocation of productive resources. My main argument is that the developmental state model of the postwar period is no longer viable in an era of science-based industries. Betting on biotech, I argue, requires a decision making calculus altogether different, politically and economically, from that of the earlier era of state-led industrialization. This book explains how betting on biotech involves *different kinds of bets*.

Betting on Biotech

The commercial promise of health biotechnology first emerged during the 1970s, when scientists and industry rediscovered the biological "heuristic" for potential innovations in health care technology. The anticipated biotech revolution was expected to rival and ultimately surpass conventional chemistry-based approaches to the development of products and services in health care. Initially fueled in the West by government research support and followed by a proliferation of R&D institutions, venture capital, and increasingly entrepreneurial universities, biotechnology was expected to revolutionize how human therapies were developed, screened, marketed, and delivered. Biotech would be a game changer for the health industry, even if the possibilities and promise of the sector were (and still are) open-ended and undefined. But it was precisely biotech's untapped and seemingly endless commercial potential that drew industrial nations, including in Asia, into the life sciences sector. The move into biotech and other science-based industries also came precisely as Korea, Taiwan, and Singapore began to face stiff competition from later developers in South and Southeast Asia, as well as China. At the time, the imperatives to upgrade industrially were unequivocal. By the 1990s, it had become clear that Korea, Taiwan, and Singapore needed to diversify their industrial economies by moving further up the commercial and technology value chains. Politically, decision makers saw the commercial promise of biotech and the scientific prestige associated with cutting-edge research in the life sciences as important sources of political capital, both at home and abroad. It was in this political economic context that biotech emerged as a key industry to develop.

Other forces were at play. Choosing to move closer to the frontier of the knowledge economy reflected a gradual, though significant, shift in the allocation of resources for innovation-driven R&D, particularly in knowledge-intensive industries such as biotech, advanced informatics and electronics, materials engineering, and nanotechnology. Total R&D spending rose during the 1990s in Korea, Taiwan, and Singapore, with the private sector, and not government, leading the way. Firms began to conduct in-house research. Collaboration among private and public R&D actors increasingly focused on basic science research and downstream linkages toward commercialization. Universities also played a more substantial role in producing new knowledge, and they emerged as key players in the knowledge economy. This more general shift in policies and priorities promoting science and technology development, combined with the hype and promise surrounding the purported revolution in the life sciences, prompted decision makers in Korea, Taiwan, and Singapore to identify biotech as a viable next-generation technology—in other words, a good bet to make. What is more, decision makers were confident, at least initially, that they could adapt for biotech the same strategies and institutions that had facilitated the rapid growth of the information technologies industry a decade earlier.

Many strategic decision makers in Korea, Taiwan, and Singapore also saw biotech as a good fit between their economies and the presumed requisites for developing a commercially viable sector. The absence of previous R&D and industry experience in the life sciences sector notwithstanding, stakeholders in Korea, Taiwan, and Singapore reasoned that their industrial economies possessed important features that were suited for growing new biotech industries, even from scratch. Governments there understood, for instance, the political and economic rationale for massive loss-leader investments in high-tech sectors, a style of industrial upgrading that decision makers had long accepted as the norm during the developmental state era. More specifically, Taiwan's postwar experience in nurturing small and medium-sized enterprises (SMEs) was seen as a key comparative advantage, particularly as the new sector's engine seemed to center on small and agile biotech venture firms. Korea's economic policy efforts during the 1990s to facilitate the growth of technology-intensive SMEs, combined with the prior existence of huge, diversified, and technologically savvy conglomerate (*chaebol*) enterprises, provided a strong foundation for investment and interfirm R&D collaboration. For Singapore, historical linkages with multinational firms, including big pharmaceutical companies, bolstered the city-state's locational advantages for the development of new knowledge-intensive industries.

Locational advantages specific to Asia were an important political economic consideration in all three cases. Strategic decision makers in Korea, Taiwan, and Singapore envisioned their economies as biotech hubs for the region, and more specifically as "gateways" or "springboards" into the massive Chinese economy. With strong legal systems already in place, greater institutional transparency, world-class university systems, a legacy of technology learning and transfer, and an established record of good international business practices, decision makers in all three economies were confident that they could, in varying ways, attract R&D talent and global firms to invest and in turn to foster international R&D collaboration. They figured their economies were in a strategic position to effectively lead, in different ways, biotech development and life sciences innovation in China and the rest of the region by leveraging their locational advantages.

Most important, however, was the fact that economic planners in Korea, Taiwan, and Singapore understood the international playing field in the biotech sector to be relatively even. They recognized that there were global leaders such as the United States and notable labs in the United Kingdom, Germany, and Japan, especially in upstream basic research in life sciences. However, decision makers also reasoned that despite the head start enjoyed by some nations, the lead was not significant, or at least not insurmountable. They rightly understood that no national economy had, as yet, come to dominate the commercial biotech sector, and they correctly foresaw an extraordinarily expansive value chain in life sciences innovation. Simply put, they recognized that latecomers would enjoy plenty of opportunities to succeed in the biotech sector. Though prospects in biotech were uncertain, they were not appreciably more uncertain for these dynamic Asian economies than they were for others already in the race.

Korea, Taiwan, and Singapore were willing to pay to get ahead in the race. Since the 1980s, total R&D spending in Korea and Taiwan has increased fivefold, and Singapore, historically a laggard in science and technology development, has seen nearly an eightfold increase in spending, putting the R&D commitments of these three economies on a par with global leaders in Europe, North America, and Japan. Not surprisingly, growth rates in R&D spending in these three cases rank among the fastest globally. Governments in Korea, Taiwan, and Singapore have invested heavily in life sciences R&D, with amounts in line with or even greater than in most advanced industrial economies. Most notably, during the middle of the first decade of the 2000s, Taiwan and Singapore allocated approximately one-third of total government R&D spending for life sciences. Private spending in biotech has similarly been on the rise, increasing at a far more rapid pace than in other technology-intensive sectors. In each of the three nations, new public and private R&D institutions dedicated to biotech have been created over the last two decades. Comprehensive regulatory infrastructures, critical to the development of the life sciences industry, are also being put in place. Universities have been restructured and reoriented toward upstream basic research and downstream commercialization in the life sciences field. And stakeholders in Korea, Taiwan, and Singapore are increasingly encouraged to collaborate more internationally, in an effort to curb their preexisting technonationalist impulses in ways that complement the technoglobalist realities of life sciences innovation.

These enormous bets on biotech have not, to date, paid off. Some economic gains have been realized as a consequence of massive efforts to grow the biotech sector since the early 1990s, but nowhere near the amount invested. Output has fallen well short of expectations. Ratios of sales revenues to R&D investment have likewise been very low in all three economies, and much lower than in other technology industries. Furthermore, firms are not surviving and the sector overall has been contracting rather than growing. Investment interest has cooled in recent years, as investors wait for a blockbuster product or a star firm to reinvigorate the flow of risk capital. Meanwhile, the governments in Korea, Taiwan, and Singapore, which have leveraged extraordinary economic and political resources on the promise of life sciences R&D and biotech commercialization, have been put on the defensive as citizens question the long-term prospects of biotech industries. National appetites for biotech have begun to wane.

This is not unique to Asia. Prognostications from global industry observers are, at best, measured, if not pessimistic. As of 2003, there were nearly

1,500 biotech firms in the United States, though fewer than 200 biotech products or services had been commercialized. And present indicators suggest that prospects in the sector have not improved. According to life sciences industry insiders, the odds of bringing new biotech products to market are getting worse, not better. Not surprisingly, through the early 2000s, profitability in the biotech sector was flat, a point reaffirmed when the *Wall Street Journal* reported in 2004 that over the previous two decades the rate of returns on investments in biotech was lower than it had been on U.S. Treasury bonds.[1] But if we look beyond measures of economic returns, we find that the sector has also failed to produce the anticipated clinical impact, in the form of health technology and new drugs. Gary Pisano's 2006 study of the U.S. biotech industry shows, for instance, that R&D productivity in the sector had essentially flatlined, and that revenues earned per dollar of R&D investment in biotech were still much lower than in the conventional pharmaceutical sector during the early 2000s.[2] A 2008 study of the sector draws an even more pessimistic conclusion, emphatically stating that the expectations of a global biotech revolution were "misplaced."[3]

The lesson is quite simple: betting on biotech, whether in Asia or the rest of the world, is an extremely high-stakes gamble with very low returns in the near and medium terms. A huge payoff is always possible, but that possibility remains terribly remote and, as I contend in this book, *inherently uncertain;* the fact that the global biotech sector has performed so poorly, and its impact both clinically and economically has been so underwhelming, only reinforces this uncertainty.

Uncertainty and Biotech

I suggest that there are three interrelated sources of uncertainty in biotech. First, the promise of innovation remains *technologically uncertain.* Notwithstanding important insights into the biological heuristic learned from basic research over the past several decades, it is still unclear if, how, and which

---

1. Only a handful of biotech firms, notably U.S.-based Amgen and Genentech, were in positive cash-flow positions as of 2005, and nearly three-quarters of American biotech firms operate with less than the equivalent of five years of cash reserves. Around one-quarter of U.S.-based life sciences firms operate with less than one year in cash reserves. See Gary Pisano, *Science Business: The Promise, the Reality and the Future of Biotech* (Boston: Harvard Business School Press, 2006), 112. See also Ernst and Young, *Beyond Borders: Global Biotechnology Report, 2008* (Cleveland: Ernst and Young, 2008).

2. Pisano, *Science Business,* 121–122.

3. Michael Hopkins, Paul Martin, Paul Nightingale, Alison Kraft, and Surya Mahdi, "The Myth of the Biotech Revolution: An Assessment of Technological, Clinical and Organizational Change," *Research Policy* 36 (2007), 584.

biotechnological techniques and applications can work to improve human health. Biotechnology, decades after the biotech revolution was supposed to have started, is still not a "mature technology," and as a consequence, viable health applications remain in their infancy. Second, there is tremendous *economic uncertainty* surrounding the commercial value of biotech in the development of health technology. Industry observers postulate that the value chain in biotech is very long, presumably with several potential entry points for prospective bio-entrepreneurs. However, the slow pace of commercialization in the sector means that markets remain undeveloped and open-ended, and thus the economic valuation of new applications continues to be uncertain. The commercial value chain is still characterized by its endless possibilities, as it was over thirty years ago, rather than by concrete, targetable products and services with assured market value. Third, the underwhelming performance of the global sector to date has intensified the *temporal uncertainty* associated with cutting-edge, first-order innovation. The distance between laboratory and market continues to be very long, unpredictable, and fraught with unforeseeable snags along the way, including regulatory constraints, clinical obstacles, and market uncertainties. It remains unclear even today, for instance, how long it will be before the commercial promise of biotech is fully realized. The political economic implications of temporal uncertainty have shaped how decision makers rationalize their bets on biotech.

We have learned a great deal about the science of biotech since the 1970s. Still, there remains tremendous uncertainty about the applicability of life sciences innovations and the commercial potential of biotech. Writing in the *Harvard Business Review* in 2000, nearly three decades after the biotech revolution was supposedly unleashed, Juan Enriquez and Ray Goldberg observe that while biotech firms came to embrace how "unlocking life's code opens up virtually unlimited commercial possibilities," firms nonetheless found that "operating within this new industry presents a raft of wrenchingly difficult challenges. They must rethink their business, financial and M&A [mergers and acquisitions] strategies, often from scratch. They must make vast R&D investments with distant and uncertain payoffs. They must enter into complex partnerships and affiliations, sometimes with direct competitors. And perhaps most difficult of all, they must contend with a public that is uncomfortable with even the thought of genetic engineering, much less its practices."[4] As Enriquez and Goldberg suggest, not only do the odds of commercial success remain unknowable, but there is still no road map, no

---

4. Juan Enriquez and Ray A. Goldberg, "Transforming Life, Transforming Business: The Life-Science Revolution," *Harvard Business Review*, March/April 2000, 97.

tried-and-true industry model for success in the life sciences sector. In other words, decision makers have little basis on which to make sound choices, little to guide them in making better bets.

Uncertainty is the key concept for this book. Uncertainty and innovation go hand in hand. Innovation is a process of discovering and adapting what was previously unknown. Because innovative outcomes are, by definition, novel and unprecedented, the processes of innovation are unpredictable and uncertain and the probability of failure is always high. It is precisely this pervasive uncertainty that confronts decision makers in Korea, Taiwan, and Singapore as they attempt to transform their industrial economies. Their success was initially built on imitating others' innovations; they now seek to generate novel and commercially viable products and services. I do not suggest that betting on biotech is necessarily a bad bet. Rather, I stress that betting on biotech entails *bets different in kind* from those that decision makers had routinely considered during the postwar period.

The postwar developmental state was adept at picking and making winners. They bet well. They nurtured productive industrial sectors as a whole, and they also helped grow winning firms, first as domestic producers and later for the international market. Their choices did not always pay off. The failed auto sector in Taiwan is a well-known example of one of the poorer decisions made by the developmental state. But this and other failed initiatives were nonetheless exceptions that prove a more general rule about the political economy of industrial upgrading in postwar Asia: the state intervened in the economy in ways that catalyzed industrial growth by making industrial winners. Several factors accounted for the state's transformative capacity in industrial upgrading, among them the hierarchical organization of the state apparatus; the meritocratic bureaucracy at the heart of the developmental state; the state's relative autonomy from, and yet embeddedness in, productive sectors within society; the transformative goals of decision makers and stakeholders inside the state; and of course the capacity of the developmental state apparatus to coordinate and strategically allocate public and private resources toward productive ends.

However, making winners was only part of the story of Asia's developmental success. The prior decision to pick winners, I contend, was far more risky and captures more accurately what we mean by the logic of state-led development. When Robert Wade writes about "big leadership" or Linda Weiss about "state guidance," they are pointing to both the capacity and the willingness of the developmental state to gamble, to make the hard choices that might ultimately lead to industrial winners. Put another way, making winners by channeling resources toward a specific company or a particular technology is one thing; picking potential winners in the first place involves an altogether different strategic calculus. To make winners you need to pick them, and this entails difficult choices.

Betting on potential winners was not a risk-free proposition. There was always the risk of failure. And yet strategic decision makers inside the Asian developmental state tended to bet well; the many studies of the developmental state tell us about the strategic rationale for how bets were made and winners picked. First, targeted industries, technologies, or even firms were selected for their complementarities with existing bases of expertise and knowledge. A history of electronics manufacturing, for instance, paved the way for the development of information technologies industries in Taiwan, just as domestic steel and electronics industries provided a viable route to auto making in South Korea. Second, strategic bets on potential winners were informed by market demand as well as by the ease of entry for domestic firms into specific niches in what were already defined global value chains. For example, moving into semiconductor manufacturing in Korea and Taiwan was a decision pulled as much by global demand as it was pushed by supply capabilities, just as the growth of the hard disk drive industry in Singapore was shaped by its locational advantages and the global market demand for computer peripherals. Third, economic planners selected particular sectors and industries that were relatively close to market or would generate returns in the near term. Taiwan and Korea, for instance, specialized in the design and manufacture of integrated circuits, knowing that ready buyers were on hand. Meanwhile, Singapore focused on the back-end manufacturing and distribution of consumer electronics during the 1980s and 1990s to supply booming consumer markets in the West. In all three cases, not only were economic returns on bets relatively certain, they were quick. Thus, while industrial upgrading during the postwar period entailed massive risk, industrial winners were picked from among firms and technologies that enjoyed, at least from the perspective of decision makers, a fair degree of technological and economic certainty.

By picking and making winners, the developmental state effectively mitigated the risks of industrial upgrading, and specifically those risks that otherwise the private sector would have had to bear alone. However, in science-based industries such as biotech, where technological, economic, and temporal uncertainties are still so pronounced, it is difficult, if not impossible, to strategically pick winners.[5] Primary uncertainty in commercial biotech innovation entails a sort of randomness that is inconsistent with the purposive

5. Johan Brink, Maureen McKelvey, and Keith Smith, "Conceptualizing and Measuring Modern Biotechnology," in *The Economic Dynamics of Modern Biotechnology,* ed. Maureen McKelvey, Annika Rickne, and Jens Laage-Hellman (Cheltenham, U.K.: Edward Elgar, 2004), 25.

decision-making practices of the postwar developmental state. It involves a different strategic calculus or logic, reflecting an altogether different kind of bet than those made during the postwar period of catch-up industrialization in Asia. As I argue in Chapter 1, if the postwar developmental state was about *mitigating risk,* then the future of science-based development is about *managing uncertainty.*

The challenges of managing technological and economic uncertainty, according to economists, are not insurmountable. One way to overcome biotech's uncertainties is to focus on those areas in which you have comparative expertise. Given the vastly unintegrated nature of the biotech value chain— its many points of entry at which to generate value—leveraging existing strengths might reveal, over time, a strategic niche within the sector. This makes sense. The problem for Korea, Taiwan, and Singapore, however, is that all three possessed very little experience in life sciences R&D before the 1990s. Because they are all relatively recent entrants, they have had in effect to start from scratch, with few existing strengths in life science research and industry to build on. When Korea, Taiwan, and Singapore entered the sector during the 1990s, they had little idea about what they might be good at.

The other way to mitigate the problems of uncertainty in biotech innovation, economists tell us, is through economies of scale and the ability to bet widely. The U.S. biotech industry, for instance, is the global leader in part because the private sector and government provide huge amounts of resources for upstream research and downstream commercialization, and vastly more than their competitors. The U.S. National Institutes of Health and the National Science Foundation disburse upward of US$30 billion each year for upstream life sciences R&D, which is about forty times more than in Korea and Taiwan and eighty times more than in Singapore. Private sector spending in biotech R&D in the United States is also off the charts when compared with places such as Korea, Taiwan, and Singapore.[6] Stelios Papadopoulos of SG Cowen investors elaborates on this point when he observes how European biotech industries will unlikely be able to compete with the United States, not because of the quality of European scientific output but rather because "Europe simply does not have the sufficient density of

---

6. To put into perspective the scale implications of this disparity, consider that U.S.-based researchers published close to 60,000 papers in the field of health-related biotech between 1991 and 2002, with Japan coming in a distant second with just over 18,000 publications. With just over 2,000 papers and 1,000 papers respectively, Korea and Taiwan ranked fourteenth and twenty-third. Singapore ranked thirty-sixth with 326 publications. See Halla Thorsteinsdottir, Abdallah Daar, and Peter Singer, "Health Biotechnology Publishing Takes-off in Developing Countries," *International Journal of Biotechnology* 8 (2006), 31.

academic scientists with commercial expertise, experienced entrepreneurs who understand how to bootstrap operations and grow companies, and local capital markets for post-venture financing."[7] Massive scale allows decision makers to bet widely, to some extent indiscriminately, thus essentially covering their bets. Scale of this magnitude is absent in the cases I examine here as well as in most of the world's industrial economies.

The challenges faced by those betting on biotech in places such as Korea, Taiwan, and Singapore are clear: these economies not only lack preexisting strengths and expertise in the life sciences industry; they are also without the scale and density that might allow decision makers to bet indiscriminately in order to identify potential winners. Decision makers in Korea, Taiwan, and Singapore can neither mitigate risk by choosing probable (if still risky) winners as they had done in the past nor bet widely on a broad range of potential winners with a degree of confidence that some will eventually emerge as successful. To put a finer point on this distinction between past practices and present-day challenges, Chin-Tay Shih, former president of the Industrial Technology Research Institute and instrumental in spearheading Taiwan's semiconductor sector, emphatically asserts that Taiwan "cannot simply use and copy its past IT model" for the development of biotech industry. He goes on to explain that because the biotech industry is highly regulated, has a long commercial gestation, is a scientific field in which Asians have little experience, and requires the integration of different fields of expertise, growing successful biotech firms eludes the state-led, hierarchically coordinated industrial strategies that were once used to develop East Asia's information technologies sector.[8] Simply put, betting on the eventual success of the semiconductor sector in Taiwan and Korea or on computer peripherals in Singapore is not the same as betting on biotech.

Organizing Biotech

But if not the postwar developmental state, then what do these political economies look like in the era of science-based industrialization? One of my aims is to provide empirical details about how the state and bio-industrial stakeholders have allocated public and private resources to grow life sciences industries in Korea, Taiwan, and Singapore. Chapters 2 and 3 examine the (re-)organization of the state and of bio-industry and how resources have

---

7. Wharton Business School, *Wharton Healthcare Leadership Exchange* (Philadelphia: Wharton Business School, February 2005), 12.

8. Author interview, Taipei, Taiwan, September 27, 2007.

been allocated. In Korea, the sector has been organized to create a discernible division of labor among a wide variety of actors and experts. Thus while Korea's bio-industrial strategy rests on the expectation that giant conglomerate firms such as LG and Samsung will eventually emerge as national champions in the biopharmaceutical sector, stakeholders there have also recognized the importance of surrounding the chaebols with a vast supporting cast of publicly funded R&D institutions, public-private biotech transfer mechanisms, and research-intensive venture firms.

Taiwan, in contrast, has chosen to leverage its experience in growing small and medium-sized enterprises as the foundation of its emerging biotech sector. As in the postwar period, the allocation of public and private resources has continued to foster a "hit-and-miss" logic of industrial selection, featuring SMEs and multiple state-sponsored technology transfer mechanisms. Taiwan's approach to biotech development hinges on the normalization of failure, on the one hand, though with the expectation, on the other, that through the seeding of "many sprouts," some firms will survive and thus identify specific niches in the biotech value chain that can be exploited through further investment. If the Korean approach bets big on the chaebols to successfully capture significant market share in the global biotech sector, the Taiwanese strategy is about spreading bets as widely as possible with the hope that despite many misses and failures, some lucrative hits will eventually be made as well.

The Singaporean approach reflects its structural disadvantages in size and its small talent pool. Decision makers there have pursued a more outward-looking, international strategy, leveraging Singapore's locational advantages and government investments in the life sciences sector to attract global firms to locate in the city-state. Unlike in Korea and Taiwan, where we see the dispersion and diffusion of resources allocated for biotech development, in Singapore the Economic Development Board, as well as the functional equivalent of its science ministry, have concentrated their allocative authorities in order to position Singapore as an attractive biomedical hub for global talent, firms, and investment capital. The expectation—the bet—is that bringing global biomedical firms to Singapore, and along with them high value-added R&D activities as well as bio-industrial manufacturing, will result in positive externalities for domestic life sciences industries.

Those familiar with regional variations in postwar Asian development will know that what I have briefly described here reflects significant continuities in the ways in which states and stakeholders have organized their biotech sectors. These nationally distinctive continuities, I argue, have been shaped by existing power relations among actors, institutional legacies of the developmental state era, and different heuristic biases shared by strategic decision makers about how best to manage uncertainty. We know, for instance, that Korea's industrialization program has always centered on the chaebols, just as Taiwan's postwar economic miracle harnessed the entrepreneurial savvy of SMEs. We also know that Singapore, by virtue of its scale-related constraints, relies on its locational advantages and government commitments to attract global industrial activity to the tiny city-state. When faced with the uncertain prospects and processes of biotech innovation, decision makers in each of the three places have essentially reverted to tried-and-true strategies.

Yet we would be wrong to assume that the story of biotech development in industrial Asia is merely one of continuity. When we closely examine the specific rationales for these choices, we find that in fact the notion of state leadership in Korea, Taiwan, and even Singapore has fundamentally changed. Apparent continuities notwithstanding, the arguments developed in this book reveal that under the surface, a fundamental transformation has been going on—a transformation, I argue, that has seen the strategic retreat of the postwar developmental state.

Beyond the Developmental State

In addition to describing how the biotech sector is organized in Korea, Taiwan, and Singapore, Chapters 2 and 3 explain how the decentralization of functional expertise within the state, combined with the multidisciplinary challenges of commercializing biotech innovation, has left the state increasingly unable to cope with the sector's myriad uncertainties. Chapter 5, which focuses on regulatory reform, carries this functionalist argument further by exposing the obstacles facing the state as it attempts to develop and coordinate new regulatory regimes. Contention among seemingly irreconcilable political interests over regulating the biotech sector has undermined the once coherent developmental state. The consequence, I believe, is that the coordinative capacity of the state has weakened, forcing it to retreat from its postwar leadership role.

Chapter 4 examines the retreat of the developmental state from a political vantage point. It focuses on the always-looming prospects of failure in the sector and how this has in turn weakened national appetites in Korea, Taiwan, and Singapore for the uncertainties inherent in first-order commercial biotech innovation. Despite efforts described in Chapter 4 to resuscitate enthusiasm for the high-risk, high-reward realities of biotech, and despite creative efforts to recalibrate popular expectations about the industry to match the long-term realities of biotech innovation, the state in Korea, Taiwan, and Singapore has chosen to back away from leading efforts to succeed in biotechnology. The state has become increasingly unwilling to shoulder the political, economic, and commercial risks that come with biotech development. Both the probability and the political economic costs of failure have become prohibitively high for the state. It has opted, therefore, to retreat from picking and making winners, a strategy the postwar developmental state had once employed with considerable confidence and success.

Though the state has become both less able and less willing to intervene in the economy in ways that it once did, it has not become irrelevant in Korea, Taiwan, and Singapore; that would be the wrong conclusion to draw. What has changed is the underlying strategic logic of state intervention. The state has in fact continued to invest heavily in science-based industries such as biotech and to intervene in ways that it thinks will increase the likelihood of commercial success in the life sciences. But how and why the state intervenes has been transformed by the distant and uncertain prospects of betting on biotech and the related challenges of managing the sector's technological, economic, and temporal uncertainties. The postwar developmental state intervened to mitigate risk in targeted firms, technologies, and industrial sectors; the strategic logic of state intervention in science-based industries targets the long-term and uncertain *processes of discovering* potential winners. The distinction between then and now might appear to be subtle. Substantively, however, it is very significant. Betting on biotech, as I argue in this book, involves gambling on a more distant process of innovation, in which the results are intrinsically uncertain, rather than on a particular product, application, or firm. Bets are now being made on the uncertain potentialities of innovation instead of on proven winners. The state has not retreated into obscurity, but rather, decision makers have been forced to bet differently. The political economy of state leadership in science-based industries such as biotech has evolved beyond the postwar developmental state.

By considering the evolving role of the state as well as the transformed logic of state leadership in science-based industries, this book encourages us to think beyond the developmental state idea—beyond the developmental state not only as a model for industrial upgrading in today's science-based knowledge economy but also as a regionally bounded phenomenon. As the arguments unfold in the ensuing chapters, it becomes clear how the challenges of making strategic bets in the face of technological, economic, and temporal uncertainty are both profoundly different from those of the postwar period and also not unique to the three Asian cases. Many economies face challenges similar to those of industrial Asia. Thus, understanding the experiences of Korea, Taiwan, and Singapore allows us to learn from three important cases that increasingly represent the global norm rather than the exception.

Like most other advanced economies, Korea, Taiwan, and Singapore are rich but relatively small, so their prospects in commercializing biotech will depend on global markets, investment, and R&D collaboration. Like many others, they are late entrants into the life sciences field, and relatively inexperienced. They are also without the scale advantages we see in the United States and emerging giants such as China and India. As a result, decision makers in these three economies, like those in other places, must make strategic choices about how to allocate resources, coordinate disparate actors, and manage the uncertainties of long-term biotech innovation. They must bet carefully and strategically in the face of pervasive uncertainty and the persistent threat of colossal failure. The book's concluding chapter argues that the transformations of the developmental state in Asia are evidence that these paragons of the distinctly Asian developmental state have evolved. They are no longer exceptional, and they are becoming more normal political economies. As they bet on biotech, they share goals, challenges, and ongoing struggles with many others.

CHAPTER 1

From Mitigating Risk
to Managing Uncertainty

> Our high-tech industry has tended to adapt technologies rather than create new ones. We look up to the leaders of these companies because they are perceived to be innovators, when in fact, they haven't created anything new.
>
> —Eugene Wong, National Science Council, Taiwan, 2008

Industrial development and diversification are about taking risk. Encouraging the growth of industry in new and unfamiliar sectors is always risky. It invariably involves costs, and the rewards are uncertain. Yet it is important to consider different kinds and levels of risk in industrial upgrading. Some endeavors are relatively less risky than others. Some bets are safer than others. Potential payoffs differ as well, and the expectation of any payoffs at all is uncertain. Generally speaking, higher-risk propositions yield higher rewards, though the likelihood of success is much lower. Science-based industries and the prospects of science-based industrialization are the riskiest enterprises of all, extraordinarily high-stakes bets. Cutting-edge innovation—that is, creating something new—requires massive amounts of resources committed to a wide range of actors and R&D activities with the faint and distant hope that such efforts are technically and economically productive. Life sciences innovation and biotech commercialization are not just risky; they are inherently uncertain enterprises.

This chapter distinguishes between risk and "primary uncertainty." Typically, risk and uncertainty are thought to be synonymous, as both are defined by the absence of certainty. They both describe circumstances in which there are unknowns. However, I seek to make a more fundamental conceptual distinction between risk and uncertainty, to suggest that they are in fact distinct and thus bear different implications with respect to the organization of political economies. Risk scenarios are those in which decision makers have some prior knowledge about potential outcomes. For instance, decision makers may have some sense of the odds of a particular outcome or the range of viable choices available. Decisions are risky, but they are not uninformed. Situations of primary uncertainty, in contrast, are those in which actors possess so little (or no) information or knowledge about a decision and its consequences that they must essentially make what are uninformed choices. Put another way, whereas risk taking involves calculated if uncertain decisions about alternative choices, the notion of primary uncertainty suggests a more ambient context in which decision-making processes are obscured by the lack of alternative choices, and even before that, the information and knowledge with which to generate clear and viable alternatives.[1]

This chapter sharpens the conceptual distinction between risk and uncertainty by examining the processes of industrial upgrading in East Asia during the postwar period; it then develops an analytical framework with which to make sense of the current processes of growing biotech industries in Korea, Taiwan, and Singapore. The core argument is that the postwar political economy in Asia was one in which the state strategically intervened in the economy for the purposes of mitigating the risks of industrial upgrading. The developmental state could not guarantee industrial success, but it demonstrated the capacity to reduce the risks of upgrading and technological "catch-up," compelling firms and industry to move into sectors they otherwise would have eschewed if left on their own. The strategy of mitigating risk is less effective, however, when it comes to cutting-edge biotech. In the current state of the biotech sector, there remains such tremendous technological, economic, and long-term uncertainty that decision makers can, at best, only strive to manage and cope with such uncertainty. The distinction I draw between risk and primary uncertainty, therefore, is not one of semantics; it is intended to illuminate how decision makers make political economic bets and how they rationalize them in the face of two different modes of industrial upgrading, each with, I assert, its own set of challenges.

---

1. In the context of capital markets, Jeffrey Winters distinguishes between risk and uncertainty in the following way: "When the stakes are high, information is crucial. Investors operate well with risk, for which probabilities of different outcomes can be calculated. They do not operate well with uncertainty, which means the absence of quality information on which to base investment decisions." Winters, "The Determinants of Financial Crisis in Asia," in *The Politics of the Asian Economic Crisis,* ed. T. J. Pempel (Ithaca: Cornell University Press, 1999), 87.

Mitigating Risk and the Developmental State

The developmental state is credited with being the main engine for postwar Asia's rapid and dynamic economic growth. It set about creating comparative and competitive advantages to gain credibility in industrial sectors that had been dominated by firms in advanced nations. The model was about using state aid to develop private sector firms, transforming them into national champions and global players. Inspired by Friedrich List's theories of nationalist economic growth, the developmental state in Asia cultivated, often through authoritarian means, nationalist myths—in postcolonial Korea, self-reliance; in Taiwan, the return to China; in postcolonial Singapore, paranoia about national survival—to deepen aspirations for social and economic modernization. Asia's developmental states were motivated by lofty "transformative" goals.[2]

The bureaucracy was at the center of the developmental state model. Meritocratic recruitment ensured that the state apparatus in Korea, Taiwan, and Singapore drew from among the nation's "best and brightest." Bureaucrats were not only talented; they were well positioned in hierarchical organizations structured along clear lines of authority. The verticalization of power was afforded in part by technocrats' dependence on the authority and patronage of the ruling political elite. But the organizational structure of bureaucratic institutions contributed as well to hierarchical forms of top-down state management. Economic pilot agencies such as Korea's Economic Planning Board (EPB), the Council for Economic Planning and Development (CEPD) in Taiwan, and Singapore's Economic Development Board (EDB) coordinated the strategies and activities of government agencies responsible for industrial growth. Because few actors were involved in economic policymaking, power and authority were not only verticalized but centralized and concentrated. A small number of powerful actors allowed technocrats to resolve coordination problems within the state.[3] The institutional organization of the developmental state ensured that it remained autonomous and insulated from narrow societal interests below. It also allowed state-level decision makers to behave decisively and authoritatively.

Peter Evans reminds us, however, that the coordinative capacity of the state was not solely a function of its political structure and autonomy but

---

2. Linda Weiss, "Guiding Globalisation in East Asia: New Roles for Old Developmental States," in *States in the Global Economy: Bringing Domestic Institutions Back In,* ed. Weiss (Cambridge: Cambridge University Press, 2003).

3. Robert Wade, *Governing the Market: Economic Theory and the Role of Government in East Asian Industrialization* (Princeton, N.J.: Princeton University Press, 1990); Gregory Noble, *Collective Action in East Asia: How Ruling Parties Shape Industrial Policy* (Ithaca: Cornell University Press, 1998).

also a consequence of its strategic "embeddedness" within productive sectors, most notably industry.[4] As the literature on the developmental state goes to great lengths to emphasize, market forces were the basis of industrial growth in Asia. State and industry cooperated in the implementation of industrial policies. Information feedback loops between them were institutionalized, formally and informally, allowing the state to strategically allocate vast resources in order to coordinate industrial activity more generally. The Korean state thus "husbanded" the chaebols. The Kuomintang (KMT) party-state in Taiwan ensured that government ownership of firms in key infrastructural sectors facilitated rather than crowded out private sector industry growth. The state in Singapore was instrumental in growing government-linked corporations in tandem with the presence of multinational firms. The state's embeddedness within society did not mean the devolution of state power, however. Rather, Evans's point is that the externalities gained from the state's strategic alliance with industry actually reinforced its market-regarding role in coordinating industrial development in postwar Asia.

Theories about East Asia's postwar miracle generated over the past three decades have more or less specified the structural conditions that allowed the developmental state to effectively implement interventionist economic policies.[5] This chapter looks at the Asian developmental state from a different vantage point. In the following sections, I revisit East Asia's postwar experience in industrial upgrading from the perspective of technological and economic *risk,* and specifically the ways in which the developmental state in Korea, Taiwan, and Singapore was instrumental in mitigating the risks of early industrialization and later industrial upgrading and diversification.

Industrial Upgrading

Industrial upgrading in Korea was led by large, diversified, and export-oriented conglomerate business groups, or chaebols.[6] They benefited from

---

4. Peter Evans, *Embedded Autonomy: States and Industrial Transformation* (Princeton, N.J.: Princeton University Press, 1995).

5. Dan Breznitz observes, rightly in my view, that theorists of the developmental state and the neodevelopmental state essentially "advance an argument about the need for specific state structure that enables emerging economies to utilize a particular strategy of development." Theories of the developmental state thus privilege the structure of the state and state-society relations as a priori conditions to effective strategic decision making and implementation. See Breznitz, *Innovation and the State: Political Choice and Strategies for Growth in Israel, Taiwan and Ireland* (New Haven, Conn.: Yale University Press, 2007), 14.

6. In 1974, earnings from the top ten chaebols equaled 15% of Korea's national product; ten years later, the top ten chaebols accounted for over 67% of GNP.

state patronage. For instance, the state received, brokered, and distributed foreign technology licenses and managed the transfer and diffusion of commercial know-how.[7] The chaebols gained domestic first-mover advantages in technology development because competition was "oligopolistic," limited to a select handful of national industrial champions.[8] Just as important, the state leveraged its financial capacity to allocate investment credit to favored firms.[9] The banking sector was nationalized in the early 1960s, and the distribution of domestic and foreign capital allowed the state to discipline and reward firms according to national economic plans and targets.[10] Essentially bankrolled by the state, Korea's chaebols enjoyed economies of both scale and scope. Scale ensured competitive prices in global markets. The chaebols' "brand" gave Korea's export-oriented companies global commercial exposure that far exceeded the market recognition of any Taiwan-based or Singaporean firm. Meanwhile, economies of scope were achieved with diversification inside firms, facilitating the internal transfer of capital, technology, and management best practices.

The development of Korea's semiconductor industry illustrates the productivity of this state-chaebol strategy for industrial upgrading. Korea's entry into VLSI (very large scale integration) chip fabrication in 1978 was prompted when a technology transfer agreement was brokered between Silicon Valley's VLSI Technology and the publicly funded Korean Institute of Electronic Technology. The big push into the industry came during the 1980s when the government invested US$400 million in semiconductor R&D. The parastatal Electronics and Telecommunications Research Institute (ETRI) coordinated a DRAM (memory chip) R&D consortium, which

7. Linsu Kim, *Imitation to Innovation: The Dynamics of Korea's Technological Learning* (Boston: Harvard Business School Press, 1997); Kim, "Crisis, National Innovation and Reform in South Korea," MIT Japan Program, Working Paper 01.01, 2001; Larry Westphal, Linsu Kim, and Carl Dahlman, "Reflections on the Republic of Korea's Acquisition of Technological Capability," in *International Technology Transfer: Concepts, Measures and Comparisons,* ed. Nathan Rosenberg and Claudio Frischtak (New York: Praeger, 1985).

8. Alice Amsden, *Asia's Next Giant: South Korea and Late Industrialization* (New York: Oxford University Press, 1989), 116–130.

9. Jung-En Woo, *Race to the Swift: State and Finance in Korean Industrialization* (New York: Columbia University Press, 1991); Karl Fields, *Enterprise and the State in Korea and Taiwan* (Ithaca: Cornell University Press, 1995); Evans, *Embedded Autonomy.*

10. According to Eun Mee Kim, nearly 50% of all commercial loans invested during the 1960s and 1970s were allocated to just six targeted industrial sectors, most of which were guaranteed by the government in terms of repayment. The six sectors were steel, nonferrous metals, machinery, shipbuilding, electrical appliances and electronics, and chemicals. See Eun Mee Kim, *Big Business, Strong State: Collusion and Conflict in South Korean Development, 1960–1990* (Albany: SUNY Press, 1997), 110.

was concentrated among a few chaebols.[11] In 1982, Samsung announced a then unprecedented US$130 million (100 billion won) investment in VLSI development. This sparked similarly significant investments from chaebol competitors Goldstar and Hyundai. From U.S.-based Micron and Japan's Sharp, Samsung acquired DRAM design and processing technologies, which enabled it to develop the more advanced 64K DRAM in 1983.[12] It is important to point out that supply-side push in the informatics sector was matched with demand-side pull. Domestic demand for such technology was high, as was foreign demand.[13] The U.S.-Japan Semiconductor Trade Agreement of 1986 and the revaluation of the yen after the Plaza Accord a year earlier weakened Japan's export dominance in the sector, increasing global market share for Korean producers. There was little uncertainty about demand. Indeed, only five years after Samsung made its historic announcement during the early 1980s, Korea's DRAM technologies neared the cutting edge and were competitive in the global marketplace.[14]

Whereas the Korean approach to technological and industrial upgrading centered primarily on national champions "husbanded" by the state, Taiwan's developmental state favored the growth of small and medium-sized enterprises into eventual global competitors. Politically motivated to prevent a concentration of industrial activity within a few firms, industrial policy planners in Taiwan eschewed the economies-of-scale logic pursued in Korea, opting for an industry-wide economies-of-scope approach.[15] Firms were nimble and flexible, and they tended to focus on specific niches.[16] Nurturing small firms, as opposed to large ones, meant that investments into specific initiatives were less concentrated. It also meant that industrial firms required less

11. Evans, *Embedded Autonomy*, 141; Mariko Sakakibara and Dong-Sung Cho, "Cooperative R&D in Japan and Korea: A Comparison of Industrial Policy," *Research Policy* 31 (2002), 685; William Keller and Louis Pauly, "Crisis and Adaptation in Taiwan and South Korea: The Political Economy of Semiconductors," in *Crisis and Innovation in Asian Technology*, ed. William Keller and Richard Samuels (Cambridge: Cambridge University Press, 2003).

12. John Matthews and Dong-Sung Cho, *Tiger Technology: The Creation of a Semiconductor Industry in East Asia* (Cambridge: Cambridge University Press, 2000), 121–123.

13. Evans, *Embedded Autonomy*, 142.

14. Linsu Kim, "National Systems of Industrial Innovation: Dynamics of Capability Building in Korea," in *National Innovation Systems: A Comparative Analysis*, ed. Richard Nelson (New York: Oxford University Press, 1993), 377.

15. Yongping Wu, *A Political Explanation of Economic Growth: State Survival, Bureaucratic Politics, and Private Enterprises in the Making of Taiwan's Economy, 1950–1985* (Cambridge, Mass.: Harvard University Press, 2005); Breznitz, *Innovation and the State*; Fields, *Enterprise and the State*.

16. Suzanne Berger and Richard Lester, eds., *Global Taiwan: Building Competitive Strengths in a New International Economy* (Armonk, N.Y.: M. E. Sharpe, 2005); Vincent Wang, "Developing the Information Industry in Taiwan: Entrepreneurial State, Guerilla Capitalists and Accommodative Technologists," *Pacific Affairs* 68 (1995).

direct investment from public coffers. Unlike in Korea, the KMT party-state in Taiwan was without the financial resources to invest in large-scale diversified firms; Taiwan's largest firms were tiny compared with Korea's chaebols. Taiwan instead relied on fiscal-based incentives and the state's coordinative leadership to nudge firms into higher-tech sectors and to offset the costs and risks of industrial upgrading.[17] Firms adapted by devising strategies to bootstrap and take advantage of the informal financial sector.

Technological and industrial upgrading flowed out of the commercialization efforts of publicly funded labs. Technology acquisition and development, and the risks associated with these midstream processes, were concentrated within parastatal labs and then transferred to the private sector. The Industrial Technology Research Institute (ITRI) was critical in developing the state's midstream capabilities. The ITRI adhered to a "license-in, license-out" model of technology acquisition, development, and private sector commercialization. The ITRI's role in midstream technology development thus effectively delivered near-market technologies to otherwise risk-averse firms. During the mid-1970s, the Taiwan government brokered a licensing agreement with U.S.-based RCA to acquire what was then its already obsolete integrated circuit (IC) technology. This was assimilated into the ITRI and specifically its Electronics Research Service Organization (ERSO). The technology was reverse-engineered, and a pilot plant for manufacturing was established soon after. Because private sector firms were hesitant to invest in IC technology, initial funding for the RCA deal came largely from public sources. The state assumed the role of what John Matthews and Dong-Sung Cho refer to as "collective entrepreneur"[18] when it spun out United Microelectronics Corporation (UMC) during the late 1970s.[19]

The ITRI and the ERSO continued to play a similar leadership role when the government decided during the early 1980s to further upgrade its electronics sector by developing Taiwan's VLSI manufacturing capabilities. Between 1983 and 1988, more than US$72 million of government

---

17. Tun-Jen Cheng, "Political Regimes and Development Strategies: South Korea and Taiwan," in *Manufacturing Miracles: Paths of Industrialization in Latin America and East Asia,* ed. Gary Gereffi and Donald Wyman (Princeton, N.J.: Princeton University Press, 1990); Fields, *Enterprise and the State.*

18. Matthews and Cho, *Tiger Technology,* 167; see also Constance Squires Meaney, "State Policy and the Development of Taiwan's Semiconductor Industry," in *The Role of the State in Taiwan's Development,* ed. Joel Aberbach, David Dollar, and Kenneth Sokoloff (Armonk, N.Y.: M. E. Sharpe, 1994).

19. Despite firms' initial reluctance to invest in Taiwan's IC manufacturing sector, the state resisted forming a wholly state-owned firm, opting instead to use its "direct influence" to organize a broad investment consortium of private firms, which in the end accounted for 51% equity in UMC. See Breznitz, *Innovation and the State,* 107.

funds was allocated for microelectronics R&D, the bulk of which was channeled to the ERSO.[20] UMC initially sought to lead the VLSI project, though
the state resisted the overconcentration of resources and market share in a
single firm.[21] Consequently, the ERSO formed an R&D partnership with
U.S.-based Vitelic to develop DRAM chip technology. The ERSO intended
to spin out a private firm in 1986, though again, local entrepreneurs were
hesitant to lead the investment. The Taiwan Semiconductor Manufacturing
Corporation (TSMC) was eventually formed, with 48% of the firm's initial
investment coming from public sources, about the same proportion of government funds for the UMC deal a few years earlier.[22] TSMC's pioneering
pure-play foundry model allowed it to fabricate chips economically and to
specific design requirements, and the firm quickly captured significant market share in a key segment of the IT value chain. As experts such as Douglas
Fuller note, IT's value chain is "granular" and "decomposed into distinct
functional parts," which allowed TSMC to target and eventually to dominate
a particular value-added niche in IT manufacturing.[23]

Singapore's industrial development followed a different pathway. Its
economic vulnerability after independence fomented a "discourse of survivalism."[24] Human capital was Singapore's primary economic resource, and
economic development was driven by a full-employment industrial strategy.
Job creation was the main priority, not technological upgrading per se. During the 1970s, state planners looked to strengthen Singapore's technology
base, specifically in "skill-intensive, higher value-added export industries."
However, a mid-1970s recession forced the government to revert to its earlier strategy of wage restraints and the continued growth of labor-intensive
sectors.[25] The overwhelming importance of job creation and labor market

---

20. Breznitz, *Innovation and the State,* 109.

21. Doug Fuller, Charles Sodini, and Akintunde Akinwande, "Leading, Following or Cooked
Goose? Innovation Successes and Failures in Taiwan's Electronics Industry," in *Global Taiwan: Building
Competitive Strengths in a New International Economy,* ed. Suzanne Berger and Richard Lester (Armonk,
N.Y.: M. E. Sharpe, 2005).

22. Philips, the multinational Dutch electronics firm, made up 28% of TSMC's initial investment, which, combined with the government's 48%, meant that less than one-quarter of the firm's
investment came from local private sources.

23. Fuller, Sodini, and Akinwande, "Leading, Following or Cooked Goose?," 77; Annalee Saxenian and Jinn-Yuh Hsu, "The Silicon Valley–Hsinchu Connection: Technical Communities and
Industrial Upgrading," *Industrial and Corporate Change* 10 (2001).

24. Henry Wai-Chung Yeung, "State Intervention and Neoliberalism in the Globalizing World
Economy: Lessons from Singapore's Regionalization Program," *Pacific Review* 13 (2001), 146; see also
David Chang, "Nation-Building in Singapore," *Asian Survey* 8 (1968).

25. Mike Hobday, *Innovation in East Asia: The Challenge to Japan* (Brookfield, Vt.: Edward Elgar,
1995), 140; Linda Lim, "Singapore's Success: The Myth of the Free Market Economy," *Asian Survey*
23 (1983), 757.

absorption was also reflected in the growth of government-linked corporations (GLCs), de facto state-owned enterprises. GLCs fostered infrastructural
development in Singapore. They were also "in competition and partnership
with foreign and local private enterprise," which meant that even into the
late 1970s most of Singapore's industrial base was tied to the government.[26]
It is estimated that during the early 1980s, there were almost five hundred
wholly or partially government-owned firms in Singapore.[27] As a result,
growing local private firms was not a priority for economic planners.[28] In
fact, Linda Low contends that the Singaporean state "maintained a certain
distance if not outright antipathy toward the local private sector."[29]

The other pillar of Singapore's postindependence industrialization strategy was the inflow of foreign direct investment (FDI), especially the location of multinational corporations (MNCs) in Singapore. During the 1980s,
Singapore received more FDI than any other economy in the developing
world.[30] The MNC strategy was viewed by policymakers as less risky, or a
way to off-load risk. Multinational companies, by virtue of their scale and
credibility, ensured access to global markets. And most important, they created jobs. In 1998, MNCs and GLCs together accounted for over half of
Singapore's national product.[31] MNCs alone captured the largest share of the
city-state's exports. In 1994, foreign enterprises contributed to about 75%
of Singapore's manufacturing output, 70% of value-added production, and
roughly 85% of exports.[32] During the 1990s, foreign sources accounted for
over 27% of Singapore's fixed capital, a share that dwarfed fixed capital stocks
in Korea and Taiwan, at 0.8% and 2.6%, respectively.[33]

---

26. Lim, "Singapore's Success," 755.

27. W. G. Huff, "The Developmental State, Government and Singapore's Economic Development since 1960," *World Development* 23 (1995), 1428.

28. According to Lee Kuan Yew, "the only reason the government moved in was that no entrepreneur had the guts and the gumption and the capital to go in on his own. . . . And we are prepared
to go into the more high-risk areas where Singaporean entrepreneurs are unable to carry that risk,
either for lack of daring or for lack of capital." Cited in Florian von Alten, *The Role of Government in
the Singapore Economy* (Frankfurt: Peter Lang, 1995), 200.

29. Linda Low, "The Singapore Developmental State in the New Economy and Polity," *Pacific
Review* 14 (2001), 146. See also Alexius Pereira, "Whither the Developmental State? Explaining
Singapore's Continued Developmentalism," *Third World Quarterly* 29 (2008).

30. Huff, "Developmental State," 1425.

31. Gavin Peebles and Peter Wilson, *Economic Growth and Development in Singapore* (Cheltenham,
U.K.: Edward Elgar, 2002), 14.

32. Kai-Sun Kwong, "Singapore: Dominance of Multinational Corporations," in *Industrial Development in Singapore, Taiwan and South Korea,* ed. Kwong et al. (Hackensack, N.J.: World Scientific
Press, 2001), 10.

33. Peebles and Wilson, *Economic Growth,* 171.

The Economic Development Board (EDB) of the Ministry of Trade and Industry was instrumental in attracting foreign firms to Singapore, highlighting the city-state's "locational advantages," including low-wage skilled labor, investment in manufacturing infrastructure, transparent policies, and strong regulatory regimes.[34] The EDB strategy paid off in electronics components and IT, which became two of Singapore's largest export sectors. U.S.-based hard disk drive firms, initially led by Silicon Valley's Seagate, located manufacturing plants in Singapore during the early 1980s. Other MNCs, notably Texas Instruments, set up chip assembly plants as early as the 1970s. These early efforts paved the way for a joint venture between the GLC Singapore Technology Group and American firms National Semiconductor and Sierra Semiconductor. The presence of foreign electronics and IT firms stimulated the growth of local SMEs, which primarily serviced the MNC sector through supply chain linkages. The large presence of MNCs was also intended to be a "conduit for transfer of advanced technology" into Singapore. Results were mixed, however, on that front. Some upward R&D spillover was realized (i.e., the development of R&D capacities),[35] though the state was unable to compel or stipulate that foreign firms be required to promote technology transfer for the purposes of local commercialization.[36] Singapore was suited for skilled manufacturing.[37]

Mitigating Risk

The postwar developmental state was effective at mitigating the risks of industrial upgrading. As Evans puts it, the developmental state nurtured "entrepreneurial perspectives among private elites by increasing incentives to engage in transformative investments and lowering the risks involved in such investments."[38] East Asian political economist Yun-Han Chu goes so far as to

---

34. David McKendrick, Richard Doner, and Stephan Haggard, *From Silicon Valley to Singapore: Location and Competitive Advantage in the Hard Disk Drive Industry* (Stanford, Calif.: Stanford University Press, 2000), 37.

35. Alice Amsden and F. Ted Tschang, "A New Approach to Assessing the Technological Complexity of Different Categories of R&D (with examples from Singapore)," *Research Policy* 32 (2003).

36. Matthews and Cho, *Tiger Technology*, 211–220.

37. In their study of the hard disk drive sector, David McKendrick, Richard Doner, and Stephan Haggard make a distinction between "operational" and "technological" clusters. Singapore was selected to be an operational cluster for the HDD sector, while the industry's technological cluster by and large remained in the United States. See McKendrick, Doner, and Haggard, *From Silicon Valley to Singapore*. This observation is also emphasized in Amsden and Tschang, "New Approach."

38. Peter Evans, "Predatory, Developmental and Other Apparatuses: A Comparative Political Economy Perspective on the Third World State," *Sociological Forum* 4 (1989), 562–563.

say that in Korea the "chaebol were able to expand rapidly and aggressively because they faced a basically risk-free environment."[39] But what exactly is meant by risk? Economists understand risk to be a quantifiable calculation of the likelihood of a certain outcome. Risk is conceived as a probability distribution. Risk calculations therefore presuppose that one has a most preferred outcome and that one attaches values to a range of potential outcomes, even if the likelihood of such outcomes is far from certain. It is because of this that economists see risk as an intrinsic characteristic of the market economy. Indeed, imperfect information and knowledge among actors (both buyers and sellers) limits certainty. Contingencies have to be accounted for. Risk is so ubiquitous in the market that firms build risk into their business models as a fixed cost. Mitigating risk, therefore, is about *knowing, and if possible increasing, the probability of success.*

What makes a proposition risky is the unknown, to be sure. Yet economists remind us that in all risk scenarios there are many things one does in fact know, which helps decision makers calculate the probability or odds of certain outcomes. First, risk entails what Frank Knight referred to as "known unknowns," that is to say, the decision maker or risk taker is at least aware of what she does not know or about what he has imperfect information. Such awareness, for obvious reasons, is critical. Second, decision makers know what are the preferred outcomes of any risk scenario, knowledge that is derived from a prior valuation of the range of potential outcomes. And third, because risk is conceptualized as a probability distribution, decision makers can use existing information to estimate the likelihood of certain outcomes, to have some sense of the odds—good or bad—of preferred outcomes.[40] Data and technical knowledge, for instance, are important for evaluating risk propositions because they help risk takers better understand the causal relationships they are attempting to forecast.[41] Knowing the science involved in a technological breakthrough, building on existing knowledge, and devising a theoretical model for a particular application of a technology are forms of relevant information that help one calculate the probability of, for example, a successful commercial outcome. While in real-world situations risk

---

39. Yun-Han Chu, "Surviving the East Asian Financial Storm," in *The Politics of the Asian Economic Crisis*, ed. T. J. Pempel (Ithaca: Cornell University Press, 1999), 201.

40. Frank Knight, *Risk, Uncertainty and Profit* (New York: Houghton Mifflin, 1921).

41. As Lewis Branscomb and Philip Auerswald explain, "it is not possible...to talk meaningfully about a given project having a 'ten percent probability of success' in the absence of some accumulated prior experience (such as a sample of similar projects of which nine in ten were failures)." See Branscomb and Auerswald, *Taking Technical Risks: How Innovators, Executives and Investors Manage High-Tech Risks* (Cambridge, Mass.: MIT Press, 2001), 44.

takers can only roughly estimate the probability of certain outcomes, theirs are nonetheless educated guesses about the future informed by the past and relevant knowledge. Risk propositions are those for which decisions are not complete shots in the dark.

Thinking about the Asian postwar experience from the perspective of risk, then, one can argue that the growth of the electronics and information technologies sectors in Korea, Taiwan, and Singapore was facilitated by what I have described as the postwar developmental state's efforts to mitigate risk. Despite key variations among the three cases, the strategic approach each took was very similar: the state was central in mitigating the risks of entry for firms and technologists in new sectors. The absence of complete certainty notwithstanding, strategic decision makers in Korea, Taiwan, and Singapore enjoyed a significant amount of knowledge about their prospects for successfully entering the electronics and IT sectors. Alice Amsden and Wan-Wen Chu offer an important observation about Taiwan—an observation that can be extended to other economies in the region—when they suggest that there was a fair degree of technological certainty in Taiwan's efforts to industrially upgrade during the postwar period. By technological certainty, Amsden and Chu mean that Taiwan by and large imported proven technologies from abroad, which were then copied, reverse-engineered, and in time improved on for export.[42] Taiwan and other late developers in the region, such as Korea and Singapore, benefited from second-mover advantages; they exploited "mature technologies."[43] Moreover, technology acquisition also centered on sectors for which there was a preexisting "pathway of learning" among engineers and entrepreneurs.[44] The adoption of advanced informatics, for instance, was built on already accumulated expertise in the electronics sector and more rudimentary experience in the IT sector. High-tech industrialization in Korea, Taiwan, and Singapore was afforded by the accumulation of existing knowledge rather than the assimilation of completely new knowledge bases; in short, they copied.[45]

The risks of industrial upgrading in East Asia were due to what Amsden and Chu call the economic unknown. What was unknown to decision makers

---

42. Alice Amsden and Wan-Wen Chu, *Beyond Late Development: Taiwan's Upgrading Policies* (Cambridge, Mass.: MIT Press, 2003).

43. Marie Anchordoguy, *Reprogramming Japan: The High-Tech Crisis under Communitarian Capitalism* (Ithaca: Cornell University Press, 2005).

44. Amsden and Chu, *Beyond Late Development*.

45. Vincent Wang explains that Taiwan's entry into the information and communication technologies sector was "an outgrowth of previous successive development strategies," not a "detached "new" sector...without any links to the economy at large. Wang, "Developing the Information Industry," 552.

was whether investments in specific sectors or technologies or even firms would create timely economic returns. There was, in other words, economic risk. However, several factors mitigated this risk. First, market demand was relatively clear. The auto sector, electronics components, and semiconductors were proven markets. As Poh-Kam Wong reasons, the fact that technology upgrading in East Asia was based on a strategy of reverse engineering existing technologies and products meant that markets were effectively guaranteed.[46] Dan Breznitz, in his study on innovation and the state, argues that late movers enjoyed the "double advantages of knowing the market, and accordingly being able to predict needs fairly accurately."[47] Second, industrial upgrading focused on niche areas on the value chain that were relatively close to market, such as in skilled manufacturing or the production side of high-tech industry. The producer's distance to market was narrowed because development centered on engineering problems rather than commercializing novel technologies. Near-market technology development strategies also ensured that economic returns would generally be quick. Not only were investments recouped in the nearer term, but failed upgrading initiatives could be identified relatively quickly and adjustments made. Stakeholders could exit without having sunk overwhelming resources into a losing sector, technology, or firm.

Third, and perhaps most important, the centralized postwar developmental state coordinated the allocation of public resources to lower firms' costs of entry into technology-based industries. In doing so, it absorbed, manipulated, and mitigated the risks of industrial upgrading. The state, for instance, subsidized fiscal and credit-based incentives to lower firms' up-front investments and other loss-leader transaction costs. Industrial technology R&D was by and large funded from public sources. The state was the primary investor in industrial infrastructure with direct investments or indirectly through state-owned enterprises and government-linked corporations. It leveraged its credibility and resources to acquire technologies from abroad. The state also structured domestic competition in order to manufacture winners. It coordinated the development of supply chain networks among firms, in effect creating markets at home and globally. As Amsden famously remarked, the state essentially got the prices "wrong," both to correct for anticipated market failures and to construct markets for potentially enterprising firms.[48]

---

46. Poh-Kam Wong, "Singapore's Technology Strategy," in *The Emerging Technological Trajectory in the Pacific Rim,* ed. Denis Fred Simon (Armonk, N.Y.: M. E. Sharpe, 1995).

47. Breznitz, *Innovation and the State,* 13.

48. Alice Amsden, *Asia's Next Giant: South Korea and Late Industrialization* (New York: Oxford University Press, 1989).

In other words, the state picked and made winners, not by eliminating risk but by mitigating it, and by increasing the probability of success for chosen sectors, technologies, and even firms.

Thus, when Samsung boldly announced its intention to enter the competitive semiconductor industry during the early 1980s, it was a move that of course entailed risk. But stakeholders there had some sense of the likelihood of Korea's eventual success in the sector. They knew they had a technology that worked. They were relatively certain that there was demand for their goods, especially after the yen was revalued in 1985, pricing Japanese exports out of the market. They also knew that wage restraints and the economies of scale in chaebol firms allowed them to manufacture chips at competitive prices. And they were assured by the state that it would "husband" Samsung's entry into the sector. Though the move was risky, stakeholders in Korea had enough information—relative certainties, as it were—to reasonably forecast the probability of success and increase that probability through strategic state interventions.

The key point is not that the process of industrial upgrading into high-tech sectors was easy, nor was it a foregone conclusion by any stretch in postwar Korea, Taiwan, and Singapore. If it had been, then late-developing countries in other regions would have similarly climbed the industrial value chain. Rather, while the prospect of successful industrial upgrading was always a high-risk bet, the developmental state was both willing and able to strategically intervene in ways that increased the chances of success, such that the odds were stacked more favorably.[49] The allocation of state resources lowered the entry barriers for industry by offsetting costs and absorbing the potential costs of risk taking. In short, picking winners to make meant that the state created relatively surer bets.

Biotechnology and Uncertainty

Betting on biotech is different. The cutting-edge frontier of the knowledge economy—whether in biotechnology, nanotechnology, advanced information and communication technologies, or other science-based businesses—and the ability to forecast innovative outcomes in these industries are characterized less by risk and more by primary uncertainty.[50] On the supply side,

---

49. Kim, "National Systems of Industrial Innovation," 376–377.

50. Gary Pisano, *Science Business: The Promise, the Reality and the Future of Biotech* (Boston: Harvard Business School Press, 2006), 7–8. Pisano elaborates: "In science-based business, R&D confronts fundamental questions about technical feasibility. Is it possible to express a protein in a bacteria cell? Is it possible to culture mammalian cells in vitro? What genes are involved in depression? Which biochemical pathways are involved in inflammation?...These are the types of questions with which science-based business in biotechnology have had to grapple. Not only are such questions difficult

for instance, there is tremendous technological uncertainty in first-order innovation. Upstream knowledge is too raw, unrefined, and far from market to provide clues about how scientific discoveries might translate into real-world commercial applications.[51] Similarly, on the demand side, tremendous economic uncertainty surrounds potential commercial applications of new knowledge and technologies. Demand-side uncertainty rests in the difficulties by which market actors are able to forecast the economic value of basic research. Economists have long shown that the appropriability and economic valuation of new upstream discoveries are inherently prone to market failure.[52] The long distance to market of new knowledge confounds prospective market demand.

Primary uncertainty is not simply a matter of higher and greater risk, however. Rather, my point is that this sort of uncertainty eludes from the start the calculability of risk. Conditions of uncertainty in first-order innovation, unlike risk propositions in technological upgrading, are those for which very little data, theory, or even a sense of eventual value exist from which to infer the probability of certain outcomes. Stakeholders in Korea, Taiwan, and Singapore have scant sense of the probability of success in commercial biotech, never mind any confidence about how to increase that probability. Biotech innovation thus entails conditions of uncertainty that are qualitatively different from those of risk scenarios, demanding qualitatively different bets by stakeholders and decision makers. Put simply, risk can be mitigated while uncertainty cannot. Picking winners in risk scenarios is an informed bet based on calculable probabilities, whereas picking winners in completely uncertain circumstances is more or less a game of chance, or as Knight put it, "pure guesswork."[53] Success in new science-based industries is about "possibility rather than probability."[54]

---

to answer, but the attempt to answer them leads, in all likelihood, to more questions—or to unexpected results."

51. Johan Brink, Maureen McKelvey, and Keith Smith, "Conceptualizing and Measuring Modern Biotechnology," in *The Economic Dynamics of Modern Biotechnology*, ed. Maureen McKelvey, Annika Rickne, and Jens Laage-Hellman (Northampton, Mass.: Edward Elgar, 2004).

52. See John Kay, "Technology and Wealth Creation: Where We Are and Where We're Going," *Other,* December 19, 2000; J. S. Metcalfe, "Science Policy and Technology Policy in a Competitive Economy," *International Journal of Social Economics* 24 (1997), 728; Kevin Murphy and Robert Topel, eds., *Measuring the Gains from Medical Research: An Economic Approach* (Chicago: University of Chicago Press, 2003); Partha Dasgupta and Paul David, "Toward a New Economics of Science," *Research Policy* 23 (1994), 490; Kenneth Arrow, "Economic Welfare and the Allocation of Resources for Inventions," in *The Rate and Direction of Inventive Activity,* ed. Richard Nelson (Princeton, N.J.: Princeton University Press, 1962); Evan Berman, "The Economic Impact of Industry-Funded University R&D," *Research Policy* 19 (1990).

53. Knight, *Risk,* 250.

54. Seongjae Yu, "Korea's High Technology Thrust," in *The Emerging Technological Trajectory of the Pacific Rim,* ed. Denis Simon (Armonk, N.Y.: M. E. Sharpe, 1995), 85.

Uncertainty in biotech commercialization is exacerbated by the under-whelming performance of the global biotech sector to date. The promise of health biotech first emerged during the 1970s, when scientists anticipated that the biological rather than the synthetic chemistry "heuristic" would allow researchers to better understand the biomechanisms of illness and dis-ease. This turn marked the beginning of what innovation scholars call a new "technological paradigm."[55] New ways of diagnosing disease were explored, and it was thought that genomic techniques would enable researchers to identify and match drug targets and compounds. The completion of the human genome project in 2003 unveiled the most comprehensive map of the genetic make-up of humans. The further development of recombinant DNA (rDNA) technology meant that proteins could be synthesized in the lab for drug therapies. Knowing the biological structure of disease and ill-ness raised the possibility that drug screening could be rational, targeted, and efficient, an approach believed to be superior to the existing model of random screening, or "molecular roulette."[56] Health biotech and the bio-logical heuristic were envisioned as the new platform or enabling technol-ogy for rapid advancements in health and the health care industry. The health care industry was to be revolutionized, and governments, researchers, entrepreneurs, venture capitalists, and popular hype fueled the commercial biotech race.

Despite such promise, biotech has failed to live up to the lofty expecta-tions of the 1970s and 1980s. Both R&D and industrial performance in the sector have been underwhelming. For instance, R&D productivity and new drug discovery through biotechnology techniques have been much lower than expected. Biotech-facilitated candidates have not fared as well in clinical trials as initially predicted. Biotech's clinical efficacy also remains uncertain. While the prospects of commercial biotech prompted the re-structuring of the pharmaceutical industry—notably the rapid growth of small biotech firms providing leads for established drug firms—the com-mercial returns from biotech have been much slower than expected and very small compared with the rate and size of investment in the sector. In fact, as of 2005, relatively few biotech products had come to market and profitability in the American-based industry had flatlined.[57] As Michael

---

55. G. Dosi, "Technological Paradigms and Technological Trajectories: A Suggested Interpreta-tion of the Determinants and Directions of Technological Change," *Research Policy* 11 (1982).

56. Michael Hopkins, Paul Martin, Paul Nightingale, Alison Kraft, and Surya Mahdi, "The Myth of the Biotech Revolution: An Assessment of Technological, Clinical and Organisational Change," *Research Policy* 36 (2007), 568.

57. Pisano, *Science Business,* 112–115.

Hopkins and his colleagues put it, "widely held expectations about the impact of biotechnology are over-optimistic."[58]

Global trends in commercial biotech development mirror trends in industrial Asia. As relatively recent entrants in the life sciences field, Korea, Taiwan, and Singapore have understandably struggled in their efforts to grow their bio-industries. The cutting edge of bio-industry there is contracting. Innovative firms are not surviving. Risk capital has become very cautious, a position that was accentuated after the 2001 dot-com bust. And stakeholders there, increasingly frustrated with the slow rate of return, are beginning to question the viability of the long-term bet on biotech. Indeed, the underwhelming performance of the sector globally and domestically has inspired less and less confidence among stakeholders, exacerbating the uncertainties surrounding innovative commercial biotech. Prospects are bleak even after two decades of investment. Stakeholders have little sense of which R&D and business models work best. They have little to go on with respect to due diligence or even the means for benchmarking and measuring progress. There are few models to emulate, given the lack of blockbusters in the industry. In other words, the poor performance of the sector has provided so little clarity about the sector that decision makers are not able to get any feel for the probability of success, and they have even less sense of how to increase that probability.

The challenges of managing uncertainty in commercial biotech innovation are derived, I contend, from the nature of the science itself. As with other science-based industries, biotech's uncertainties are technological, economic, and temporal. The basis of *technological uncertainty* in biotech innovation stems from the unintegrated, multidisciplinary nature of the field. Biotech innovation requires expertise from different scientific fields (biology, chemistry, physics), engineering (applied problem solving), and industry, including intellectual property management, venture firm strategy, legal policy, and regulatory sciences. Its multidisciplinarity also means that specialized skills and expertise are institutionally disparate, divided among many stakeholders.[59] And yet innovative biotech R&D demands interaction and collaboration among these disparate groups of expert stakeholders. The fact that biotech is considered an enabling or platform technology for both upstream researchers and downstream entrepreneurs means that the biotech R&D process is neither linear nor unidirectional. Rather, bio-industrial R&D continually

---

58. Hopkins et al., "Myth of the Biotech Revolution," 584.
59. Branscomb and Auerswald, *Taking Technical Risks.*

moves up, down, and across various R&D agendas, making the likelihood of a technological breakthrough even more uncertain.[60]

Biotechnology's demand-side *economic uncertainties* are equally pronounced. As with all science-based industries, commercializing biotech, a technology that is far from mature, encounters the inherent problems of valuing knowledge, identifying market demand, and forecasting market potential for such knowledge.[61] Gary Pisano notes: "Consider the problem of valuation. Existing financial modeling methodologies are of little help: they rely on an analysis of historical earnings and earnings potential. Most biotech companies have no earnings (let alone an earnings history), and with nearest products several years away and facing enormous technical and commercial uncertainty, it is hard to construct any reasonable valuation model."[62] What Pisano means is that the commercial biotech market remains undeveloped. The array of industrial applications of biotech is vast. The potential value chain in commercial biotech is exceptionally long and, as yet, relatively undefined. Identifying commercially viable markets thus remains an open-ended endeavor.

Furthermore, because of the complexity and unintegrated nature of biotech innovation, the structure of the commercial biotech industry is one in which firms and labs are highly specialized and narrow in their R&D operations. On their own, these firms create little commercial value. Successful commercialization rests on the integration of these different bases of expertise with bits and pieces of knowledge. As an enabling technology in health care, for instance, biotech is useful insofar as there are applications that it can help deliver. As a platform technology, biotech can realize its integrative potential only if there are firms and labs working on biotech applications that can use this platform. Commercializing innovation thus requires not only the cultivation of disparate specialized knowledge but also the eventual integration of decentralized expertise in ways that "fit." The reality is that much of the innovative work in commercializing biotech takes place long

---

60. See Maureen McKelvey, Annika Rickne, and Jens Laage-Hellman, eds., *The Economic Dynamics of Modern Biotechnology* (Northampton, Mass.: Edward Elgar, 2004); Robert Kaiser and Heiko Prange, "The Reconfiguration of National Innovation Systems: The Example of German Biotechnology," *Research Policy* 33 (2004); Susanne Giesecke, "The Contrasting Roles of Government in the Development of Biotechnology Industry in the US and Germany," *Research Policy* 29 (2000).

61. The fact that, according to Luigi Orsenigo, market predictions during the 1990s for the biotech sector ranged from US$10 billion to US$60 billion reflects the problem of forecasting biotechnology's market potential. Orsenigo, "The Dynamics of Competition in a Science-Based Technology: The Case of Biotechnology," in *Technology and the Wealth of Nations*, ed. Dominique Foray and Christopher Freeman (New York: Pinter, 1993), 43.

62. Pisano, *Science Business,* 143.

before the technology is even considered market-ready. Biotech's distance to market exacerbates economic uncertainty.

The story of Celera Genomics illustrates the problem. Based in the United States, Celera was the first private firm to map the human genome. The firm developed in tandem, and indeed in competition, with the U.S. government's efforts in leading the worldwide human genome project. When the human genome map was completed, Celera was sure customers would demand access to this new genetic knowledge. Celera quickly learned, however, that its original business plan to sell its proprietary genomic information was flawed. Though the firm was on the cutting edge of life sciences R&D, too few customers were buying Celera's product. The information business of life sciences, which made good commercial sense in the abstract, failed. Despite forecasts to the contrary, Celera's product commanded little market value. In 2000, Celera shares sold for US$200. By the end of 2002, share prices had fallen to just US$20, one-tenth the value. Even what seemed to be the most commercially certain of enterprises, a good bet backed by good science, succumbed to commercial biotech's economic uncertainty.[63]

Biotech's long distance to market is a source of *temporal uncertainty*. Commercializing innovative biotech is a very long-term enterprise, and success is a long shot. And for recent entrants to the sector such as Korea, Taiwan, and Singapore, the temporal horizon looms even longer. The implications of distance to market exacerbate biotech's uncertainties in several ways. For one, the regulatory demands of the sector mean that premarket regulatory regimes governing ethics, standards, R&D, and product development not only lengthen biotech's distance to market but also add to the potential obstacles to the commercialization of new biotech products and services. The problem of regulatory obstacles is compounded, I argue in Chapter 5, if regulatory policies are not coherent and consistently enforced. Second, and from a more political point of view, the sector's long distance to market continually tests stakeholders' commitment to growing innovative bio-industries. As alluded to above, the sector's poor performance in Korea, Taiwan, and Singapore has dampened people's confidence about its prospects and exacerbated its uncertainties. Coping with such uncertainty indefinitely is inconceivable and, more precisely, as I show in Chapter 4, politically unfeasible. Thus, biotech innovation requires political strategies to sustain a nation's appetite for uncertainty over the *very* long term. It requires that strategic stakeholders manage expectations, rationalize sunk investments and year-over-year losses, and,

---

63. See Ingrid Wickelgren, *The Gene Masters: How a New Breed of Scientific Entrepreneurs Races for the Biggest Prize in Biology* (New York: Times Books, 2002).

most pressing, normalize failure in bio-industrial endeavors. All the while, stakeholders are confronted with the question, "How long is long enough?" Betting on biotech means that decision makers have to gauge when the time is right to cut their losses, admit failure, and move on, a choice that has rarely been explored in the experience of the postwar developmental state.

Managing Uncertainty

Betting on the biotech sector more broadly is one thing, but making specific bets in what is a technologically, economically, and temporally uncertain industry is another. As I have argued, conceiving of biotech innovation in terms of primary uncertainty implies that decision makers have little to go on in how they make strategic choices. Which technologies in the life sciences ought to be targeted and how? What R&D capacities need to be facilitated? What regulatory policies should be implemented and by what criteria? How should resources be allocated and according to what rationale? Primary uncertainty obscures clarity with respect to these core questions of policy, resource allocation, and industrial strategy. In other words, managing uncertainty is a tall order because primary uncertainty precludes such manageability.

Economists tell us that one plausible way out of this conundrum is to leverage the economies of scope and scale. Economic actors should allocate resources broadly and indiscriminately, diversifying the scope of activity across an entire industrial field and diffusing the costs of such activity among many actors. From this process, universes of "like cases" can be assembled, out of which relevant data and knowledge are gathered. Specialization, diversification, diffusion, and then consolidation in uncertain ventures provide a history that decision makers can use to infer ways to manage uncertainty. Scale is essential, however. The ability to bet indiscriminately is also critical. But the reality is that it is also inconceivable in many economies, the exceptions being perhaps the United States and giant latecomers such as China. Rather, the challenge for Korea, Taiwan, and Singapore, and virtually all other aspirants in the biotech sector, is to bet *discriminately* and thus strategically. But how?

Despite an enormous—and still growing—multidisciplinary literature on technology innovation, theory provides few answers about how decision makers can go about dealing with the uncertainties inherent in first-order innovation. The national innovation systems framework provides considerable insight into the process of connecting disparate actors and experts to bridge the gaps in translating science into applied technologies, in long-term financing of new inventive products and services, and in people-to-people social networks and clusters.[64] Innovation, we know, is an intensely interactive enterprise, and one that is determined by people and the institutional complexes that shape people's behaviors, their incentives, and their interactions.[65] Interactions are also local and global.[66] However, innovation systems theory tends to be empirically rich and analytically descriptive rather than predictive-theoretical. To correct this, the varieties-of-capitalism framework developed by Peter Hall and David Soskice attempts to provide some causal claims between certain institutional designs and innovation outcomes.[67] And while their assertions intuitively make sense—for instance, the basis of financial markets determines incremental versus radical innovations—the empirical evidence does not hold up across all sectors and all national contexts.[68] In other words, theory does not inform confident claims about how to bet on innovation and specifically on biotech innovation.

Indeed, the inherent uncertainties of first-order innovation obscure theoretical and prescriptive precision. Instinctively, for example, intellectual property (IP) protection might seem to be an institutional foundation for any innovation system, though empirical studies have shown that the effect of IP regimes varies by sector. The presumed positive effects of the 1980 Bayh-Dole Act, a landmark policy initiative that permits closer commercial linkages to be formed between the academy and industry, have also been brought into question.[69] In the commercial biotech sector specifically, stakeholders are increasingly questioning the relevance and applicability of the venture financing model developed in the information technology sector, just as strategic planners inside global pharmaceutical firms increasingly wonder

---

64. See Richard Nelson, ed., *National Innovation Systems* (New York: Oxford University Press, 1993); Donald Stokes, *Pasteur's Quadrant: Basic Science and Technological Innovation* (Washington, D.C.: Brookings Institution, 1997); Branscomb and Auerswald, *Taking Technical Risks.*

65. For a more thorough review of institutional effects on technological innovation, see J. Rogers Hollingsworth, "Doing Institutional Analysis: Implications for the Study of Innovations," *Review of International Political Economy* 7 (2000).

66. See Steven Casper, *Creating Silicon Valley in Europe: Public Policy towards New Technology Industries* (New York: Oxford University Press, 2007); Daniele Archibugi and Simona Iammarino, "The Policy Implications of the Globalization of Innovation," *Research Policy* 28 (1999); Michael Porter, "Clusters and the New Economics of Competition," *Harvard Business Review,* November–December 1998.

67. Peter Hall and David Soskice, eds., *Varieties of Capitalism: The Institutional Foundations of Comparative Advantage* (New York: Oxford University Press, 2001).

68. See, for instance, Mark Zachary Taylor, "Empirical Evidence against Varieties of Capitalism's Theory of Technological Innovation," *International Organization* 58 (2004); Dirk Akkermans, Carolina Castaldi, and Bart Los, "Do 'Liberal Market Economies' Really Innovate More Radically than 'Coordinated Market Economies'? Hall and Soskice Reconsidered," *Research Policy* 38 (2009).

69. David Mowery, Richard Nelson, Bhaven Sampat, and Arvids Ziedonis, eds., *Ivory Tower and Industrial Innovation: University-Industry Technology Transfer Before and After the Bayh-Dole Act in the United States* (Stanford, Calif.: Stanford University Press, 2004).

about firm best practices regarding the development or acquisition of biotech leads. Susanne Giesecke captures this conundrum when she observes that

> [biotechnology's] specific features include the length and especially the uncertainty of races to find new compounds. This search involves extensive time horizons that are due to strict safety regulations and thereby cause high capital intensity. At the same time, biotechnology is a high-risk technology, economically as well as technically. Thus, an enabling institutional arrangement has to provide for the maximum containment of those economic, technical and safety risks. These specific features—time intensity, uncertainty, capital intensity and risks— are inherent to the path of biotechnical development.[70]

The point is that biotech's uncertainties—and the inherent uncertainty of science-based industries more generally—beget further organizational, institutional, and strategic uncertainties. Theories thus provide important analytical guideposts, but in the end, adapting to the realities of uncertainty and the innovation economy involves continual experimentation and learning among decision makers and stakeholders.[71] As Bengt-Ake Lundvall puts it, it is the "ongoing processes of learning, searching and exploring which result in new products, new techniques, new forms of organization and new markets."[72] Dani Rodrik similarly asserts that technology innovation systems and innovation best practices cannot simply be imported from abroad and transposed and replicated at home. Rather, he argues, the strategic and institutional bases of an innovation system are ultimately shaped "locally, relying on hands-on experience, local knowledge and experimentation."[73] To experiment and to gain experience means that strategic decision makers have *to do something* and they have to *rationalize their decisions*. Doing nothing is not an option; they have to make choices.

70. Giesecke, "Contrasting Roles of Government," 209–210.

71. In her study of the origins of life sciences technology transfer at Stanford University, Jeannette Colyvas contends that the early institutionalization of Stanford's program resulted from experimentation with four contending organizational models, reflecting different interests and understandings of research collaboration. See Jeannette Colyvas, "From Divergent Meanings to Common Practices: The Early Institutionalization of Technology Transfer in the Life Sciences at Stanford University," *Research Policy* 36 (2007), 474.

72. Bengt-Ake Lundvall, ed., *National Systems of Innovation: Towards a Theory of Innovation and Interactive Learning* (London: Pinter, 1992), 8.

73. Dani Rodrik, *One Economics, Many Recipes: Globalization, Institutions and Economic Growth* (Princeton, N.J.: Princeton University Press, 2007), 164.

The rest of this book examines what "doing something" has actually entailed in Korea, Taiwan, and Singapore since they ramped up efforts to make it in the commercial biotech sector. The book essentially tells two stories, both of which I briefly foreground here. The first is a story of continuities. Decision makers in Korea, Taiwan, and Singapore have continued to make policies and allocate resources in ways not dissimilar to the earlier periods of industrial upgrading in the developmental state. In some respects, stakeholders have attempted to manage biotech's uncertainties by adhering to past practices in mitigating risk. The second story, however, is one of significant change and discontinuity. More specifically, the evidence from Korea, Taiwan, and Singapore reveals a fundamentally changing role of the developmentally oriented state, reflecting the ways in which first-order innovation in commercial biotech is a qualitatively different political economic endeavor than in the past and demonstrating that betting in bio-industrial development requires different strategic rationalizations.

Old Wine in New Bottles?

Decision makers in Korea, Taiwan, and Singapore are very aware of the technological, economic, and temporal uncertainties of commercial biotech innovation. Invariably, stakeholder informants in all three places (and elsewhere as well) express to me their frustration over these sorts of uncertainties and what to do about them. The fact that Korea, Taiwan, and Singapore have invested billions of dollars in the sector—an investment that in the past would have inspired great confidence for success—and have seen, as yet, relatively little economic return only exacerbates such feelings of frustration. Still, they recognize that they need to do something to facilitate commercial biotech innovation. As in the postwar period of industrial upgrading, biotech stakeholders continue to believe that the state *can* help create an environment that is conducive to the distant and unpredictable possibilities of breakthrough innovations.

The state in all three places has similarly increased its financial commitment to upstream life sciences R&D, not only with research dollars but also with major investments in infrastructure. The government in Korea, Taiwan, and Singapore has, for instance, paid significant attention to regulatory reform, from intellectual property protection to clinical regulation. It has directed resources to encourage industry to take on a larger share in the biotech R&D pie. The state has also explicitly encouraged technology transfer and the deepening of linkages between the academy and industry to narrow the research gap in technological innovation. Specifically, it has relaxed

regulations that had earlier impeded the flow of knowledge and people between the public and private sectors, and the governments in all three places
have taken an active role in creating new technology transfer mechanisms
inside public R&D institutions.

With respect to growing firms, the state in Korea, Taiwan, and Singapore
has provided myriad incentives, including fiscal and credit subsidies, to lure
private sector investment into science-based industries. In fact, as I argue in
Chapter 4, the state has invested heavily in creating biotech "stars" and national champions in industry and R&D. In all three places, public resources
have also been allocated directly and indirectly to the venture capital sector,
and state regulations have been relaxed specifically to encourage bio-venture
investment. Meanwhile, financial policies have similarly been reformed in
order to channel more private sector investment into high-risk technology
sectors: secondary stock markets have been created, mergers and acquisitions
regulations have been revised, and the initial public offering (IPO) process
has been reformed, thus providing early-stage venture investors a larger menu
of exit options.

Variations in past practices among Korea, Taiwan, and Singapore have also
persisted into the era of biotechnology. The evidence presented in Chapters 2
and 3 shows how strategic decision makers have not veered far from existing strategic repertoires of policy interventions and models of industrial
organization. Stakeholders in Korea, for example, have continued to pin the
future of commercial biotech innovation on the chaebol sector and its scale
advantages. Managing uncertainty in Taiwan has continued to rely on a hit-
and-miss strategy for identifying potential leads inside midstream technology
development centers such as the ITRI. And decision makers in Singapore
aim to continue attracting multinational firms, rather than creating homegrown innovators, by spending on and strengthening the city-state's existing
locational advantages. In each case, decision makers have approached the
challenges of managing uncertainty by reverting to existing scripts that had
helped them mitigate risk so well in the past. The legacies of the postwar
developmental state have persisted into the present, and the specific imprint
of each country's unique developmental experiences has also endured.

But this should not be surprising. An influential body of empirical research shows that under conditions of primary uncertainty, decision makers
rely on heuristic biases—beliefs, values, cognitive shortcuts, repertoires—to
help them navigate what they otherwise know little about. According to
economics Nobel laureate Daniel Kahneman, decision makers cope with uncertainty by making decisions as though they can in fact manage it. Heuristic
biases, scripts, or strategic repertoires allow decision makers to cognitively

transform otherwise unmanageable realities of primary uncertainty into what they *believe* to be more manageable risk propositions.[74] Biotech stakeholders in Korea, Taiwan, and Singapore have reverted to what they know best and what they know worked in the past to help them make strategic choices in the face of what in reality is a tremendously uncertain technical and commercial endeavor. Therefore, one way to think of this first story is that strategic decision making in the era of science-based industrialization in Korea, Taiwan, and Singapore is merely "old wine in new bottles." There is obviously some truth to that characterization, as we would be naive to think that decision makers today are working from a strategic tabula rasa.

But the evidence presented in this book also suggests that amid such continuity, there is something more fundamentally transformative going on in Korea, Taiwan, and Singapore. Decision makers, particularly those inside the state, have had to make significant adjustments and to articulate new strategic rationalizations about the role of the state in the face of such uncertainty. What has occurred over the past twenty years or so in Korea, Taiwan, and Singapore in terms of science-based industrial development is therefore not merely old wine in new bottles. The enduring scripts, strategic repertoires, and heuristic biases described above notwithstanding, there has also been a fundamental transformation in the very idea of the developmental state. The strategic logic of the postwar experience in state-led economic development has been altered.

First, in all three cases, the state has retreated from its past leadership role in directing industrial upgrading, and economic development more generally, from the top down. It continues to allocate resources to facilitate new industrial endeavors. But frankly, this sort of government intervention is not unique to places such as Korea, Taiwan, and Singapore. All states—even the leanest of the liberal market economies such as the United States—pour massive amounts of public resources into new industry development. Rather, what always stood out among the Asian cases was that the developmental state proactively picked winners and, in doing so, bore the heavy costs of risk inherent in industrial upgrading. But this, I suggest, is no longer the case. The state has strategically refrained from picking winners in commercial biotech. In fact, it has proactively shifted uncertainty to other stakeholders.

Second, the long-term realities and related uncertainties of biotech innovation have compelled decision makers in Korea, Taiwan, and Singapore to

---

74. Daniel Kahneman and Amos Tversky, "Judgment under Uncertainty: Heuristics and Biases," *Science* 185 (1974); David Moss, *When All Else Fails: Government as the Ultimate Risk Manager* (Cambridge, Mass.: Harvard University Press, 2004), 40–41.

significantly scale back past practices in actively coordinating industrial activity. The hallmark of the developmental state was its capacity and willingness to coordinate actors in productive ways, using various state incentives, its close interactions with industry, and strategic industrial policies. The developmental state also actively forged linkages among public and private actors. The founding of Taiwan's TSMC is a perfect example of the developmental state's coordinative capacity for growing firms and its willingness to use it. The approach to biotech innovation, however, rests more on the long-term potentiality that such linkages will form over time than on strategic decision makers coordinating such linkages from the top down. Put another way, the state has helped put the pieces of the biotech sector in place but has left putting those pieces together to others.

Third, the retreat of the state and its diminishing capacity to coordinate reflect a more general pattern in the diminished coherence and fragmentation of the state apparatus. The postwar developmental state was vertically organized, characterized by what Evans calls its "corporate coherence." However, as the following chapters show, this is no longer the case when it comes to life sciences innovation. Biotech stakeholders in Korea, Taiwan, and Singapore in fact comprise a wide range of actors with specialized knowledge and expertise, interests and priorities, both inside and outside the state apparatus. Corporate coherence has given way to greater fragmentation, institutional disparateness, contested policy agendas, and varied bases of expertise, which have, I argue, reshaped the processes of decision making.

The main objective of this chapter was to lay out a conceptual distinction between risk and uncertainty. Some may think the distinction, as I have argued it here, is a bit overstated. It is not as though we know *nothing* about biotechnology; and in reality, biotech's prospects are not what Knight theoretically saw as primary uncertainty. This is true. But as the basis for a framework, the distinction provides tremendous analytical utility. The reality for decision makers in Korea, Taiwan, and Singapore is that they themselves understand their current circumstances to be vastly different from what they confronted during earlier modes of industrial upgrading in the postwar period. They have experienced the prospects of growing bio-industry as profoundly uncertain. Whereas in the past, industrial upgrading centered on mature technologies with defined applications and market demand, biotech innovation entails an as yet undeveloped technology with very unclear market signals. The framework I have presented here thus helps illuminate how stakeholders and decision makers in Korea, Taiwan, and Singapore have had to make choices, make strategic bets, and articulate new rationalizations of those bets in their efforts to succeed in commercial biotech innovation. Indeed, without such a conceptual distinction between risk and primary uncertainty, one might see the empirical evidence in Asia as solely path-dependent continuities of past practices in mitigating risk—old wine in new bottles. And while this is one of the stories of biotech innovation in Korea, Taiwan, and Singapore, the distinction between risk and uncertainty permits a deeper story about a more fundamental transformation beyond the developmental state in the current era of science-based industrialization.

CHAPTER 2

Reorganizing the State

The postwar economic miracles in Korea, Taiwan, and Singapore were facilitated by the developmental state's strategic capacity and willingness to coordinate the allocation of resources in order to mitigate risk. By mitigating the risks of industrial upgrading, the state encouraged otherwise risk-averse entrepreneurs to develop new industrial competencies and competitive advantages in global markets. This chapter looks at the state in the specific context of biotech innovation and examines the extent to which earlier patterns of state intervention and state organization have endured in the current era of knowledge-based industrial development. The short answer is yes and no.

On the one hand, the state in Korea, Taiwan, and Singapore continues to allocate tremendous amounts of resources to the biotech sector and science-based industrial development. In terms of public sector inputs, the state's role has not diminished. With respect to biotech development, the state's share of the total R&D resource pie is disproportionately larger than in other technology sectors. In other words, patterns of state intervention have endured in terms of committing resources to facilitate the development of new industries such as commercial biotech. Current patterns of resource allocation by the state also reflect earlier state strategies distinctive to each of the three cases, an indicator of strategic continuity among them. Korea has continued to "go big," Taiwan has chosen to "go small," and Singapore has continued to "go global." In Korea, the state has maintained its strategy of providing a wealth of resources up and down the technology chain, from basic research to downstream commercialization. The government in Taiwan has stayed focused on midstream R&D, most notably in public research institutes (PRIs) such as the Industrial Technology Research Institute (ITRI). And the Singaporean state has continued to allocate public R&D resources to accentuate the city-state's locational advantages and to strengthen its domestic bio-industrial capacity with the goal of becoming an R&D hub for transnational biomedical firms. Decision makers tend to adhere to cognitive scripts and existing strategic repertoires when making difficult choices, especially when they are confronted with extraordinarily uncertain circumstances.

On the other hand, we see significant change and discontinuity in *how* resources are allocated, that is, the processes by which state-level stakeholders decide where resources are to be allocated and for what purposes. Unlike in the past, when decision-making processes and the strategic rationalizations for public resource allocation were centralized and concentrated among a few actors, the allocative process in biotech has become considerably more contested among stakeholders. This pattern is especially clear in Korea and Taiwan and is becoming increasingly evident in Singapore as well. The transformation is not insignificant with respect to the notion of strategic state leadership. Specifically, examining changes in how resources have been allocated for the development of biotech allows us to see how the state's coordinative capacity has diminished and how rationalizations about the state's "guiding" role have been transformed. Even in Singapore, where conventional wisdom suggests that decision-making processes remain concentrated and centralized, emerging conflicts over resource allocation in biomedical industry development are reshaping the state apparatus and the strategic role played by state-level decision makers; even there, the state is being reorganized in profound ways.

Dan Breznitz, in his study of innovation-based industrialization, asserts that the "state should no longer methodically plan the development of strategic industries by choosing specific products and product niches."[1] His observation is not merely an assertion about the IT sector; it also reflects the empirical evidence about biotech. But whereas Breznitz argues the state *should not* pick winners, my argument suggests that the diminishing coordinative capacity of the state in Korea, Taiwan, and Singapore means that it *cannot* pick winners any longer. More specifically, this chapter demonstrates

---

1. Dan Breznitz, *Innovation and the State: Political Choice and Strategies for Growth in Israel, Taiwan and Ireland* (New Haven, Conn.: Yale University Press, 2008), 29.

how the reorganization of the state's apparatus and its retreat from coordinating the biotech sector stems from (1) the decentralization of expertise among state-level actors, (2) the absence of institutional leadership inside the state apparatus, and (3) the articulation of new strategic rationalizations about the state's more modest role in managing biotech industry's technological, economic, and temporal uncertainties.

Laggard to Leader

We can get a better sense of patterns of continuity and change in the organization of the state in the era of biotech innovation and science-based industrialization by recalling the growth of science and technology capacity in Korea, Taiwan, and Singapore, a transformation that has seen these economies evolve from imitative followers to potential technology leaders. They have come a long way. During the immediate postwar period, there was little to speak of in terms of science and technology capacity in Korea, Taiwan, and Singapore. At that time, economic activity in all three places centered on labor-intensive, low value-added manufacturing, and there were no economic imperatives for deepening science and technology capacity. But by the 1980s, as we know, these economies had evolved into skillful technology absorbers. They had become adept technology imitators, leveraging their skills in engineering by assimilating second-generation technologies from abroad. More recently, Korea, Taiwan, and Singapore have shifted their science and technology focus toward becoming innovators, creators of cutting-edge technologies and applications, and ultimately generators of new markets. In all this, the state has maintained a critical supply-side role.

Inputs

Before the 1980s, when Korea, Taiwan, and Singapore had just begun to upgrade into higher-technology industrial sectors, total R&D spending was near zero. In fact, even by the early 1980s, total R&D spending ranged from between just 0.31% of GDP (Singapore) to 0.62% of GDP (Korea). To put these figures in comparative perspective, at that time, leading industrial nations such as the United States and Germany were already spending in excess of 2% of GDP on R&D.[2] But throughout the 1990s, R&D expenditure

2. Suni Mani, *Government, Innovation and Technology Policy: An International Comparative Analysis* (Northampton, Mass.: Edward Elgar, 2002), 91; Walter Arnold, "Science and Technology Development in Taiwan and South Korea," *Asian Survey* 28 (1988), 439; Science Council of Singapore,

growth rates in Asia were among the fastest in the world, such that by about 2005, R&D spending in Korea had reached 2.99% of GDP, in Taiwan 2.58%, and in Singapore 2.39%. While the private sector's share of R&D investment increased significantly during this time, accounting for between two-thirds and three-quarters of total spending in recent years, the public sector's absolute share of R&D spending grew considerably as well.

Such efforts have paid off. On virtually every measure, public inputs into science and technology development have contributed to significant gains in outputs. The number of research scientists and engineers (RSEs) has increased many times over in all three places. With respect to publications, Korea and Taiwan ranked among the world's top 20 in the Science Citation Index by around 2005 and Singapore stood at 29. Global rankings in the Engineering Citation Index demonstrate a similar pattern; in 2006, all three were ranked among or near the world's top 20. In terms of technological output measured in U.S. patents awarded, Taiwan and Korea were, respectively, fourth and fifth globally.[3] On most global ranking schemes, Singapore has lagged, to be sure, but when measured in terms of output (i.e., publications, patents) per capita, Singapore's R&D output performance has been equally strong, if not stronger than that of its larger comparators.

R&D spending is only one important input in the development of domestic science and technology capacity. An equally critical variable for the growth of a knowledge economy, and industrial upgrading more generally, is human capital development and the creation of talent. During the catch-up developmental phase in the postwar period, the state invested in human capital by universalizing primary education and making high school education more accessible.[4] In Korea, Taiwan, and Singapore, state-led efforts in educational reform and increased funding contributed to rapid enrollment growth

---

National Survey of R&D Expenditures and Manpower, 1981/2 (Singapore: Science Council of Singapore, 1983).

3. Data collected from A*STAR, *National Survey of R&D in Singapore, 2006* (Singapore: A*STAR, 2007); National Science Council (NSC), *Indicators of Science and Technology, 2007* (Taipei: NSC, 2007).

4. The World Bank shows that between 1960 and 1985, primary education was "by far the single largest contributor" to high economic growth rates in postwar Asia. World Bank, *The East Asian Miracle: Economic Growth and Public Policy* (New York: Oxford University Press, 1993), 52. During the immediate postindependence period in Singapore (early 1960s), for instance, education accounted for 27% of all social development expenditures, second only to public housing and greater than expenditures for health and social welfare combined. David Ng Foo Seong, "Strategic Management of Educational Development in Singapore (1965–2005)," in *Toward a Better Future: Education and Training for Economic Development in Singapore since 1965,* ed. Sing Kong Lee et al. (Washington, D.C.: World Bank, 2008).

throughout the 1960s and 1970s.[5] By the 1980s, greater emphasis was placed on postsecondary education and skills development, and enrollments sky-rocketed.[6] In Taiwan, for instance, enrollment rates in higher education increased from just 1.4% of the national population during the 1950s to nearly 39% in 1992.[7] A disproportionate number of university and college students in Korea, Taiwan, and Singapore favored and continue to favor engineering as their main field of study.[8] Solely domestic efforts to grow talent such as these are not enough, however. Having relatively small populations means that growing the talent pool domestically is a strategy that has its limits, a problem that can be exacerbated by the inevitability of brain drain. To deal with these scale-related problems, Taiwan has since the early 1980s proactively lured back skilled overseas Taiwanese.[9] Singapore's National Technology Plans of 1991 and 1996 were explicit about the imperatives of attracting foreign re-

---

5. Robert Wade, *Governing the Market: Economic Theory and the Role of Government in East Asian Industrialization* (Princeton, N.J.: Princeton University Press, 1990), 64; Alice Amsden, *Asia's Next Giant: South Korea and Late Industrialization* (New York: Oxford University Press, 1989), 218.

6. Molly Webb, *South Korea: Mass Innovation Comes of Age* (London: Demos, 2007), 23; see also Larry Westphal, Linsu Kim, and Carl Dahlman, "Reflections on the Republic of Korea's Acquisition of Technological Capability," in *International Technology Transfer: Concepts, Measure and Comparisons*, ed. Nathan Rosenberg and Claudio Frischtak (New York: Praeger, 1985), table 6.3.

7. Haider Khan, *Interpreting East Asian Growth and Innovation: The Future of Miracles* (New York: Palgrave Macmillan, 2004), 79.

8. Chng Meng Kng, Linda Low, Tay Boon Nga, and Amina Tyabji, *Technology and Skills in Singapore* (Singapore: Institute of Southeast Asian Studies, 1986), 41; Council for Economic Planning and Development, *Taiwan Statistical Data Book* (Taipei: CEPD, 1999), 275; Science Council of Singapore, *National Survey*, 41; Ministry of Education, Science, and Technology, Korea.

9. According to data compiled by AnnaLee Saxenian, only 407 overseas Taiwanese returned to Taiwan in 1970. In 1980, the figure had increased to 640. It grew rapidly thereafter, and in 1990, close to 2,900 Taiwanese returned. The return rate increased rapidly again during the early 1990s, peaking in 1994 with over 6,500 returnees, a trend that was driven by the weakening U.S. economy but also by government incentives and proactive recruiting efforts. AnnaLee Saxenian, "Taiwan's Hsinchu Region: Imitator and Partner for Silicon Valley," SIEPR Discussion Paper, No. 00-44, 2001, 47. See also Cheng-Fen Chen and Graham Sewell, "Strategies for Technological Development in South Korea and Taiwan: The Case of Semiconductors," *Research Policy* 25 (1996), 771; Kuen-Hung Tsai and Jiann-Chyuan Wang, "An Examination of Taiwan's Innovation Policy Measures and Their Effects," *International Journal of Technology and Globalization* 1 (2005), 242. Yun-Han Chu reports that the government sponsored the Monte Jade Association, which set up offices in Silicon Valley, Boston's Route 128, and the Austin, Texas, area. The association was established to gain information about new technology developments in leading clusters in the United States, as well as to recruit Taiwanese engineers, scientists, and entrepreneurs back to Taiwan. See Yun-Han Chu, "Re-engineering the Developmental State in an Age of Globalization: Taiwan in Defiance of Neo-liberalism," *China Review* 2 (2002), 42; see also Wen-Hsiung Lee and Wei-Tzen Yang, "The Cradle of Taiwan High Technology Industry Development: Hsinchu Science Park," *Technovation* 20 (2000), 55.

search talent.[10] Even ardently technonationalist South Korea has been forced to look globally for talent.[11]

The transition from science and technology laggard was hastened by the state's efforts to build physical R&D infrastructure and strategically allocate R&D resources. The role that public research institutes (as opposed to firms) played in R&D in Korea, Taiwan, and Singapore was critical, and their centrality in the development of new technologies and applications persists today. Perhaps the most noted public research institute is Taiwan's Industrial Technology Research Institute. Formed in 1973, the ITRI received nearly two-thirds of all Science and Technology Programs funds allocated by the Ministry of Economic Affairs.[12] Government research institutes in Korea, such as the Korean Institute of Science and Technology (KIST) and the Korean Advanced Institute of Science (KAIS), received similar disproportionately large allocations from the state; in the 1970s, PRIs in Korea accounted for about 84% of all R&D expenditures, and even into the 1980s, the PRI share of total national R&D spending still amounted to approximately half the entire budget.[13] In Singapore, though the PRI sector has accounted for a smaller slice of the R&D resource pie, its share has increased more rapidly than in Korea and Taiwan. In addition to the state's capital investments in physical infrastructure, such as the construction of the Biopolis complex and other new R&D clusters, research budgets and human capital resources for Singapore's PRIs more than doubled during the 1990s, and by the end of that decade, PRIs drew in a greater share of public R&D resources than did the university sector.[14]

---

10. Govindan Parayil, "From Silicon Island to Biopolis of Asia: Innovation Policy and Shifting Competitive Strategy in Singapore," *California Management Review* 47 (2005), 66; Alexius Pereira, "Whither the Developmental State? Explaining Singapore's Continued Developmentalism," *Third World Quarterly* 29 (2008), 1196.

11. In 2008, the Korean government unveiled its 825-billion-won (over US$650 million) "World Class University" project, which was "designed to recruit top-notch researchers from abroad, who will collaborate with [their] Korean counterparts to activate research in key growth-generating fields [including life sciences], and contribute to enhancing the capacity of Korean universities." Ministry of Education, Science, and Technology, press release, June 20, 2008.

12. Jiann-Chyuan Wang, "The Industrial Policy of Taiwan, ROC," in *Industrial Policies in East Asia,* ed. Seiichi Masuyama, Donna Vandenbrink, and Siow Yue Chia (Tokyo: Nomura Research Institute, 1997), 76; John Matthews, "The Origins and Dynamics of Taiwan's R&D Consortia," *Research Policy* 31 (2002), 635; Chiung-Wen Hsu and Hsueh-Chiao Chiang, "The Government Strategy for the Upgrading of Industrial Technology in Taiwan," *Technovation* 21 (2001), 124; Vincent Wang, "Developing the Information Industry in Taiwan: Entrepreneurial State, Guerilla Capitalists and Accommodative Technologists," *Pacific Affairs* 68 (1995).

13. Mani, *Government, Innovation and Technology Policy,* 96.

14. Poh Kam Wong, "From Using to Creating Technology: The Evolution of Singapore's National Innovation System and the Changing Role of Public Policy," in *Competitiveness, FDI and*

Governments in all three places have also refined public policies in order to facilitate cutting-edge technology innovation, notably regulation policies regarding patient safety, manufacturing standards, and clinical R&D. Intellectual property regimes were reorganized as well during the late 1990s to meet global standards in legislation and enforcement, reforms that have increased not only domestic R&D but also patenting activity among foreign inventors.[15] And while the private sector's share on the input side has increased dramatically over the past two decades or so, especially in R&D spending, the state's commitment to industry remains sizable. This is especially pronounced in life sciences R&D and commercial biotech. For instance, between 1998 and 2002, Taiwan's Executive Yuan Development Fund allocated over US$660 million for downstream investments in biotech firms.[16] The Singaporean government created the Bio*One venture capital fund, which by 2007 managed close to US$800 million earmarked for commercial investment in biomedical industries; Bio*One is the largest such fund in all of Asia.[17] As Table 2.1 indicates, overall public spending on biotech R&D in Korea, Taiwan, and Singapore is comparable with or even higher than that in other advanced industrial countries. Moreover, biotech R&D expenditures alone account for about 30% of total public R&D spending in Taiwan and Singapore, an extraordinarily large proportion, and 15% in Korea, a still comparatively high share.

Over the past decade, upstream basic research has become an integral part of plans for science and technology development in Korea, Taiwan, and Singapore. Aspirations in biotech, a science-based industry, have necessitated

Technology Activity in East Asia, ed. Sanjaya Lall and Shujiro Urata (Northampton, Mass.: Edward Elgar, 2003), 203.

15. See Susan Sell, *Private Power and Public Law: The Globalization of Intellectual Property Rights* (New York: Cambridge University Press, 2003), 79; Keith Maskus, *Intellectual Property Rights in the Global Economy* (Washington, D.C.: Institute for International Economics, 2000), 93. In the field of biotech and pharmaceuticals, 85% of patent activity in Taiwan during 2003 was accounted for by foreign nationals. See Taiwan Intellectual Property Office (TIPO), *2003 Annual Report* (Taipei: Ministry of Economic Affairs, TIPO, May 2004 [in Chinese]), 70–71. In Korea, this figure amounted to 30%. Author interview, Daejon, Korea, May 27, 2003. Overall, between 30% and 40% of all patent applications early in the first decade of the 2000s came from foreign inventors. National Science Council (NSC), *Indicators of Science and Technology, ROC, 2002* (Taipei: NSC, 2002), 88–89; Taiwan Intellectual Property Office, *2003 Annual Report,* 53; Korean Intellectual Property Office, *Statistical Data Book* (Daejon: Korean Intellectual Property Office, 2001), 102.

16. Government funds designated for commercial investments are managed by private sector fund managers. According to government officials in Taiwan, public sector decision makers are without the expertise and capacity for industry due diligence to invest strategically in biotech.

17. Singapore's Bio*One fund was created in 1990, initially with modest capital investments amounting to approximately US$26 million. In 1998, it was expanded with a second, $46 million fund. When the Biomedical Science Initiative was launched in 2001, Bio*One raised an additional US$660 million, and by 2007, it managed close to US$800 million, all of which was slated for investment in the biomedical sector.

Table 2.1   Public Spending on Biotechnology R&D (2003)

COUNTRY	US$ MILLIONS	AS % OF TOTAL PUBLIC R&D SPENDING
Korea	727	15
Taiwan (2006)	618	31
Canada	549	12
Spain	453	n.a.
Singapore (2005)	360	28
United Kingdom	212	2
New Zealand	149	24
Denmark	131	10
Finland	105	7
Norway	90	6
Sweden	29	1

Sources: Brigitte van Beuzekom and Anthony Arundel, *OECD Biotechnology Statistics—2006* (Paris: OECD, 2006); National Science Council (NSC), *Indicators of Science and Technology, 2007* (Taipei: NSC, 2007); Agency for Science, Technology, and Research (A*STAR), *National Survey of R&D in Singapore, 2006* (Singapore: A*STAR, 2007).

such a shift. It is important to stress that this emphasis on science (rather than on technology development) and the open-endedness of basic research is new to policymakers in Korea, Taiwan, and Singapore, and marks an abrupt change from past practices in "catch-up" technology assimilation and development, particularly in information technologies. As a senior Singaporean official once remarked during the late 1970s, while "pure or basic research to enlarge the frontiers of knowledge without conscious applicable goals is not wasteful...a developing nation like Singapore has neither the financial nor human resources to indulge in it. Our efforts have to be primarily in that area of research more properly termed development."[18] Three decades ago, upstream research was viewed as an indulgence; currently, basic research is understood to be the lifeline of cutting-edge biotech industries.

To that end, in all three places more and more R&D resources have been allocated to the university sector and explicitly designated for upstream research. In Korea, research budgets for universities increased fivefold between 1990 and 1998, from US$341 million to $1.6 billion, and nearly doubled again by 2005. University research personnel more than tripled over the same time period, while the number of university-based research centers grew from just 13 in 1990 to 45 in 1997.[19] Consequently, between 1999 and 2002,

18. Chor Boon Goh, "Science and Technology in Singapore: The Mindset of the Engineering Undergraduate," *Asia Pacific Journal of Education* 18 (1998), 63.

19. National Science Council (NSC), *Indicators of Science and Technology, 2007* (Taipei: NSC, 2007), 38; see also Webb, *South Korea: Mass Innovation,* 24; Ministry of Science and Technology/Korea

the average yearly growth in the number of academic papers published in the field of health biotech by South Korean researchers increased by nearly 12%; in contrast, leading countries such as Germany, the United States, Japan, and the United Kingdom experienced negative growth in publications, ranging from −2.5% to −7.8%.[20] The shift toward basic research has been most pronounced in Singapore, where between 2000 and 2005 the share of R&D resources allocated for basic research nearly doubled, from around 11% of total spending to near 21%. The creation of the National Research Fund and the Academic Research Fund in 2007 resulted in even larger allocations to upstream R&D activities. Universities in Singapore have also gained greater autonomy, being increasingly free from government and bureaucratic interference in carrying out research programs. Funding streams and the design of research programs have been similarly reorganized to free university researchers from bureaucratic meddling and to promote more sustained collaboration among upstream researchers.[21]

Coordinating Science and Technology

On the input side, the state has mattered and continues to matter in advancing science and technology development in Korea, Taiwan, and Singapore. The state's commitment and the allocation of tremendous amounts of public resources have transformed these late developers from science and technology laggards to potential leaders at technology's cutting edge. But state "leadership" was not solely about supplying resources. Leadership, as understood in the era of the postwar developmental state, was also about the state's coordinative role in allocating these resources, processes that were by and large institutionally centralized and concentrated among a few powerful actors. As I described in Chapter 1, decision-making processes and policy implementation were shaped by hierarchical lines of authority. Science ministries were relatively autonomous and generally supported by economic policy–related

---

Institute of Science and Technology Evaluation and Planning (MOST/KISTEP), *The 21st Century Frontier R&D Program* (Seoul: MOST/KISTEP, 2002).

20. Halla Thorsteinsdottir, Abdallah Daar, and Peter Singer, "Health Biotechnology Publishing Takes-off in Developing Countries," *International Journal of Biotechnology* 8 (2006), 30.

21. Winston Koh and Poh Kam Wong, "Competing at the Frontier: The Changing Role of Technology Policy in Singapore's Economic Strategy," *Technological Forecasting and Social Change* 72 (2005), 269–270; see Goh, "Science and Technology in Singapore," 65–66; see also Chor Boon Goh, "The Role of State and Society in the Development of Science and Technology in Singapore" (PhD diss., University of New South Wales, 1995), 236; Parayil, "From Silicon Island," 57; National Science and Technology Board (NSTB), *National Science and Technology Plan, 1996* (Singapore: NSTB, 1996), 12, 41.

agencies within the state. And even in Singapore, where the Ministry of Science and Technology was unceremoniously disbanded in 1981 for its ineffectiveness, the National Science and Technology Board (NSTB) was established less than a decade later, and from the start wielded considerable power and authority inside the state. Coordinative capacity within the hierarchically organized state apparatus allowed decision makers to authoritatively allocate public resources in ways that facilitated catch-up technology development generally in Korea, Taiwan, and Singapore, shaping different national styles of industrial upgrading in each of the three cases.

The rest of this chapter examines the allocation of state resources for life sciences innovation and commercial biotech development in Korea, Taiwan, and Singapore. I argue that despite the continued commitment of the state to supply inputs for the biotech innovation process, the state's top-down coordinative capacities to pick and make winners have diminished quite considerably, marking a significant departure from the postwar developmental state. What was once viewed as a coherent developmental state apparatus endowed with a hierarchically organized bureaucracy has been transformed into what one industry observer aptly characterizes as a "bureaucratic labyrinth."[22] The uncertainties of biotech innovation have undermined the state's capacity to pick winners.

Korea

The developmental state in Korea was lauded for its extraordinary coordinative capacity. It was the closest approximation anywhere of the Japanese capitalist developmental state. The allocation of state resources was purposive and strategic, intended explicitly to mitigate the risk of industrial upgrading. Resources were channeled in ways that increased the probability that higher value-added sectors could be mastered by Korean firms. The state turned long shots into surer bets. Internal coordination was afforded by the vertically organized state. In the bureaucratic hierarchy, the Economic Planning Board (EPB) was at the apex of state power, its position strengthened by the political support of the presidential Blue House. However, hierarchy and the centralization of coordinative power have proven to be no longer sustainable in the era of science-based industrialization. With respect to biotech, there is much less top-down coordination in the allocation of public resources. Power and authority within the state have become progressively horizontalized.

---

22. Author interview, Taipei, Taiwan, April 23, 2002.

In the past, only a few actors were involved in promoting industrial growth. Upgrading into the electronics and information technologies sector, for instance, was led by the industry ministry and its electronics engineering research institute. With few actors, the EPB could effectively coordinate from above. The biotech sector is constituted differently, however, with many more actors invested from the start in the sector's development. Seven ministries were involved in life sciences industry development when the government promulgated its 1994 biotechnology promotion plan.[23] Given the multidisciplinary and fragmented nature of the biotech innovation process, it made sense that the number of ministerial stakeholders would increase at the outset. The functional imperatives of biotech innovation forced the decentralization of specialized knowledge among ministerial actors. Each could rightly claim legitimate expertise and thus the specialized knowledge to help deal with the challenges of biotech innovation.

Interministerial Conflict

Claims of specialization by ministerial stakeholders did not, at least initially, prevent overlap and jurisdictional duplication. The Ministry of Science and Technology (MOST) and the Ministry of Education (MOE) clashed over which was responsible for science education and human capital development in Korea's university system. The Ministry of Commerce, Industry, and Energy (MOCIE) and MOST waged similar jurisdictional battles. The MOCIE focused on industry development and was responsible for all industry-related R&D, especially that which was directed at commercialization. Yet universities and public research institutes funded by the MOST established technology-licensing offices during the 1990s for the purposes of commercialization as well, and in the case of the Korean Research Institute of Bioscience and Biotechnology (KRIBB), its own bioventure incubation facility. The MOCIE thus felt the MOST was looking too far downstream and had encroached on MOCIE's R&D programs.[24] The Ministry of Health and Welfare (MOHW), meanwhile, claimed the development of health biotech applications to be its chief responsibility. In 1999, the MOHW established the Korean Health Industry Development Institute (KHIDI), its biobusiness development arm. It also continued to fund upstream R&D. Consequently, the MOHW's R&D programs were perceived to have crowded the efforts

---

23. The Ministries of Science and Technology; Commerce, Industry, and Energy; Health and Welfare; Education; Agriculture and Forestry; Environment; and Maritime Affairs and Fisheries.

24. The Korean Research Institute for Bioscience and Biotechnology is the largest MOST-funded public research institute dedicated to life sciences R&D.

of both the MOCIE and the MOST. The lines demarcating upstream and downstream activities and priorities were increasingly blurred.

Internal bureaucratic conflict ensued, especially over the allocation of R&D resources. In many contexts, such conflict over the distribution of public resources can be mitigated or preempted, especially when the pool of committed resources expands. If it is expected that all stakeholders will increase their respective stock of resources, then cooperation rather than conflict should ensue.[25] This reasoning might be intuitively correct. However, in the case of Korea (and as we will see, in Taiwan as well), the expansion of the resource pool contributed to conflict. There are several reasons for this. First, the amount of resources dedicated to the sector grew so rapidly after biotech was initially identified as a future pillar industry that state actors viewed the expanding pool of resources in intensely competitive terms, precluding, at least initially, the opportunity for more cooperative and collaborative terms to be negotiated. Not only did overall government R&D expenditures steeply increase, from just US$120 million in 1976 to almost US$9 billion in 2006, but government spending in biotech R&D grew more rapidly than in other sectors, drastically raising the stakes for contending ministries.[26]

Second, resources that had been earmarked for biotech development were viewed by stakeholders as a new and thus separate budget line. In this respect, competition was a function not so much of a growing resource pie, but rather of what was perceived to be an *entirely new* pie to be parceled out among ministerial stakeholders. Third, claims of specialized expertise notwithstanding, the fact of the matter was that state actors themselves were unsure, at least initially, about what roles each would or could play in the development of biotech and bio-industries, so much so that state officials worried that the multiplication and duplication of ministerial stakeholders would lead to the inefficient allocation of public R&D resources. The sector's technological and economic uncertainties precluded a clear division of labor at the outset, and actors were essentially defending their respective "turf," the boundaries of which they had yet to work out. But as a preemptive move, it made more sense for them to compete than to concede because the stakes were potentially very high. And finally, interministerial conflict was exacerbated by the absence of an effective overarching pilot agency within the state apparatus

---

25. This important observation was raised by one of the anonymous reviewers of the manuscript of this book.

26. Ministry of Science and Technology (MOST), *National Science and Technology Statistical Indicators* (Seoul: MOST, 2002), and *Innovation for the Future: Science and Technology in Korea* (Seoul: MOST, 2007).

capable of coordinating R&D programs from the top down. The EPB proved ineffective in this role. It was later replaced by the "super" Ministry of Finance and Economy during the late 1990s, which, as it turned out, similarly lacked the expertise and authority to coordinate interministerial efforts in biotech development.

The elected National Assembly approves the government's total R&D budget, though actual resource allocation decisions for the various ministries are made by the Ministry of Planning and Budget (MPB). The MPB is a powerful ministry, given its control of the government's purse strings, though it too proved ineffective in coordinating the allocation of R&D resources in science-based initiatives such as in biotech. The MPB lacks the scientific and industrial expertise with which to adjudicate ministerial claims from below. It is a budgeting ministry after all, concerned more about the government's overall fiscal circumstances than about evaluating specific R&D programs. Furthermore, R&D spending represented only one portion of the government's total budget, and comparatively speaking, a relatively small share of the national budget. The MPB thus tended to defer to ministerial claims on the national R&D budget, which intensified interministerial competition.

This did not mean the MPB was negligent in its budgeting responsibilities, nor did it eschew the advice of experts when it came to evaluating ministerial research plans. The MPB relied on the Korean Institute of Science and Technology Evaluation and Planning (KISTEP), an organization closely affiliated the MOST, to evaluate ministerial budget proposals. This arrangement made sense to some, as the MOST (and KISTEP) possessed the expertise required to properly evaluate science and technology R&D plans. Yet for many others, the MPB's reliance on KISTEP raised concerns about the budgeting ministry's impartiality. Many pointed out that the MOST benefited disproportionately from this arrangement, and went so far as to suggest that the institutional arrangement was unfair and came at the expense of other, equally vital ministerial units. Thus, the MPB's legitimacy, credibility, and ultimately its ability to allocate R&D resources were undermined, which again exacerbated rather than mitigated ministerial conflict. The high-profile National Science and Technology Council (NSTC) was formed in 1999 by the Presidential Office, in large part to manage conflict and reduce ministerial duplication by advising the MPB in R&D budgeting matters. But it suffered a similar legitimacy problem, as it was co-chaired by the minister of science and technology.[27] The NSTC was seen as partial.

27. Author interview, Seoul, Korea, July 10, 2003.

Conflict was compounded by the fact that there were no institutional mechanisms to facilitate interministerial or interagency planning for the purposes of reducing overlap and jurisdictional duplication. The R&D budgeting process involved little, if any, formal discussion among the ministries regarding their respective R&D plans. Budget deliberations took place directly between the line ministry and the MPB. Thus, ministries negotiated their respective R&D budget allocations in parallel with one another and bilaterally with the MBP. Communication was low. Trust, necessary for cooperation, was minimal.[28] The absence of such mechanisms further undermined the MPB's capacity to coordinate the allocation of R&D resources from above.[29]

Dividing the Labor

The functional imperatives of the biotech sector altered the internal dynamics of Korea's postwar developmental state, specifically the decentralization of relevant expertise among actors. Interministerial conflict during the 1990s transformed the basis of coordination and the mechanisms that determined the allocation of resources. It became clear that any semblance of top-down coordination was no longer feasible. However, learning ensued and the internal dynamics of the state were reorganized again into the 2000s. Most significantly, interministerial competition in the Korean state provided over time the basis for implicit coordination and accommodation. In the first decade of the 2000s, interministerial competition and conflict had evolved into a more discernible division of labor among the ministerial stakeholders. They had worked things out by establishing their R&D specializations and articulating them as such. They gained the resources to further develop their research programs, and they did so without explicit coordination from above. They adapted in order to complement one another.

To differentiate itself from the MOST, the MOCIE focused on sponsoring R&D in applied technologies that could be assimilated quickly by firms. In recent years, the MOCIE has partnered with small and medium-sized enterprises in new technology sectors.[30] MOCIE projects have tended to be relatively short term, lasting usually between three and five years. Outside of targeted R&D projects, the MOCIE has invested in industry-related infrastructure, allocating over 50% of its budget to industry development

28. Joseph Wong, "From Learning to Creating: Biotechnology and the Postindustrial Developmental State in Korea," *Journal of East Asian Studies* 4 (2004).

29. Author interview, Seoul, Korea, July 11, 2003.

30. Author interview, Seoul, Korea, July 11, 2003.

initiatives. The MOST, in contrast, has committed over 90% of its budgetary resources to strictly research programs.[31] MOST research schemes, such as the well-funded 21st Century Frontier Development Program (which includes life sciences and biotech), have by and large been directed at universities and government research institutes rather than firms.[32] Research funding from the MOST has also tended to be longer term, lasting usually up to ten years.[33] About half the MOST's R&D projects are mission-oriented, broadly targeting, for example, upstream genomics or novel drug discovery. The other half is dedicated to "open call" projects initiated by researchers themselves.[34] MOST research programs thus tend to be more open-ended than those of the MOCIE.

The MOHW has continued to focus on the development of health-related applications of biotech. It has dedicated R&D resources to upstream research as well as to midstream and downstream commercialization programs. Unlike the MOCIE and the MOST, however, the MOHW has targeted a particular subsector of the biotech industry.[35] Over 90% of MOHW research resources are directed at four interrelated applications of biotech R&D: new drug development, health care delivery, the development of medical device technology, and the strengthening of clinical R&D infrastructure.[36] The ministry's biobusiness development institute, KHIDI, and its health technology transfer office also recently proposed the creation of a midstream mechanism aimed at "accelerating new drug development." The plan, which was to be implemented by 2009, would establish a government-funded R&D center that would purchase "raw technologies" (drug candidates) from local and foreign sources, further develop potential leads and conduct preclinical tests in-house, and license out candidates to Korean pharmaceutical firms. Health policymakers in the MOHW, by deepening both upstream and downstream R&D capacities, envision capturing a critical segment of the pharmaceutical

---

31. In 2005, 93% of MOST R&D resources were allocated as research grants, with the remaining 7% directed at infrastructure. The MOCIE, on the other hand, allocated 58% of its R&D resources for infrastructural development, with the balance distributed in the form of industry-focused R&D grants. See Biotech Policy Research Center, *Status of Biotechnology in Korea* (Daejon: Biotech Policy Research Center, 2006), 40.

32. It should be noted that as of 2008, the MOST and the Ministry of Education were merged to form the single Ministry of Science, Education, and Technology, emphasizing further the upstream orientation of the MOST's research programs.

33. MOST/KISTEP, *21st Century Frontier.*

34. Korea Science and Engineering Foundation (KOSEF), *Paving the Way to the Future of Korea's Science and Technology* (Daejon: KOSEF, 2007).

35. Author interview, Seoul, Korea, July 8, 2003.

36. Biotech Policy Research Center, *Status of Biotechnology,* 68.

value chain, supporting Korea's national industrial champions in drug development.[37]

This emergent division of labor was eventually reflected in the allocation of R&D resources dedicated to the life sciences. During the late 1990s, the MOST accounted for the vast majority of government R&D spending in biotech. This was in line with claims that the MPB model of R&D budgeting favored the MOST. Early in the first decade of the 2000s, however, the R&D budget began to take on a new shape. The MOST's share decreased considerably, down to one-third of the biotech R&D budget in 2004–2005. Meanwhile, the MOCIE's share increased from just 4% during the first phase (mid-1990s) to 15% in Phase 3 of the government's biotech plan. In fact, between 2004 and 2005, the MOCIE's *actual* budget allocation grew from 21% to 27%, far exceeding the government plan (see Table 2.2). The MOHW's share in 2004–2005 represented 19% of the budget, which similarly exceeded the government's plan. The MOST, MOCIE, and MOHW accounted for 80% of all government R&D spending in biotech, though the resource gap narrowed considerably among them.

The point is that interministerial competition during the 1990s did not prohibit eventual accommodation among the ministries in the early 2000s. A complementary division of labor based on different roles was formulated, with the MOST responsible for upstream basic research, the MOCIE for midstream technology development and commercialization, and the MOHW for a biotech subsector related to the management of health technology and health care delivery. How did the ministries work things out and arrive at this complementary arrangement, and how exactly did they achieve that in the absence of top-down coordination?

First, the MOST indirectly shaped this division of labor. Even though its share of government R&D resources decreased over time, it still accounted for around half the overall R&D budget during the late 1990s. It was at this time that the MOST increasingly dedicated its resources to midstream and upstream capacity building rather than further developing the downstream R&D activities it had initiated during the 1980s and early 1990s. It devised more open-ended funding sources for university and public lab researchers. By deliberately staking out a narrower and defined research mandate, the MOST compelled other key ministerial actors, notably the MOCIE and MOHW, to adapt and carve out their own R&D niches. They were in effect forced to define their own specialized research programs in relation to the

---

37. Author interview, Seoul, Korea, September 14, 2007.

Table 2.2.   Distribution of Biotechnology Funding in Korea, Government Sources
(% of total budget)

MINISTRY	PHASE 1 (1994–1997)	PHASE 2 (1998–2001)	PHASE 3 (2002–2007)
Science and Technology	56	51	44
Education	5	10	9
Agriculture and Forestry	19	10	13
Commerce, Industry, Energy	4	15	15
Health and Welfare	12	10	14
Environment	2	2	3
Maritime Affairs and Fisheries	2	2	2
Total	100	100	100

Source: Biotechnology Promotion Plan (internal government document, Seoul, April 2003).

MOST's initiatives. Consequently, the MOCIE developed new programs for midstream and downstream R&D, while the MOHW focused its R&D resources on specific health biotech applications. They accommodated by complementing one another.

Second, ministerial stakeholders increased their lines of informal communication. Policymakers explain that it was in their collective interest to do so. Early in the first decade of the 2000s, ministerial stakeholders realized that duplication and overlap were not beneficial either to their own ministerial interests or to the larger goal of growing a vibrant biotech sector. Resources were being wasted. Conflict had also proven counterproductive. Thus, through the iterated budgeting process, ministries came to identify their presumed strengths (and weaknesses) and competencies in life sciences R&D. They had also learned that, in the end, their collective interests to accommodate one another by dividing the labor of R&D along differentiated rather than duplicative research programs served their specific ministerial interests. Put another way, ministerial stakeholders recognized that by formulating a division of R&D labor, each could claim a piece of the new resource pie. The various stakeholders were encouraged to engage in informal interministerial dialogue. They learned about one another's R&D plans and adapted accordingly.

Third, new institutional initiatives were promulgated by the state during the middle of the first decade of the 2000s to ensure that such complementarities were sustained over the long term. In 2004, the government created the Office of Science and Technology Innovation (OSTI). Though technically the executive office of the National Science and Technology Council (NSTC), the OSTI enjoys considerable autonomy from other government agencies. Because it receives and reviews all annual ministerial R&D

budget proposals, the OSTI has a more expansive view than the ministries do of the resource pool and the management of ministerial R&D programs. The OSTI also has the power to unilaterally shift resources from one ministry to another. But what is particularly interesting is that even though the OSTI is headed up by one of the two vice-ministers of science and technology, it is nonetheless perceived by ministerial stakeholders as a legitimate and impartial R&D budgeting institution. The OSTI has somehow overcome the legitimacy problems associated with the MPB and NSTC. It is seen as capable and staffed with expert consultants who understand the science of technological innovation. Unlike the MPB, the OSTI is regarded as having the legitimacy to plan the nation's science and technology development programs.

Specifically, the OSTI is perceived to function independently of the MOST, even though it is chaired by a senior MOST official. This is due in large part to the transformation of the MOST itself. During the early 2000s, the MOST was reorganized into two distinct sections, each headed by a vice-minister. One section continued to plan and execute the ministry's R&D programs and to advocate for the ministry's specific interests. The other was responsible for R&D planning for all government ministries. The vice-minister in charge of planning heads up the OSTI. The two organizational halves of the MOST work independently, creating institutional distance between the ministry's specific interests, on the one hand, and its more general planning role, on the other. Stakeholders tell me that this distance has mitigated prevailing concerns about the perceived lack of impartiality in national R&D budgeting. The fact that the MOST's share of R&D resources declined into the middle of the first decade of the 2000s, to the benefit primarily of the MOCIE and MOHW, reinforced this perception. And finally, the OSTI was created (in 2004) *after* ministerial stakeholders had already begun to accommodate one another. In other words, the complementary division of R&D labor described above was not created by the OSTI. Rather, the OSTI was established to sustain that arrangement, to ensure, for instance, that the MOST continued to focus on upstream basic research and the MOCIE developed R&D programs aimed at midstream and commercialization. In this respect, the OSTI's "planning" role has had less to do with coordinating from above and more with sustaining and indirectly facilitating potential complementarities among various ministerial stakeholders.[38] From a strategic point of view, the OSTI's role has been critical in ensuring that the allocation of

---

38. Author interviews, Seoul, Korea, September 13 and 14, 2007.

resources in Korea continues to span the entire spectrum of R&D activities, upstream and downstream.

Taiwan

As in Korea, policymakers in Taiwan were confronted early on with the multidisciplinary challenges of biotech development and science-based industrialization. Taiwan's entry into the biotech sector, like that of Korea, revealed an institutional mismatch between past practices of centralized planning and the new realities of cutting-edge technological innovation. And as in Korea, industrial upgrading into the biotech sector increased the number of relevant bureaucratic actors, each of which claimed specialized expertise in the life sciences field. Stakeholders included ministerial-level actors such as the National Science Council, the Ministry of Economic Affairs, the Department of Health, the Council on Agriculture, and the Academia Sinica.[39]

Similar to the Korean experience, expertise inside the Taiwanese state was decentralized and the power to coordinate was horizontalized. The National Science Council (NSC) claimed that it was the most capable agency for science and technology policy planning. The Department of Health (DOH) possessed expertise in the design and implementation of clinical R&D programs. Meanwhile, the Ministry of Economic Affairs (MOEA) had proven effective in promoting industrial investment and new venture developments. The Council on Agriculture (COA) claimed ownership of Taiwan's R&D capabilities in agricultural biotech and the implementation of food and agro-biotech regulations. State-level stakeholders, all "experts" in their own right, vied for government resources earmarked for life sciences R&D. The fact that the government's budget for biotech R&D grew substantially, from 18% of national R&D expenditures in 1998 to almost 30% in 2002, meant that the competitive stakes had increased considerably and over a very short period of time.[40] As was the case in Korea, the lines of contestation were exacerbated because of the steep increase in public resources allocated for biotech, the understanding that such resources constituted a new dedicated (rather than expanded) budget line, and the absence of institutional leadership over a fragmented state.

---

39. Unlike other research institutes in Taiwan, the Academia Sinica is not funded through a ministerial budget line. Rather, it is funded directly by the president's office and enjoys a status and powers similar to those of a line ministry.

40. Biotechnology and Pharmaceutical Industries Program Office (BPIPO), *Introduction to Investment in the Biotechnology and Pharmaceutical Industries in Taiwan* (Taipei: BPIPO, 2003), 22.

Pilot agencies such as the Council for Economic Planning and Development (CEPD) were without the authority and legitimacy to effectively lead. Technocratic "generalists" were increasingly perceived to be ill-suited for coordinating cutting-edge biotech R&D. Science-based agencies fared no better. For instance, even though the Science and Technology Advisory Group (STAG) of the NSC, and more recently the cabinet-level Biotechnology Steering Committee (BSC), were expected to coordinate development efforts, their authority and influence were limited. The head of the STAG and the BSC is a minister without portfolio, which in the state's bureaucratic hierarchy ranks lower than the heads of the other line ministries. He lacks power. Moreover, unlike in the past, when technocratic "strong men" were able to marshal the resources and political will to jump-start Taiwan's process of industrial upgrading into high-tech sectors,[41] no similarly compelling or charismatic leader has emerged for the biotech sector.[42] For these reasons, top-down coordination has proven to be increasingly unworkable. Stakeholders in Taiwan's biotech sector characterize the innovation system there as a conductorless "jazz band," with different players improvising and "doing their own thing." As in Korea, uncertainty in science-based industrialization forced the state in Taiwan to reorganize. What informed this adaptive process?

Despite tremendous uncertainty surrounding Taiwan's future in the biotech sector, stakeholders were certain of three things. First, Taiwan had a strong record in midstream technology development and in successfully bringing technologies closer to market for commercialization. Its record in biotech was virtually nonexistent at that point, to be sure, but researchers and industrial policymakers had considerable experience in technology transfer and forming commercially viable ventures. Second, though it was uncertain exactly where local innovators might develop comparative advantages in the biotech sector, decision makers understood that commercial biotech entailed a very long and fragmented value chain, comprising many potential entry points for entrepreneurial firms. Third, Taiwanese policymakers were very aware of their resource constraints. Though the amount of public and

41. Yongping Wu, *A Political Explanation of Economic Growth: State Survival, Bureaucratic Politics, and Private Enterprises in the Making of Taiwan's Economy* (Cambridge, Mass.: Harvard University Press, 2005).

42. K. T. Li is considered the architect of Taiwan's industrial miracle. Though Li was a minister without portfolio, his leadership style, vision, and political capital allowed him to overcome his relatively low ranking in the bureaucratic hierarchy. In fact, that he was not attached to any one ministry gave him the political latitude within which to coordinate state efforts at rapid industrial upgrading.

private capital in Taiwan intended for biotech was not insignificant, the resources there (especially from the private sector) paled in comparison to those available in other advanced industrial economies—or even Korea, for that matter. Amid uncertainty and the realities of resource constraints, it was at least certain, or perceived as such, that Taiwan's best shot at making it in the biotech sector was to identify and develop specific niches in the life sciences value chain.

Looking Downstream

Whereas the Korean approach is to allocate sufficient resources to foster a vertical division of labor in upstream and downstream R&D activities in the life sciences field, Taiwan's approach has favored a more horizontal division of labor centered on the downstream. Rather than dedicate state resources to develop fully complementary capabilities in upstream, midstream, and downstream biotech R&D, as in Korea, decision makers in Taiwan have spread a disproportionate amount of R&D resources to efforts in downstream commercialization. Thus, while the absolute resource commitment to upstream basic research has grown in Taiwan, it has actually decreased as a proportion of overall R&D resources. In 2005, over three-quarters of public R&D expenditures were directed at applied and experimental technology development.[43] The National Science Council, nominally tasked with promoting upstream research, decreased its funding for basic research considerably during the first decade of the 2000s. And even though the NSC allocated nearly 70% of its budget to support academic research, the majority of university R&D has in fact been directed at midstream research and commercialization.[44] Technology licensing and venture business development offices have been established in virtually all of Taiwan's nominally upstream research institutions. University researchers have also been given incentives to pursue patents on their work, an output measure increasingly used to evaluate professors' productivity. Upstream researchers are expected to become technopreneurs.

Taiwan's strategy of spreading resources downstream in biotech development has flattened the state's R&D budget commitments among the various stakeholders. As Table 2.3 shows, the distribution of R&D funding in

---

43. National Science Council (NSC), *Indicators of Science and Technology, 2006* (Taipei: NSC, 2006).

44. See NSC, *Indicators, 2006.* Approximately one-sixth of the NSC's 2006 budget was invested in the development of industrial parks, a further indication of the council's emphasis on facilitating downstream industrial output.

biotech gradually converged across the ministries between 1998 and 2001 and has stayed the same since. Generally speaking, funding for the NSC and MOEA decreased while resources allocated to the DOH and the COA increased proportionately. In 2002, 20% of government R&D spending was allocated to the National Genome Project, an interministerial initiative that shared funding for the NSC, the Academia Sinica, the DOH, the COA, and the MOEA.[45]

Taiwan's is essentially a hit-and-miss strategy. A flattened R&D budget ensures that ministerial stakeholders involved in biotech innovation efforts are allocated adequate, if not overwhelming, resources to develop potential R&D niches. Spreading, as opposed to concentrating, state resources across different ministries has diversified the potential sources of commercial output and diffused the costs of expected failures, both of which are intended to increase the probabilities of some potentially innovative outcomes, no matter how small. It should be emphasized that Taiwan's hit-and-miss approach is not one in which potential winners are picked from the top down, but rather one in which "hits" are ultimately to be identified through continual experimentation from below. Identifying the "misses" would also be significant, for obvious reasons.

This process was further institutionalized in 2004, when the STAG imposed performance benchmarks for all publicly funded research centers. When the Strategic Review Board (SRB) of the STAG produced its 2004 report, there was a sense of panic and growing impatience regarding the slow pace of commercial biotech output.[46] According to the SRB's annual report, public R&D units were expected to spin out a total of eighteen commercial "success cases" by 2010. There was debate about the usefulness of the STAG's benchmarking exercise: those implicated by the STAG's plan expressed concern about measuring output, and critics stressed the economic and technological uncertainties of biotech innovation as well as the long gestation period required to translate upstream discoveries into commercially viable outputs. They also pointed to the underperformance of the commercial biotech sector globally. Ministries worried about failing to meet their targets, concerned that the STAG's implicit emphasis on ministerial competition would mean that their resources would decrease if they came up short. They

---

45. Executive Yuan, *Action Plan for Biotechnology Industry*, revised October 2001, government document, 7.

46. Science and Technology Advisory Group—Strategic Review Board (STAG—SRB), *Observations and Recommendations* (Taipei: STAG—SRB, Executive Yuan, 2004 [in Chinese]).

Table 2.3.   Distribution of Biotechnology and Pharmaceutical R&D Funding in
Taiwan, Government Sources (%)

	1998	1999	2000	2001	2002
National Science Council	26.9	28.6	31.5	25.3	23.9
Department of Health	16.4	17.1	17.6	20.6	15.6
Ministry of Economic Affairs	21.5	18.7	17.6	15.0	12.4
Academia Sinica	12.7	13.5	12.0	11.0	7.8
Council on Agriculture	11.5	22.1	21.3	24.7	19.5
Genome	—	—	—	—	20.1

Source: Biotechnology and Pharmaceutical Industries Program Office (BPIPO), *Status of Taiwan Biotech* (Taipei: BPIPO, 2003).

also feared that such a short time frame would compel R&D labs to forgo longer-term innovative research for less cutting-edge output.

After some consultation, the STAG agreed that targets would be proportional to the amount of R&D funding each institute received from public sources. A successful firm was defined as one that was commercially viable and revenue generating, though not necessarily profit making.[47] The ITRI and the Development Center for Biotechnology were expected to produce four success cases each, while the National Health Research Institute and the COA were targeted to spin out two firms. Research centers such as Academia Sinica were expected to create three biotech firms, as was the university sector funded by the NSC. There was no directive, however, as to what types of biotechnologies were to be commercialized; that was left up to the individual labs. Though in the end the benchmarks were met with skepticism, the initiative informally institutionalized expectations regarding the growth of commercial biotech in Taiwan.[48] It also reinforced the downstream orientation of publicly funded research institutes and their ministerial patrons. And even though the STAG was without the leverage to reward or punish research labs, the imposition of these "soft" targets informally heightened the sense of competition among ministerial stakeholders. Simply put, the STAG's initiatives confirmed Taiwan's hit-and-miss approach to biotech commercialization.

47. More specifically, a successful firm would have to achieve a market capitalization five times its initial investment and employ at least fifty R&D staff. Author interview, Hsinchu, Taiwan, October 12, 2004.

48. Senior researchers and institute directors I spoke to described the STAG initiative as "childish," "nonpunitive," and "counterproductive to collaboration."

Institutional Reproduction

The allocation and spread of state resources toward downstream R&D activities contributed to the institutional reproduction of ITRI-like technology transfer mechanisms. The ITRI, under the MOEA's jurisdiction, became the institutional model for biotech development. Beginning in the mid-1990s, the ITRI turned its attention to life sciences industry growth. The president of the ITRI during the first decade of the 2000s, Johnsee Lee, came from a biochemistry background, and he initially headed up the ITRI's Biomedical Engineering Center (BMEC) before being promoted to president in 2004. As before, the ITRI looked to develop promising technologies and technological applications in-house and then deliver the technology to the private sector. The BMEC initially focused on biopharmaceutical R&D with an emphasis on gene-based technologies. However, it quickly became apparent that drug discovery did not match well with the ITRI's experience and strengths in engineering. Though the ITRI did not abandon its drug research programs entirely, it reallocated resources toward developing commercially viable technology transfer programs in medical devices, biochips, and health diagnostic kits. This focus was emphasized even more after the ITRI began to develop some promising leads in these areas. As intended, the ITRI had started to carve out potentially viable niches, and it continued to shift resources in that direction. Taiwan's hit-and-miss strategy seemed to be working.

What is most interesting is not so much that the ITRI has continued to play an important prospecting role in biotech innovation, just as it did in other technology sectors, but that the institutional investments made by other units inside the state replicate the ITRI midstream model. The MOEA's Development Center for Biotechnology (DCB) is a good example. The DCB was created in 1984, though it was relatively inactive during its early years, when it floundered because of a lack of funding and the dearth of bio-industrial activity in Taiwan. The DCB was originally intended to be an upstream research facility, but given the weak base of domestic R&D talent in the life sciences, it was unable to assemble a deep enough pool of research talent. Beginning in the early 2000s, however, it was revived when its mission was redefined by the MOEA. It began to move away from basic research toward more midstream and commercially oriented life sciences R&D. For instance, the various presidents of the DCB during the first decade of the 2000s came back to Taiwan with years of overseas pharmaceutical industry experience. They were encouraged to return to help grow Taiwan's biotech industries. And while the DCB has continued to focus its research efforts on drug development, it has reoriented its R&D programs further down-stream. It runs a "biofronts" program that identifies promising candidates in the United States and Europe for the DCB to acquire and develop. With toxicology testing facilities on site, the DCB's research increasingly focuses on preclinical drug development. Its pharmaceutical pilot plant was upgraded to meet U.S. Food and Drug Administration (FDA) regulations, allowing the DCB to work even more closely with industry to identify and develop preclinical drug candidates.

The Department of Health adopted a similar institutional strategy when it created the National Health Research Institute (NHRI) in 1995. The NHRI is based in Miaoli County, about an hour from Taipei by train. Like the ITRI and the DCB, the NHRI has focused its R&D efforts on downstream-oriented research, though as Yu-Sheng Chao, one of the NHRI's directors, explains, the NHRI has tended to allocate resources to the research side of R&D, leaving the development to firms and the private sector. Still, the NHRI's primary objective, as it was articulated by Chao himself, is to "build up firms' pipelines" through the codevelopment of new drug compounds.[49] Like the DCB and the ITRI, the NHRI works closely with industry with an eye toward downstream commercialization. The Biotechnology Division, for example, partners with local firms to form biopharmaceutical technol-ogy transfer schemes structured around multifirm, premarket R&D consor-tia (discussed in the next chapter). The rationale, according to Chao, is to bring researchers from industry and the NHRI closer together and foster the transfer of R&D expertise both upward and downward.[50] Like the DCB and the ITRI, the NHRI is leveraging its R&D expertise to develop Taiwan's downstream potential.

In sum, resources within the state in Taiwan are being allocated in decen-tralized ways in order to nurture multiple research agendas among parastatal labs with the hope that one or more commercially viable niches can be identified. Where such niches might eventually emerge and when, however, remain unknown. Thus, as in the case of Korea, Taiwan's strategy is open-ended and flexible. But whereas the Korean state has allocated resources and reorganized institutions to vertically develop complementary R&D capabili-ties that span upstream and downstream research activities, Taiwan's logic of resource allocation has focused on midstream and downstream commercial-ization and a logic that is driven by implicit competition among units. Both

---

49. Author interview, Nankang, Taiwan, April 29, 2002.

50. Author interview, Nankang, Taiwan, April 29, 2002, and Miaoli, Taiwan, September 17, 2007.

Korea and Taiwan have refrained from picking winners through the allocation of public resources, however. Confronted with biotech's myriad uncertainties, they have both gambled, albeit in distinct ways, on the *potentiality* that
some winners might eventually emerge. Growing biotech in Taiwan is driven
by a hit-and-miss logic in which the avoidance of big financial bets remains a
key strategy. Decision makers have rationalized a strategic approach centered
on continual experimentation, intermural competition, and learning through
trial and error among commercially oriented labs. Late in the first decade of
the 2000s, it appeared that the hit-and-miss approach had begun to clarify
a more commercially oriented division of labor among state-sponsored labs;
one observer suggests that the ITRI is best suited for medical device design, the NHRI for vaccine development, and the DCB for drug discovery
and the business of clinical R&D.[51] What is important to reiterate, however,
is that this division of labor has emerged in Taiwan in the absence of top-
down coordination.

Singapore

The Singaporean state, unlike Korea and Taiwan, was reorganized to facilitate
even *greater* coordination in the allocation of public resources for biotech.
Whereas resources have been spread among different ministerial stakeholders
in Korea and Taiwan, power and authority to allocate such resources in Singapore were further concentrated within the state apparatus. Public resource
allocation for biotech was considerably more targeted and coordinated. This
does not mean, however, that uncertainty has been less pronounced in Singapore, nor should patterns of state reorganization there be interpreted as
greater confidence among decision makers in their ability to plan. Rather,
it is just the opposite. The state understood that it needed to coordinate the
allocation of resources to compensate for Singapore's deficiencies in life sciences innovation, in effect to bear some of the up-front costs that individual
researchers or entrepreneurs would understandably eschew as late entrants
in bio-industrial upgrading.[52] For instance, Singapore's size means that its

---

51. Author interview, Taipei, Taiwan, September 19, 2007.
52. Edgar Schein notes that "one of the original motivators for government involvement in
economic development was the shortage of entrepreneurs willing to bear some of the risks of development." Philip Yeo, the former cochairman of the EDB and the chairman of the A*STAR, was
quoted in the *Financial Times* in 1994 as saying, "Government is the great worrier. No individual has
the resources to do what a government can do. When government abdicates, individuals suffer." See
Edgar Schein, *Strategic Pragmatism: The Culture of Singapore's Economic Development Board* (Cambridge,
Mass.: MIT Press, 1996), 163.

talent pool is comparatively small.[53] Its science and technology capabilities—
measured in terms of university research, R&D infrastructure and spending,
and personnel—initially lagged far behind other latecomers such as Korea
and Taiwan. Singapore, in these respects, was *really* late. And because Singapore had relied so heavily on foreign direct investment for its early industrialization, it had failed to develop an indigenous industrial base, particularly
in innovative firms capable of absorbing, never mind creating, cutting-edge
biotechnologies.

Therefore, the Singaporean strategy for growing its biomedical industry
was from the outset based on two interrelated objectives. First, stakeholders understood that foreign firms, especially multinational pharmaceutical
firms, were needed to jump-start Singapore's biomedical industry drive.
Global firms would entail positive externalities, including employment, investment, technological spillover, and the local assimilation of biobusiness
know-how. Second, stakeholders recognized that attracting such firms to
Singapore required that it rapidly develop its domestic R&D capabilities.
Attracting foreign firms was no longer simply about creating jobs at home;
instead, the intention was to create higher value-added jobs to make Singapore a global biomedical R&D hub. The objectives were thus clear in the
minds of decision makers. They understood that to achieve such objectives
required purposive coordination. And to that end, power and authority were
concentrated in the Economic Development Board (EDB) of the Ministry
of Trade and Industry (MTI), and the Agency for Science, Technology and
Research (A*STAR).[54]

Rescaling Authority

The National Science and Technology Board, the institutional precursor to
the A*STAR, was created in 1991 to spearhead Singapore's efforts in industrial R&D capacity building. According to the 1991 National Technology
Plan, the NSTB was intended to be an equal partner with the Ministry
of Education (MOE) and the Ministry of Health (MOH) in administering
and coordinating national R&D plans. Not unlike in Korea, there was at
least initially an implied division of labor and thus division of power among

---

53. In 2005, there were 810 R&D personnel in Singapore's bio-industrial sector and 3,221 R&D
personnel in both public and private life sciences labs. See A*STAR, *National Survey*, 12. In 2003 in
Korea, there were 5,248 researchers in industry alone. See Biotech Policy Research Center, *Status
of Biotechnology*, 102. LG Life Sciences, one of Korea's largest pharmaceutical firms, employed 340
researchers, or the equivalent of 42% of the bio-industry R&D personnel in all of Singapore.

54. Author interview, Singapore, June 22, 2004.

ministerial stakeholders. The MOE, for instance, was mandated to develop upstream academic research through its administrative control over Singapore's two national universities. The MOE was also responsible for funding all public research institutes (PRIs). The Ministry of Health developed R&D capabilities in health technology research. Meanwhile, the NSTB, which was under the jurisdiction of the MTI, was tasked with administering public resources aimed at "industry-driven" R&D.[55] In other words, the NSTB was not intended, at least at the beginning, to be the state's principal coordinative body in the management and allocation of public R&D resources. However, by the conclusion of the first National Technology Plan in 1996, the NSTB was explicitly identified as the "lead government agency driving medium to long-term technological development" in Singapore.[56] In other words, by the mid-1990s, the NSTB had assumed a much greater coordinative role inside the state, a leadership role that was strengthened when the board was transformed into the A★STAR in 2001. Authority had been rescaled. How do we explain this change?

Several developments during the 1990s and into the early 2000s contributed to the rescaling of authority in the state apparatus. First, the NSTB gained control of the funding of PRIs, including the Institute for Molecular and Cell Biology (IMCB), Singapore's largest public lab dedicated to biotech. Before the establishment of the NSTB, PRIs were administered by the National University of Singapore and the Nanyang Technological University. Research budgets were set by the universities and thus came under MOE funding. During the early 1990s, however, the power to allocate resources to the PRIs was centralized within the NSTB. This diminished the authority of the MOE while strengthening the coordinative capacity of the NSTB. The NSTB was in charge of allocating S$2 billion for R&D over the course of the first National Technology Plan, S$4 billion between 1996 and 2000, and S$7 billion from 2001 to 2005.[57] In the life sciences field, the IMCB was the single largest recipient of public R&D funds administered by the NSTB.

Second, the government initiated a thorough administrative reorganization of the state apparatus during the late 1990s. Economic restructuring and new socioeconomic pressures entailed increasingly complex policy problems for decision makers. The 1997 financial crisis emphasized the imperatives of

55. National Science and Technology Board (NSTB), *National Technology Plan, 1991* (Singapore: NSTB, 1991), 21–22.

56. National Science and Technology Board (NSTB), *National Science and Technology Plan, 1996* (Singapore: NSTB, 1996), 8.

57. NSTB, *National Science and Technology Plan, 1996*, 22.

efficient public administration. Inspired by new public management theory and the promise of greater administrative efficiency, the government undertook a process of administrative "decentralization." Eliza Lee and Shamsul Haque describe decentralization as the "agencification" of authority within the state apparatus. Leadership, authority, and strategic planning were scaled from the ministries to specialized agencies within them, such as the EDB and the NSTB, both of which are a part of the MTI.[58] Specialization via agencification was intended to streamline the bureaucracy and to prevent the sort of jurisdictional overlap, duplication, and conflict that we saw early on in Korea and Taiwan. But scaling downward in effect translated into the further concentration of authority. It was in this context that the NSTB was elevated in de facto status as the specialized agency in charge of developing Singapore's science and technology base. The NSTB's authority was further augmented when it was reconstituted in 2001 as the overarching Agency for Science, Technology and Research, or A*STAR.

Third, rescaling authority within the state apparatus was effectively finalized when the 2001 Biomedical Sciences Initiative (BMSI) formally empowered the A*STAR and the EDB as the two leading government agencies in charge of Singapore's biomedical industry development. Without a strong domestic R&D base, it was reasoned, global firms were less likely to locate their operations in Singapore. Likewise, the absence of a foreign industry presence slowed the process of domestic R&D capacity building. The objectives of the A*STAR and the EDB were thus interconnected.

The EDB actually drafted Singapore's first national biotech program as early as 1988, and it was revised into the biotech "master plan" in 1990.[59] The EDB formed the biomedical sciences (BMS) Group during the early 1990s. This high-level group is headed by the cochairman of the EDB and is dedicated to attracting investment from life sciences MNCs. Over the past several years, virtually every major pharmaceutical firm has relocated a part of its operations to Singapore. To achieve this, the BMS Group has drawn on its extensive network of global firms and research institutes, offering lucrative incentives to prospective partners. It also oversees the Bio*One venture capital fund, the investment arm of the EDB.[60] In 2007, the fund's total

---

58. Eliza Lee and M. Shamsul Haque, "The New Public Management Reform and Governance in Asian NICs: A Comparison of Hong Kong and Singapore," *Governance* 19 (2006), 612–613.

59. Economic Development Board (EDB), *Biotechnology: A Growing Industry, Focus for Tomorrow* (Singapore: EDB, 1992).

60. The Bio*One manages four funds: the Singapore Bio-Innovations Fund, the PharmBio-Growth Fund, the Life Sciences Investment Fund, and the Biomedical Sciences Investment Fund (BMSIF). The BMSIF equals approximately US$660 million, making it the largest of the four.

capitalization equaled approximately US$800 million, the largest such fund in the Asia region. The EDB also adopted a "boomerang" policy, whereby outward Bio★One investments were conditional on the expectation that invested firms abroad would eventually bring some of their operations to Singapore. To complement the EDB, the A★STAR, like the NSTB before it, continued to develop Singapore's domestic R&D capabilities. The A★STAR leadership actually comprises only two councils, the Science and Engineering Research Council (SERC) and the Biomedical Research Council (BMRC).[61] The BMRC manages and allocates public R&D funds to the seven life sciences PRIs and five research consortia.[62] Its share of such resources is not insignificant; in 2005, for instance, over half of all R&D funds allocated to the PRIs were in the area of biomedical research, almost all of which (amounting to S$322 million) was administered by the A★STAR.[63]

The Bases of Coordination

The power and authority afforded to the EDB and A★STAR were extraordinary. Some observers put it in the following way: if Taiwan's biotech innovation system is analogous to an improvisational jazz band (the implication being the absence of strong central leadership), then Singapore's is a disciplined symphony orchestra with the EDB and A★STAR costarring as the conductor. To be sure, the concentration of authority within the state apparatus went beyond the formal empowerment of the two agencies in biotech policy matters as described above; the bases of coordination were resource-based and institutional in nature.

The A★STAR and EDB were responsible for allocating the vast majority of R&D funding for and investment in Singapore's biomedical sector. Unlike in Korea and Taiwan, where public R&D resources were allocated among several ministerial stakeholders, the A★STAR alone was in charge of distributing virtually all R&D funds in Singapore. Given the size of the life sciences R&D budget, this was not a trivial stock of resources. In most other sectors, the private sector tends to account for over half of all R&D investment.

61. The BMRC was established in 2000, under what was then the National Science and Technology Board.

62. The seven PRIs are the Institute of Molecular and Cell Biology, Bioinformatics Institute, Bioprocessing Technology Institute, Genome Institute of Singapore, Institute of Bioengineering and Nanotechnology, Institute for Medical Biology, and Singapore Institute for Clinical Sciences. The five research consortia are the Singapore Cancer Syndicate, Bioimaging Consortium, Stem Cell Consortium, Immunology Network, and Singapore Consortium for Cohort Studies.

63. Agency for Science, Technology, and Research (A★STAR), *National Survey of R&D in Singapore, 2005* (Singapore: A★STAR, 2006), 15.

In Singapore, for instance, the private sector's share in *overall* R&D funding increased to about two-thirds during the 1990s and early 2000s, a portion consistent with other industrial countries. However, in the area of biomedical R&D, which accounts for one-fifth of Singapore's total R&D spending, public funds (government, higher education, and PRIs) made up 65% of R&D resources, the mirror image of the public-private share in total R&D spending. In other words, given weak private sector investment in Singapore in biomedical research, the state, and specifically the A★STAR, has had to compensate. In 2005, A★STAR-funded PRIs accounted for 38% of total biomedical R&D spending, more than the entire private sector (see Table 2.4).

The EDB's control over resource allocation has been more indirect than that of the A★STAR, though no less significant. The Bio★One fund, for instance, made up for the relative dearth of domestic venture capital by injecting hundreds of millions of dollars into domestic R&D efforts. Moreover, the EDB's leadership role in brokering foreign direct investment in the biomedical industry has contributed greatly to the accumulation of R&D resources in Singapore. And even though private industry accounted for just 35% of total biomedical R&D spending during the middle of the first decade of the 2000s, the vast majority of this investment came from those MNCs that had been lured by the EDB. According to government figures, multinational companies are responsible for approximately three-quarters of all private sector R&D spending in Singapore's biomedical sector. In terms of R&D personnel, 60% of all researchers working in the biomedical industry are employed by a foreign firm.[64]

The bases of intrastate coordination extended beyond the EDB's and A★STAR's control over biomedical industry R&D resources. Indeed, what was further distinctive (in comparison with Korea and Taiwan) about the reorganization of state power in Singapore was the degree to which authority was concentrated at the individual level. More specifically, Philip Yeo, a noted senior official in the government, is credited with having been the architect of Singapore's biomedical sciences initiative. He in many ways represented the charismatic "strong man" absent in contemporary Korea and Taiwan. Yeo's leadership in the EDB spanned twenty years, during which he was EDB chairman from 1986 to 2001 and cochairman until 2006. Yeo was also chairman of A★STAR from 2000 to 2007. In other words, he simultaneously oversaw the EDB's BMS Group and the A★STAR's BMRC during Singapore's major push into the biomedical industries sector. Yeo surrounded

---

64. A★STAR, *National Survey, 2005,* 15.

Table 2.4.   Distribution of R&D Funding in Singapore by Source (S$ millions and %)

	PRIVATE SECTOR	GOVERNMENT SECTOR	HIGHER EDUCATION	PUBLIC RESEARCH INSTITUTES	TOTAL
Total R&D expenditure	3,031 (66%)	442 (10%)	477 (10%)	630 (14%)	4,580 (100%)
Biomedical R&D expenditure	299 (35%)	102 (12%)	132 (15%)	322 (38%)	855 (100%)

Source: Agency for Science, Technology and Research (A*STAR), *National Survey of R&D in Singapore, 2005* (Singapore: A*STAR, 2006), 15.

himself with an international advisory board of the world's most respected scientists. Being positioned in leadership roles in the two government agencies explicitly tasked with growing Singapore's biomedical sector meant that Yeo more easily marshaled domestic resources. He also provided a credible and respected face to the international investment and scientific communities. And he enjoyed an institutional vantage point from which to effectively coordinate the two agencies.

The relatively small number of actors involved in facilitating the growth of the biomedical sector contributed to the high coordinative capacity of the Singaporean state, and Philip Yeo was clearly at the center of the decision-making process. Unlike in Korea and Taiwan, where varied ministries of relatively equal power and expertise vied for allocative authority, in Singapore the processes of bureaucratic agencification resulted in the opposite, such that fewer, not more, actors were involved in planning and decision making. Strategic alignment among government stakeholders was easier to achieve. The deeper, more normative underpinnings of the state remained hierarchical: as Edgar Schein notes in his study of the EDB, systems of "nonhierarchic hierarchy" and "participatory autocracy" are reinforced by "strong patterns of deference to authority."[65] The authority, in this case, was unequivocally Philip Yeo.

New Directions?

The Singaporean experience appears to be the outlier with respect to how the state has been reorganized in the Asian cases examined in this book. A greater concentration of power and authority within the state apparatus and thus the persistence of hierarchical means for intrastate coordination seem to

---

65. See Schein, *Strategic Pragmatism,* 112. For reference to the term "participatory autocracy," see Schein, *Strategic Pragmatism,* chap. 1.

trend in the opposite direction of the organizational changes we see in Korea and Taiwan. A compelling explanation for this divergence might rest with the nondemocratic nature of the Singaporean state. It is often assumed that the institutional flux that comes with the processes of democratic transition, such as we saw in Korea and Taiwan during the early 1990s, inevitably leads to the deconcentration of power and authority.[66] In Singapore, the absence of democratic reform and the continued dominance of the People's Action Party (PAP) prevent the devolution of power within the state apparatus.[67] Indeed, when Philip Yeo headed the EDB and the A*STAR between 2000 and 2006, he exercised a tremendous amount of individual and institutional power. He consulted very broadly, but he was also reportedly predisposed to marginalizing those within the ranks of the EDB and the A*STAR who were not in line with his strategic vision.

Change may be afoot, however, in the organization of Singapore's science and technology innovation system, change that provides a potentially powerful counterpoint to the "nondemocratic" conventional wisdom. Specifically, recent developments in Singapore suggest a nascent process of state reorganization that has been motivated by the overwhelming uncertainties of science-based industrialization, a process that has prompted a shift away from the prevailing strategy of attracting MNCs and toward a more open-ended and institutionally disparate approach that more fully captures the broad spectrum of R&D activities required for biotech development. As explained above, before 2007 virtually all R&D funds were administered through the Ministry of Trade and Industry (MTI), specifically its two key agencies, the EDB and the A*STAR. Things began to change after 2007, however, when the government unveiled its 2010 Science and Technology Plan (drawn up in 2006), which suggests that a significant reorganization of the Singaporean state and its coordinative style may be under way.

First, the state increased public funding for R&D in order to meet its larger goal of 3% of GDP devoted to R&D spending. Public funds were intended to supplement private sector investment, for which a significant portion is directed to the biomedical sector. On the input side, the state's commitment to growing science-based industries increased. Second, and more important, the disbursement of these new funds altered the state-level administration

---

66. Pereira, "Whither the Developmental State?"; Yu-Shan Wu, "Taiwan's Developmental State: After the Economic and Political Turmoil," *Asian Survey* 47 (2007).

67. Authoritarian states are presumed to be more capable than democracies at sustaining institutional order. As one policymaker from Taiwan succinctly put it: "Fifteen years ago we could have done what Singapore is currently doing, that is, centralizing coordination. However, in today's Taiwan, that would be impossible." Author interview, Taipei, Taiwan, October 14, 2004.

and coordination of science and technology development. In addition to earmarking more resources for R&D, the state created entirely new funding streams, thus undercutting the concentrated resource base that had afforded the EDB and A★STAR their prevailing coordinative authority within the state. Of the S$13.55 billion (or US$9 billion) that the government earmarked for national R&D, S$5 billion was to be allocated by the newly formed National Research Fund (NRF) and over S$1 billion by the Ministry of Education through its Academic Research Fund (AcRF), totaling approximately US$4.2 billion. The remaining S$7.5 billion—a sizable amount though a significantly smaller share of the total resource pie—has continued to be administered by the Ministry of Trade and Industry through the EDB and the A★STAR. Both the NRF and the AcRF are intended to target resources for more upstream, exploratory research, while the funds earmarked for the MTI have continued to be directed at more downstream R&D.[68] Organizationally, the EDB and A★STAR are no longer the only sources of R&D funds and coordinative authority inside the state.

Third, in 2007 Philip Yeo was reassigned to lead SPRING, the MTI's agency for promoting small and medium-sized enterprises. Many insider accounts of Yeo's transfer imply that he had lost out in a political struggle with senior official and rival Tony Tan, who was, incidentally, subsequently appointed to head the newly formed National Research Foundation. But beyond a political power play, the creation of new funding streams and new administrative units within the state apparatus in Singapore suggests that the distribution of authority and the allocation of resources have become increasingly horizontalized and decentralized in ways not dissimilar to what we have seen in Korea and Taiwan. And at the least, the move points to a potentially new strategic direction in Singapore with respect to the coordination of resource allocation, a move away from past practices in top-down coordination toward a more horizontally organized and decentralized management of science and technology development.

Continuity and Change

One of the key attributes of the postwar developmental state model was its strategic industrial policies, interventions in the economy that compelled otherwise risk-averse firms to enter new industrial technology sectors. The literature tells us that much of the developmental state's strategic capacity

---

68. Ministry of Trade and Industry (MTI), *Plan 2010: Science and Technology; Sustaining Innovation-Driven Growth* (Singapore: MTI, 2006).

was owed to the organization of the state apparatus. State capacity reflected an authoritative and coherent bureaucracy. Strategic decision making and policy implementation were coordinated through vertically organized institutions. And the state controlled and allocated tremendous amounts of resources. In other words, the internal organization of the developmental state was conducive to a top-down, coordinated style of resource allocation, which in turn afforded it the authority and structural capacity to pick and make winners, to target and mobilize resources around winning sectors, technologies, and even firms. I began this chapter by asking whether these patterns of coordination, strategic decision making, and resource allocation have persisted into the current era of science-based industrialization; the answer is both yes and no.

The evidence presented in this chapter confirms that there have been significant continuities in how the state is organized and in how decision makers inside the state see their guiding role in biotech development. Most obviously, the state as a whole has maintained control over a significant resource base, which it has continued to allocate broadly for the purposes of industrial technology upgrading. What is more, not only does the biotech sector account for a significant share of total government R&D spending—15% in Korea and around 30% in Taiwan and Singapore—but the state's share in total biotech R&D expenditures is comparable to, and in Singapore even greater than, private sector investments in life sciences R&D. The state has thus continued to treat commercial biotech development as a loss-leader investment, recognizing that, as was the case in the past, state leadership through the allocation of public resources remains critical to encouraging follow-on investment. In this way, the state has continued to mitigate the risks of entry for otherwise risk-averse stakeholders in the life sciences sector.

The analysis of the three cases presented in this chapter also shows that patterns of resource allocation are strikingly similar to nationally distinct practices of the past. Current patterns are in line with prevailing strategic repertoires unique to each of the three cases. In Korea, the allocation of public resources has continued to reflect a broad division of labor, including open-ended basic research in the upstream and industry-focused downstream development. The Korean pattern of resource allocation, similar to postwar efforts in industrial upgrading, continues to be comprehensive in scope, sizable in scale, and intended to capture the full spectrum of R&D activities. Meanwhile, the pattern we see in Taiwan centers on small bets spread among various state-level stakeholders. Not unlike in the past, decision makers there have continued to privilege a niche approach to bio-industrial upgrading and, most important, a continued commitment to focusing on midstream technology development. To be sure, of the three cases in this book, the shift in R&D funding to upstream basic research has been least pronounced in Taiwan. And finally, the Singaporean pattern of resource allocation reflects decision makers' proven strategy of attracting global biomedical firms in an effort to transform the city-state from technology manufacturer to viable R&D hub. As in the past, the state has allocated resources in a coordinated fashion to augment and emphasize Singapore's locational advantages, to build up domestic R&D capacity, and to seed the growth of local supporting industries.

To manage biotech's technical and economic uncertainties, decision makers in Korea, Taiwan, and Singapore have therefore reverted to past patterns of resource allocation. The evidence suggests, as theory would predict, that when confronted with such enormous and multifaceted uncertainty, strategic actors will make choices that reflect their own heuristic biases. Despite tremendous uncertainty in the biotech sector, and quite frankly extraordinary uncertainty about how the state can facilitate the growth of a sector about which it knows so little, decision makers in Korea, Taiwan, and Singapore have strategically rationalized and justified expensive allocative choices in ways that are most familiar to them. Strategic repertoires and cognitive scripts help decision makers manage uncertain prospects. In this respect, the varied and not surprising ways in which decision makers have allocated state resources in Korea, Taiwan, and Singapore are a perfect example of how strategic actors will make choices *as if uncertainty can be managed.* As I argued in the previous chapter, actors will attempt to turn uncertain prospects into risk propositions that can be mitigated.

Yet the evidence presented in this chapter suggests that there is also something more fundamentally transformative going on in all three cases, particularly with respect to how state-level decision makers exercise leadership in industrial technology upgrading. So while there are important continuities in resource allocation within states and in the supply-side impact that states have had in biotech development in Korea, Taiwan, and Singapore, there is a profoundly different strategic logic in how states there approach the challenges of growing biotech industries and facilitating life sciences innovation. To put it simply, biotech stakeholders in Korea, Taiwan, and Singapore are no longer looking to pick winners to make. Rather, in all three cases, future prospects rest on the distant, likely improbable, and unknowable *potentiality* of viable winners emerging. Korea's comprehensive approach in allocating resources hinges on the formation of potential complementary R&D linkages, just as Taiwan's hit-and-miss approach rests on the eventual identification of core competencies and potential niches in biotech markets. Likewise, despite careful planning inside the state, Singapore's hub strategy depends, in the end, on the decisions of global firms to locate higher value-added R&D operations in the city-state. Instead of strategically picking winners, state leadership in the current era of science-based industrialization is premised on betting flexibly, in recognition of the unpredictability of the emergence of eventual winners. Technological and economic uncertainty in biotech has made the developmental state strategies of picking bio-industry winners impractical.

The coordinative capacity of the state has diminished. There are two reasons for this. First, as this chapter has detailed, the multidisciplinary nature of biotech has forced a functional redistribution of authority among state actors claiming specialized expertise. The functionalist imperatives of biotechnology and science-based industrialization more generally are accentuated by the sector's technical and market uncertainties. As the cases of Korea and Taiwan clearly show, there is little sense about core competencies and prospective comparative advantages in the commercial biotech sector. Recent adjustments in Singapore suggest that different bases of expertise (other than the EDB and A*STAR) and varied research agendas across the R&D spectrum have similarly prompted a more diffuse allocation of resources. Second, the decentralization of expertise in all three cases has effectively undermined coordinative leadership within the state apparatus. Once politically powerful pilot agencies are now perceived to lack sufficient expertise to choose how resources earmarked for biotech ought to be allocated. Efforts to create high-level biotech steering committees in Korea and Taiwan have similarly been frustrated by ministerial claims from below. The EDB and A*STAR have effectively been downgraded in Singapore, their authority challenged by other viable biotech stakeholders inside the state. Simply put, a leadership void has emerged inside the state apparatus.

The combination of these two factors—the functionalist imperatives of biotech and the absence of legitimate coordinative leadership characteristic of the old developmental state model—has contributed to the structural and organizational fragmentation of the state. There is, when it comes to the biotech sector, a greater plurality of actors, interests, expectations, expertise, and priorities among varied stakeholders in Korea, Taiwan, and Singapore. The redistribution of authority has fomented competition and contestation among state actors as they vie for a rapidly expanding resource pie, and more decentralized modes of coordination are the result. No longer are coordinative processes dictated from the top down. No longer is the state apparatus—at least among the many actors involved in biotech development—organized vertically and strategic decisions determined hierarchically. No longer is the state even capable of swiftly and purposively mobilizing resources in strategic ways, as the distribution of such resources has become increasingly dispersed in Korea, Taiwan, and even Singapore. The reorganization of the state has altered the logic of state leadership in facilitating innovation-driven technological development.

CHAPTER 3

Organizing Bio-industry

Commercializing biotech is an extraordinarily complex process. It involves the generation of new knowledge in the upstream and the translation of knowledge into usable technological applications that bear market value. Marketable novel technologies need not be just cutting-edge knowledge but also include innovative business models and market savvy, as well as patient, creative, and entrepreneurial investment. The commercialization process encompasses a broad range of different actors and activities, all of which must be integrated in productive ways. Technical and economic uncertainties of biotech innovation, however, complicate this process. Commercializing biotech, as once described to me, involves many moving parts that must be combined and recombined in order to chase down many moving targets.

This chapter builds on the last one by untangling these complex processes from the perspective of the firm and the industry. Specifically, this chapter looks at how biotech industries have been organized in Korea, Taiwan, and Singapore. It identifies the core actors in the innovation system, the range of relevant supporting actors, and the strategic interactions between firms, labs, and the state. The analysis further articulates how decision makers in Korea, Taiwan, and Singapore strategically rationalize the ways in which bio-industry is organized. While they face similar challenges in betting against biotech's myriad sources of uncertainty, decision makers in Korea, Taiwan, and Singapore have organized bio-industry in different ways, revealing quite varied strategic rationales.

Data on trends in innovation are a good starting point for making some initial sense of this variation. According to Mahmood and Singh's study of overall patenting activity in Asia (a crude but still useful measure of innovative output), the specific sources of innovative activity differ markedly.[1] In Korea, large business groups, or chaebols, accounted for 81% of all patenting between 1990 and 1999, while other firms made up just 12%. Multinational firms operating in Korea were responsible for less than 1% of U.S. patents, and individual researchers (such as university professors and employees of government research institutes) accounted for just 7%. In contrast, MNCs in Singapore were awarded nearly half (46%) of all U.S. patents granted to Singaporean-based inventors. In Taiwan, MNCs and large business groups accounted for merely 5% of patenting activity, while local firms and research organizations such as the ITRI made up 36% of output.[2] The majority of patents in Taiwan (59%) were registered with individuals, universities, and small-scale industrial entrepreneurs.[3]

Mahmood and Singh also calculate the concentration of patenting activity in Asian countries. The highest levels of concentration, through the end of the 1990s, were in Korea, where 85% of all patents were granted to the top fifty patent earners, basically among the conglomerate chaebol firms. Samsung Electronics alone accounted for 36% of all patents awarded to Korean inventors between 1970 and 1999. Singapore's innovation activities have been similarly concentrated, and its top fifty patent earners accounted for 70% of all patenting activity. Taiwan's patent outputs, on the other hand, are much more diffuse, with only 26% of awarded patents concentrated among the top fifty patent earners. The bases of technological innovation in Taiwan have been spread out among multiple sources.

In many respects, Mahmood and Singh's findings are not surprising given what we know about national variations in industrial technology development among these three Asian economies. In Korea, technology development is concentrated among the chaebols, whereas in Taiwan, innovative

---

1. Their study uses U.S. patent data; patents awarded domestically (i.e., within the home country) are not included in their data set. However, given that U.S. patents are considered the most difficult to attain and usually provide the largest market access for eventual products, U.S. patent data offer an indication of the most significant and innovative outcomes. Ishtiaq Mahmood and Jasjit Singh, "Technological Dynamism in Asia," *Research Policy* 32 (2003), 1045.

2. The ITRI was Taiwan's top patent earner between 1970 and 1999, with 1,229 patents. See Mahmood and Singh, "Technological Dynamism," 1046.

3. Thanks to one of the anonymous reviewers of the manuscript of this book for pointing this out to me.

activity is diffused among public and private sources. Meanwhile, in Singapore, industrial technology development revolves around the activities of multinational corporations. Differences in both the sources and concentration of innovative activities reflect the overall organization of the respective political economies. Though not unexpected, these contrasting patterns of technological innovation are significant, for they indicate where innovative activity has been concentrated in Korea, Taiwan, and Singapore and suggest how we might expect bio-industrial innovation to evolve in the three cases. Indeed, the contrasts are so stark that it seems sensible to keep these patterns in mind as we focus on the organization of bio-industry in the three cases. To a good extent, these variable patterns of technology development have endured.

Taiwan's "Many Sprouts"

With the exception of a few U.S.-based firms, the biotech industry is dominated by small enterprises. The global biotech industry model was transformed when, beginning in the 1980s, large pharmaceutical firms opted to strategically collaborate with, or outright acquire, specialized start-ups rather than develop cutting-edge biotechnologies in-house. As the costs of translational R&D became prohibitive for big drug firms, they needed to continually fill their pipelines with prospective candidates from elsewhere.[4] They wanted to spread their bets, and small biotech start-ups were the most cost-effective way to identify potential winners. Together big and small life sciences firms formed a technological and economic "marriage of convenience."[5]

Because most biotech firms are spun out of universities or life sciences labs further upstream, they tend to focus on one or two specialized technologies and applications. On the one hand, specialization exacerbates the risks associated with biotech innovation and the likelihood of commercial failure among small firms. But on the other hand, growth in the overall number of bioventures increases the potential rewards for breakthrough technologies industry-wide and, more important, spreads the costs of failure across the entire industry. The proliferation of small firms means that there is a high probability of failure for individual ventures, but a critical mass of firms increases

---

4. Lawton Robert Burns, ed., *The Business of Healthcare Innovation* (New York: Cambridge University Press, 2005).

5. See Richard Oliver, *The Coming Biotech Age: The Business of Bio-Materials* (New York: McGraw-Hill, 2000).

the chances of success for the industry as a whole, especially as leading firms look to innovative venture firms for potential leads. This is the same strategic logic that informs Taiwan's current efforts in biotech commercialization.

Growing SMEs

Given the evolution of the structure of biotech industries, Taiwan's industrial landscape seems to fit well with the commercial uncertainties of life sciences innovation. There are no large pharmaceutical companies in Taiwan, and to the extent that there is any drug-making capacity, most is in generic manufacturing for the domestic market. Marketing, sales, and distribution are also limited to the home market. Not surprisingly, then, Taiwan's emergent biotech industry continues to be dominated by small and medium-sized enterprises, a pattern consistent with its postwar strategy of niche industrialization.[6] Unlike in Korea and Singapore, the growth of SMEs continues to be the strategic basis of industrial upgrading in postwar Taiwan.[7]

In the absence of large diversified enterprises that can absorb the costs of industrial upgrading through the economies of scale, SMEs in postwar Taiwan leveraged instead their industrial and commercial agility. Unencumbered by the organizational constraints typical of very large firms, SMEs adapted to rapidly changing markets.[8] In this respect, SMEs would appear ideal for the biotech sector, where commercial markets remain relatively uncertain. What is more, because of their scale-related constraints in financial capital, personnel, and R&D, SMEs are also more likely, out of sheer necessity, to form collaborative linkages with R&D institutes and other commercial entities. Throughout the postwar period, successful SMEs clustered around one another and in close proximity to R&D centers, notably the ITRI and the Hsinchu Science Industry Park.[9] Not surprisingly, these patterns have

---

6. Unlike in Korea, where industrial output was dominated by a handful of chaebols, approximately 98% of Taiwan's firms during the postwar era were SMEs, many of which contributed to Taiwan's export economy and its industrial value-added gains.

7. Yun-Han Chu, "Surviving the East Asian Financial Storm: The Political Foundation of Taiwan's Economic Resilience," in *The Politics of the Asian Economic Crisis,* ed. T. J. Pempel (Ithaca: Cornell University Press, 1999).

8. Danny Lam and Ian Lee, "Guerilla Capitalism and the Limits of Statist Theory: Comparing the Chinese NICs," in *The Evolving Pacific Basin in the Global Political Economy,* ed. Cal Clark and Steve Chan (Boulder, Colo.: Lynne Rienner, 1992), 111–113; Vincent Wang, "Developing the Information Industry in Taiwan: Entrepreneurial State, Guerilla Capitalists and Accommodative Technologists," *Pacific Affairs* 68 (1995), 572–574.

9. In 1998, the Hsinchu Science Industrial Park housed 272 firms. See Wen-Hsiung Lee and Wei-Tzen Yang, "The Cradle of Taiwan's High Technology Industry Development: Hsinchu Science Park (HSP)," *Technovation* 20 (2000), 570.

been replicated in Taiwan's biotech sector with the creation of dedicated clusters in Hsinchu and more recently in Tainan, Nankang, and elsewhere on the island.

Taiwan's SMEs in the postwar period required lower start-up costs and investments, which meant more manageable entry barriers for prospective entrepreneurs. This in turn lowered the costs of risk taking. Risk aversion was further overcome by means of both broad and dense networks of firms that collectively absorbed the costs of commercial failure industry-wide and maximized the economies of scope over a broad spectrum of goods and services.[10] Commercial failure became normalized in Taiwan; some firms found viable niches, though many did not. Indeed, failure came to be understood as merely a reality of industrial upgrading. But because the actual costs of failure for SMEs were minimal—when compared with the capital requirements of large firms—entrepreneurs, with the assistance of state incentives, were in the end more likely to enter potentially high-growth sectors.[11] The normalization of failure in postwar industrial upgrading in Taiwan, it would seem, suits the inherent uncertainties of biotech innovation.

Most important of all, however, is the fact that the postwar SME strategy was predicated on the segmentation, rather than intrafirm consolidation, of commercial value chains, not unlike the current global biotech industry. Taiwan's industrial SMEs are particularly well suited for more "granularized" and "dis-integrated" technologies such as IT, electronics, and, it has been argued, biotech.[12] Firms are thus focusing on specialized segments of the biotech innovation process and the commercial value chain.[13] Aspirations to grow large-scale, fully integrated biotech or biopharmaceutical firms in Taiwan were nonstarters from the beginning. Rather, Taiwan's biotech industry as a whole is conceived as "one giant firm" in which individual SMEs are expected to contribute to different though vital links of the value chain.[14]

---

10. Dan Breznitz, *Innovation and the State: Political Choice and Strategies for Growth in Israel, Taiwan and Ireland* (New Haven, Conn.: Yale University Press, 2007); Richard Nelson, ed., *National Innovation Systems: A Comparative Analysis* (New York: Oxford University Press, 1993).

11. According to AnnaLee Saxenian, 1,373 IT companies were formed in 1997 and another 1,147 (or 84%) folded that same year. AnnaLee Saxenian, "Taiwan's Hsinchu Region: Imitator and Partner for Silicon Valley," SIEPR Discussion Paper No. 00-44, 2001, 11.

12. See Suzanne Berger and Richard Lester, eds., *Global Taiwan: Building Competitive Strengths in a New International Economy* (Armonk, N.Y.: M. E. Sharpe, 2005); Alice Amsden and Wan-Wen Chu, *Beyond Late Development: Taiwan's Upgrading Policies* (Cambridge, Mass.: MIT Press, 2003); Haider Khan, *Interpreting East Asian Growth and Innovation: The Future of Miracles* (New York: Palgrave Macmillan, 2004); Saxenian, "Taiwan's Hsinchu Region."

13. Author interviews, various cities, Taiwan, December 16, April 23, and April 26, 2002.

14. Author interview, Nankang, Taiwan, April 29, 2004.

The story of ScinoPharm illustrates the SME approach to commercial biotech development. ScinoPharm was founded during the mid-1990s by two former executives and scientists at Syntex, a U.S.-based drug firm. After Syntex was acquired by Roche, Jo Shen and Hardy Chan returned to Taiwan to form ScinoPharm, a pharmaceutical ingredients firm. Its major investor was the Uni-President food conglomerate. Initially, ScinoPharm's core business was in supplying active pharmaceutical ingredients (APIs) for drug firms. Manufacturing APIs is a growth segment in the drug development industry and one that industry watchers predict will be increasingly outsourced. ScinoPharm was among the first Taiwan-based companies to have its production facilities certified by the U.S. FDA, expanding its market beyond local buyers. Though ScinoPharm's business model initially centered on a "me too" product and service, the firm's competitive advantage was realized through proprietary process innovations. Its initial business model, in other words, was based on price competition.[15]

The firm's long-term ambitions, however, are in the biotech sector proper, and not chemistry-based manufacturing and supply. ScinoPharm thus has a two-stage growth strategy. ScinoPharm Biotechnology was created in 2001 as a subsidiary of the parent company. With a small R&D staff working in research facilities near Shanghai, ScinoPharm Biotechnology quickly gained a foothold in the biopharmaceutical industry, providing contract manufacturing of biologicals, which Shen and Chan anticipated in the wake of new discoveries in genomic research and the rapid entry of major drug firms into the biopharmaceutical sector.[16] Over the longer term, however, the firm looks to develop, manufacture, and distribute biogeneric drugs. In 2006, ScinoPharm reported a 43% revenue growth from the previous year and for the first time posted net profits, almost all of which came from its API supply business.[17] The firm planned to launch an IPO soon thereafter.

The story of ScinoPharm is exemplary of Taiwan's SME strategy in biotech industry development. The firm began as a start-up. It benefited from various state incentives, including low-interest loans, though its primary equity investors came from the private sector, not the government. Like other venture firms, ScinoPharm draws on foreign expertise, specifically returnees to Taiwan who bring with them overseas industrial experience. But most important, it is understood that if ScinoPharm is to survive, it has to expand

15. Robert Yuan, "Scinopharm Focuses on Manufacturing of APIs," *Genetic Engineering News* 22 (March 15, 2002).

16. Author interviews, Tainan, Taiwan, October 15, 2004.

17. Scinopharm press release, "Scinopharm's 2006 Revenue and Net Income at Record High," February 26, 2007. See http://www.scinopharm.com (accessed March 5, 2007).

its markets in the absence of excessive government patronage. Its gradual two-stage business model was therefore necessitated by the fact that the firm is dependent on a near-term revenue stream to survive, compensating for the dearth of patient and risk capital in Taiwan's biotech sector. ScinoPharm thus delayed its entry into its core biotech business by establishing an initial market presence in a "me too" niche in the pharmaceutical supply chain. Upgrading into more innovative biotech applications has been carried out within the firm over time. ScinoPharm was not a big-bang biobusiness.

ScinoPharm's example is an important one because it is consistent with Taiwan's overall strategy for developing R&D-intensive biotech SMEs. Mirroring the "hit-and-miss" logic of resource allocation described in Chapter 2, Taiwan's approach to bio-industrial growth is to seed "many sprouts." Most are not expected to survive, but those that do might eventually grow to be successful firms.[18] Given biotech's uncertainties, it is not clear which firms will survive. Nor is there any certainty about which niches will eventually be captured by Taiwanese firms. The state has purposely steered clear of picking winners in commercial biotech. What *is* certain, however, is that struggling firms with little potential for growth cannot survive. The challenges faced by ScinoPharm and its responses are typical of a Taiwanese SME.

Investing in the Midstream

Though it is expected—and even encouraged—that the majority of Taiwanese biotech SMEs will in the end be commercial failures, firms have not had to bear the uncertainties of biotech innovation and commercialization alone. As I described in Chapter 2, the state is investing in midstream R&D to help mitigate the risks of commercializing biotechnology.[19] More precisely, the state, when compared with the state in Korea and Singapore, has allocated a disproportionately large stock of public resources to strengthening, diversifying, and multiplying biotech development and transfer mechanisms dedicated to the life sciences industry. Thus, despite the uncertainty about which of Taiwan's "many sprouts" will survive commercially, public investment in midstream activities is intended to increase, even if only marginally, the probability of some longer-term survivors in the sector.[20]

---

18. Author interview, Taipei, Taiwan, October 11, 2004.

19. Author interview, Taipei, Taiwan, September 16, 2007.

20. Author interview, Taipei, Taiwan, October 11, 2004. See also Pao-Long Chang and Chiung-Wen Hsu, "A Stage Approach for Industrial Technology Development and Implementation," *Technovation* 19 (1999).

The National Health Research Institute is a good example of this mid-stream biotech development strategy. The NHRI was established in 1995 by the Department of Health. Its annual budget is sizable by the standards of Taiwan-based research institutes, amounting to approximately US$90 million, nearly all of which comes from the state. Unlike the ITRI, the NHRI was initially intended to concentrate on upstream life sciences research, similar to the National Institutes of Health in the United States. However, the NHRI is increasingly focusing on the development of applied technologies, a reorientation that was prompted when the DOH, its ministerial patron, steered its R&D programs further downstream. Since the early part of the first decade of the 2000s, the NHRI's Biotechnology Division, headed by Yu-Sheng Chao, has focused on new drug discovery and development. According to Chao, because Taiwan has no domestic pharmaceutical industry, emerging biotech firms, especially those working on drug development, lack bio-industry and R&D experience.[21] The NHRI's primary objective, therefore, is to transfer promising drug candidates to commercial pipelines within the industry. To narrow the gap between R&D and commercialization, the NHRI is also increasingly partnering directly with industry.

In 2007, Genovate Biotechnology, a Taiwanese biotech start-up, initiated an R&D partnership with the NHRI to work on new drug leads for pre-clinical development. The partnership was subsequently transformed into a full-fledged R&D consortium made up of ten local biotech SMEs. To offset the consortium costs, the ten firms contributed just 15% of total R&D funds while the NHRI accounted for the remaining 85%. Together they conduct "precompetition" R&D. One objective of the consortium is to eventually license out NHRI-developed compounds for clinical and commercial development. Another is to promote intermural learning, in which R&D and biobusiness knowledge are transferred both up and down the research chain.[22] The consortium provides firms the opportunity to conduct early-stage, high-risk research. It has allowed firms to better "understand the science, the biochemical make-up" of potential compounds. Meanwhile, the NHRI is exposed to the needs of industry, learning how upstream discoveries are developed to match downstream applications.[23]

The manner in which the consortium was formed is significant. In the past, parastatal labs, and not firms, were the "anchor" in public-private R&D alliances. Consortia were almost always organized from the top down and

21. Author interview, Nankang, Taiwan, April 29, 2002.
22. Author interview, Zhunan, Taiwan, September 17, 2007.
23. Author interview, Zhunan, Taiwan, September 17, 2007.

usually after targeted applications had first been identified by state planners. Past R&D consortia also tended to center on engineering problems that needed to be solved, a mandate that reflected industrial policies designed explicitly to target and make winners. The origins of the NHRI consortium were different, however. For one, the consortium was initiated from the bottom up and by private sector firms.[24] Moreover, the R&D objectives of the consortium are considerably more open-ended and less targeted than in consortia of the past. As Johnsee Lee, former president of the ITRI explains, collaborative R&D in the life sciences is neither "short term" nor narrowly "project-based" in terms of organization, both of which characteristics were typical of past R&D consortia. Instead, biotech R&D collaboration is becoming more institutionalized among longer-term partners with research agendas that are more open-ended.[25]

The NHRI consortium is just one of many initiatives in Taiwan facilitating closer and longer-lasting linkages between midstream R&D centers and the private sector. The ITRI, not surprisingly, continues to play a leadership role in creating such linkages. Phalanx Biotechnology, a venture firm specializing in micro-array production for biochips, was spun out of ITRI in 2002. The initial idea for Phalanx arose in 1998, when ITRI researchers agreed that the best way forward was to leverage their engineering expertise in biomaterials, medical devices, and biochips, all of which are essentially engineering-based biotech applications. Johnsee Lee, who was at the time ITRI's vice-president and director of the Biomedical Engineering Center (BMEC), focused some of ITRI's life sciences R&D programs on micro-array technology, a specialized niche within the biochip industry.[26] There were no inducements from above to target micro-array technologies. Rather, the impetus for this new R&D agenda came from within the ITRI. Though biochip R&D in ITRI was funded by the Ministry of Economic Affairs between 1998 and 2002, funds were allocated through regular budget lines. Biochip technology, in this respect, was not targeted. It did not benefit from priority investments from the Executive Yuan Development Fund. In fact, micro-array technology was considered at the time too distant to market to be a viable commercial winner; it was merely one of many sprouts.

---

24. The transformation of R&D alliances in Taiwan is well documented by John Matthews, who argues that by the end of the 1990s, firms played "an increasingly active role" by "taking the initiative in forming [R&D] alliances." See Matthews, "The Origins and Dynamics of Taiwan's R&D Consortia," *Research Policy* 31 (2002), 635.

25. Author interview, Hsinchu, Taiwan, March 22, 2004.

26. Author interview, Hsinchu, Taiwan, March 25, 2002.

ITRI researchers nonetheless approached the development of micro-array technology with some sense of market potential. On the supply side, micro-arrays, or gene chips, which array DNA spots on a single slide for use in monitoring gene expressions, were expensive to produce. As of the late 1990s, production costs amounted to about US$2,000 per slide. There were clear supply-side pressures to reduce costs. On the demand side, however, there was uncertainty about the market potential of gene chips. Markets had been relatively sluggish because of the costs to produce the chips, and also because applied genomic research had only just begun to take off. ITRI engineers nonetheless reasoned that cost reductions in production combined with more efficient automation techniques for using DNA micro-array technologies could induce market demand. In 2000, ITRI researchers set an eventual production goal of 50,000 slides per day, at approximately one-tenth the then market price.

What was risky and uncertain was whether ITRI-developed technologies could in fact reach this production capacity. In 2002, a prototype was developed through proprietary innovations in the production of micro-arrays. Proof of concept was demonstrated thereafter. The manufacturing technology worked. Phalanx was then spun out of the ITRI and incubated in the Hsinchu Science Industrial Park. The MOEA was one of many investors in the company, though unlike in the past, the vast majority of financing came from private sector sources and not the state. China Steel and the Yu Long conglomerate led the initial investment. In fact, the ITRI and the MOEA purposely structured the first round of financing to prevent any single investor, including the government, from holding more than a 20% equity stake in the firm. This in effect diversified Phalanx's equity base, diffused risk among multiple investors, and, most important, ensured that the firm remained predominantly a private sector endeavor. Phalanx was not TSMC or UMC, which were heavily supported by the state in the days of IT sector upgrading, in that the economic uncertainty was shouldered by the firm's many industrial stakeholders and not primarily the government.[27]

Off-Loading Uncertainty

Taiwan's approach to growing bio-industry emphasizes certain features that, as we will see, diverge from those in Korea and Singapore. First, technological innovation continues to center on activities within midstream R&D labs.

---

27. Author interviews, Hsinchu, Taiwan, October 12, 2004, and December 16, 2005.

Publicly funded institutes such as the ITRI, the NHRI, and the Development Center for Biotechnology, as well as upstream labs, including Academia Sinica, continue to attempt to bring technologies closer to market in order to narrow the technology gap between science and industry.[28] Commercial biotech's technological uncertainties are thus managed by publicly funded labs.[29] However, unlike in the past, biotech R&D and commercialization are not directed by state planners but led largely by private sector firms, industrial investors, and individual researchers themselves.

Second, though the burdens of facilitating technological innovation continue to be the responsibility of parastatal labs, publicly funded R&D institutions are perceived as not commercially agile enough to take on the market risks and economic uncertainties inherent in the sector on their own. The engines for biotech commercialization are SMEs and start-up venture sectors. As one entrepreneur explains, even the ITRI, which is experienced in transferring its R&D further downstream, is viewed as "too slow and cumbersome" and too "risk-averse" for commercializing biotech.[30] Economic uncertainty is thus borne by industry, which has attempted to manage such uncertainty by seeding "many sprouts." Industry investments in the biotech sector have been intentionally spread so that areas of potential commercial growth can be identified and the costs of anticipated failures diffused.[31]

And third, Taiwan's "many sprouts" strategy demonstrates how stakeholders in Taiwan aim to capture small niche segments of biotech's vast and unintegrated commercial chain, an approach that suits Taiwan's industrial organization. The absence of scale advantages inside firms prohibits efforts to develop fully integrated biotech firms. Ventures such as ScinoPharm and Phalanx also have to operate with nearer-term horizons with respect to generating revenue streams and viable commercial outputs. Critics contend that these constraints force potentially innovative Taiwanese firms to abandon

---

28. In a recent conference paper on biotechnology clusters in Taiwan, Mark Dodgson et al. note, "Rather than organizing around multinational firms which import knowledge, the biotechnology clusters [in Taiwan] are being formed around primary research facilities with the aim of developing new knowledge." The point is that publicly funded research institutes are the institutional core of collaborative R&D and biotech commercialization. See Dodgson, John Matthews, Mei-Chih Hu, and Tim Kastelle, "The Changing Nature of Innovation Networks in Taiwan: From Imitation to Innovation?" (paper presented at the annual DRUID conference, Copenhagen, Denmark, June 18–20, 2006), 7.

29. Author interview, Taipei, Taiwan, October 11, 2004.

30. See also Min-Ping Huang, "The Cradle of Technology: The Industrial Technology Research Institute," in *The Silicon Dragon: High-Tech Industry in Taiwan,* ed. Terence Tsai and Bor-Shiuan Cheng (Northampton, Mass.: Edward Elgar, 2006).

31. Author interview, Taipei, Taiwan, March 24, 2004.

long-term R&D objectives for short-term revenues.[32] To be sure, bioventures in Taiwan are becoming less ambitious, opting for what Steven Casper refers to as "sub-sector"—meaning less lucrative and less cutting-edge—niches along biotech's commercial value chain.[33] Yet opponents to this critical view assert that Taiwan's SME approach ensures that only strong (i.e., revenue-generating, private sector investment) firms survive and that through learning and adaptation, and essentially bootstrapping, such firms have the capacity to grow and continually upgrade from within. They also reason that when commercially viable niches are identified, or when some "sprouts" have begun to show commercial promise, new resources will be allocated. Potential winners are therefore discovered over time through a hit-and-miss process—commercial trial and error among firms.

Integrating Knowledge in Korea

The industrial landscape in Korea continues to be vastly different from that of Taiwan. Korea's postwar industrialization was led by large and diversified chaebol firms such as Samsung, Hyundai, and LG. The Korean strategy for industrial upgrading looks to capture longer portions of commercial value chains and, unlike in Taiwan, ultimately the entire value chain. The scale and scope of chaebols support such aspirations. Chaebol success in the electronics, IT, and automobiles sectors is evidence of Korean firms' capacity to conduct innovative R&D and to ensure high-quality manufacturing, sales, and marketing, as well as logistics management, within a single firm. Technological innovation and private sector industrial R&D continues to center on the leadership of the chaebol sector. Patent data presented by Mahmood and Singh confirm this, as do investment data from studies of other industries.[34]

Korea's aspirations to become a global biotech producer continue to rest with the chaebol firms.[35] Industry, and not the state, has taken the lead in

---

32. Author interviews, Taipei, Taiwan, April 23, 2002, and October 13, 2004.

33. Steven Casper, *Creating Silicon Valley in Europe: Public Policy toward New Technology Industries* (New York: Oxford University Press, 2007).

34. John Matthews and Dong-Sung Cho, *Tiger Technology: The Creation of a Semiconductor Industry in East Asia* (New York: Cambridge University Press, 2000); Joonghae Suh, "Korea's Innovation System: Challenges and New Policy Agenda," INTECH Discussion Paper Series, 2000; Linsu Kim, "National Systems of Industrial Innovation: Dynamics of Capability Building in Korea," in *National Innovation Systems,* ed. Richard Nelson (New York: Oxford University Press, 1993); Mahmood and Singh, "Technological Dynamism."

35. Author interview, Daejon, Korea, May 23, 2003. The Biotech Policy Research Center's 2006 report, for instance, emphasizes how biomedicines account for 90% of resources in the global biotech

Korea, focusing firms' efforts on growing a viable domestic pharmaceutical industry—a very uncertain proposition. Drug discovery and development entails the greatest risk, the longest distance from bench to market, and the largest loss-leader investment. Yet industrial stakeholders in Korea perceive biopharmaceuticals as potentially the largest source of revenue in the sector, the big prize. The goal to capture biopharmaceutical markets reflects the bio-industry ambitions of the chaebols. They have the R&D capabilities and experience needed to bring upstream research further downstream.[36] They possess the resources to increase their manufacturing capacity to bring new drugs to market at competitive prices. The chaebols are able to leverage their global brand and marketing channels to ensure access to international markets. And they are huge; scale in gigantic firms such as LG, Samsung, and Hyundai is expected to help absorb the extraordinary costs of life sciences innovation over the long term.[37]

Chaebol Leadership

Expectations of chaebol leadership in commercial biotech were generated not out of state directives but rather from firms' own bio-industry initiatives. LG Life Sciences (LGLS) emerged as Korea's largest pharmaceutical firm during the first decade of the 2000s, though its origins date back to the mid-1980s, when the LG pharmaceutical division was first created. LGLS was spun out of its parent company, LG, in 2002, around the time that its novel antibiotic, Factive, was about to gain U.S. FDA approval. Factive is the first—and as of 2009, the only—FDA-approved drug discovered and developed in Korea. Its story raised LGLS's profile at home and internationally, and the firm was soon recognized as Korea's pioneer in new drug development.[38] Building on the momentum generated by Factive, LGLS is currently spearheading several R&D projects in biopharmaceuticals and biological drug delivery systems.

The chemistry behind Factive was developed in-house beginning in the early 1990s. LGLS funded preclinical R&D up to Phase 1 trials, but as a relative newcomer to the industry, it decided to license the compound to Glaxo, a

market, thus concluding that this particular sector is the most lucrative. Biotech Policy Research Center (BPRC), *Status of Biotechnology in Korea* (Daejon: BPRC, 2006), 21.

36. According to 2001 figures for the pharmaceutical sector, R&D expenditures per researcher in large firms (more than 300 employees) were about 50% higher than those of SMEs. Ministry of Science and Technology (MOST), *National Science and Technology Statistical Indicators* (Seoul: MOST, 2002).

37. Author interview, Seoul, Korea, September 13, 2007.

38. Author interviews, Seoul, Korea, May 26, 2003; July 11, 2003; and September 13, 2007.

foreign pharmaceutical firm, for human clinical trials during the mid-1990s. The U.S. FDA initially rejected the clinical trial results due to high toxicity levels, and Glaxo abandoned the compound soon thereafter. LGLS then licensed Factive to Genesoft, a U.S.-based biopharmaceutical firm. Genesoft reanalyzed the clinical data and reapplied for FDA approval, which it gained in 2002. As part of the licensing deal, Genesoft retained Factive's distribution rights in North American and European markets, while LGLS secured the rights to produce and distribute Factive to all other global markets, its principal targets being Japan, India, and China.[39]

The story of Factive and LGLS was received positively but also with some caution in Korea. With respect to the positive, Korea had clearly arrived on the global drug scene and LGLS's triumph demonstrated that Korean firms could succeed in drug discovery and development and could leverage their brand in forging global R&D alliances. Important lessons were also learned from the Factive story. Though the Factive project did not entail a lab-to-market product, the firm gained experience in preclinical R&D as well as in dealing with the business and regulatory imperatives of drug discovery and development. Perhaps most important was the fact that Factive was seen as not a product of state patronage, as was the case in high-technology development in the past. Rather, the case of LGLS and Factive confirmed that chaebol leadership in growing bio-industry was indeed viable.[40]

Yet the story of Factive was also received as a cautionary tale about the future prospects of Korea's life sciences industry. The fact remains that LGLS is small compared with established global drug firms.[41] What is more, though LGLS has enjoyed sizable returns from Factive, the firm has yet to successfully bring a biological drug from bench to market. Aspirations of becoming a fully integrated biopharmaceutical firm notwithstanding, the reality is that the story of LGLS failed to assuage prevailing concerns about the technological, economic, and long-term uncertainties of biopharmaceutical development, especially among other chaebol firms. To be sure, LGLS is the only chaebol to have invested significantly in life sciences innovation during the

---

39. Author interview, Seoul, Korea, July 11, 2003.

40. One contrarian view on the suitability of chaebol leadership in biotechnology notes that in the past, Korea's largest firms were primarily motivated by market share rather than profitability and real earnings. In an industry such as biotech, where recouped investments are critical for long-term product and service development, the chaebols will need to rethink prevailing business models. See Meredith Woo-Cumings, "The State, Democracy and the Reform of the Corporate Sector in Korea," in *The Politics of the Asian Economic Crisis,* ed. T. J. Pempel (Ithaca: Cornell University Press, 1999), 122, 141.

41. BPRC, *Status of Biotechnology,* 18.

1990s. Whereas Samsung's initial investment in semiconductors in the early 1980s attracted rapid follow-on investments by competitors, chaebol investment in biotech overall has been relatively slow. Bio-industry investors note, for instance, that the development of Factive spanned nearly a decade and a half, cost LGLS a huge amount of investment capital, and yet still confronted many obstacles that could have sunk the project during its development.[42] That the enormous risks and uncertainties of new drug development are shouldered almost entirely by the firm also means that entry barriers to the sector appear prohibitively high, a deterrent for even the most innovative and risk-embracing chaebol firms. Simply put, commercial biotech continues to be very far from a sure bet, both in spite of and because of LGLS's commercial success.

LGLS cannot do it alone in biotech innovation in Korea. And while it is expected that the chaebol sector will lead the growth of biotech firms, it is also clear that the lure of potential but distant profits and market share alone are not enough to draw conglomerate firms into the sector. And the state is limited in what it can do to lead biotech commercial development. For one, the state is increasingly incapable of directly shaping large firm behavior. By the 1990s, the balance of power and the nature of the relationship between the state and industry had been reversed, and the state no longer commanded industry as it had during the postwar developmental state period. The developmental state's ability to steer industry had waned.[43] But I suggest that the state's relatively weak position vis-à-vis industry was not solely a function of its diminishing capacity to coordinate from the top down; rather, the state is also less willing to take on the risks and uncertainties of coordinating science-based industrialization. The government has made clear that the technological and economic uncertainties of biotech are to be managed by industry and firms. Simply put, state planners have decided that betting on and prospecting biotech firms is the sort of gamble they are no longer willing to wager on.

---

42. The long-term nature of drug development was particularly startling for Korean firms, especially when compared with their experiences in the ICT sector. Korean firms first entered the semiconductor industry in 1983 with relatively small investments. Just five years later, Korea's four main semiconductor firms invested over $1.3 billion in new manufacturing facilities. Spending on R&D increased more than sevenfold between 1983 and 1987, and accounted for 22% of total investment in the sector. By the end of 1988, Korean firms were just half a year behind Japanese leaders in introducing the 1M DRAM chip. In short, the time horizon between a firm's initial entry into the sector to the point where it was competitive was very short. See Kim, "National Systems," 377.

43. Author interview, Seoul, Korea, May 28, 2003. See also Eun Mee Kim, *Big Business, Strong State: Collusion and Conflict in South Korean Development, 1960–1990* (Albany: SUNY Press, 1997).

The Supporting Cast

The chaebols need a supporting cast, different parts of the innovation enterprise that can be linked in productive ways with Korea's leading firms.[44] Here the state plays a critical role. As I described in Chapter 2, the state allocates significant stocks of resources to develop upstream and midstream R&D capabilities. New laws are hastening the creation of new technology transfer mechanisms in virtually all publicly funded research labs to facilitate the "diffusion of innovation" and to encourage the integration of multiple bases of knowledge.[45] In other words, the state's primary role has been to help create this supporting cast.

Venture firms, for instance, are expected to play an essential role in supporting the chaebols by discovering potential drug candidates or providing critical research services for drug development firms.[46] Once ignored by the state in favor of growing chaebol firms, technologically savvy SMEs began to benefit from government support in the 1990s. In 1996, the Ministry of Commerce, Industry, and Energy (MOCIE) created the Small and Medium Sized Business Administration (SMBA) office, which, along with other state agencies, provides R&D-intensive SMEs with a broad range of economic inducements and incentives, including investment capital and the institutionalization of technology transfer offices in all public R&D labs. Central and regional governments in Korea are also investing in the construction of new centers of R&D excellence, the revitalization of science-based industry parks, and the organization of technology clusters.[47] Regulations that had previously prohibited university professors and researchers from entering the private sector were lifted in a "special" 1997 law, a decision that was intended to spark a wave of technology spin-offs.[48] Furthermore, state initiatives have attempted to redress the dearth of industrial financing for technology-based SMEs, through such measures as the disbursement of government loans, the implementation of regulatory reforms in venture capital fund-raising, and the development of the secondary technology stock market

---

44. Author interview, Seoul, Korea, May 26, 2003.

45. Suh, "Korea's Innovation System," 29.

46. Author interviews, Seoul, Korea, May 27, 2003, and September 14, 2007. See also Suh, "Korea's Innovation System."

47. Soon Il Ahn, "A New Program in Cooperative Research between Academia and Industry in Korea, Involving Centers of Excellence," *Technovation* 15 (1995); S. Chung, "Building a National Innovation System through Regional Innovation Systems," *Technovation* 22 (2002).

48. The law was implemented in 1999 and was to expire ten years later. Macrogen's Jun-Seong Seo was the first university professor to take advantage of this law when he became Macrogen's CEO in 2000.

(KOSDAQ), as well as reforms to mergers and acquisitions regulations to encourage more interfirm collaboration.

These efforts, initiated during the late 1990s, have produced strong results. Between 1997 and 2004, SMEs accounted for nearly 90% of formal sector employment in Korea. Small firms also generated 42% of export production and more than half of all domestic manufacturing output. In the pharmaceutical sector, 87% of all R&D units in 2001 were located within SMEs and accounted for nearly two-thirds of total research personnel in the sector.[49] It is estimated that early in the first decade of the 2000s, Korea's bioventure sector comprised about 450 to 600 firms, ranking Korea among the world's leaders in newly created biotech start-ups. Even after the dot-com bust of 2001, government and industry estimates still counted more than 200 active biotech SMEs through the middle of the first decade of the 2000s.[50] Industry insiders view these figures with some optimism, as firms that survived the industry's contraction during the early 2000s are likely to be on firmer financial footing and with potentially marketable technologies in their pipelines. Before 2000, only six biotech ventures were listed on the Korean stock exchange; between 2000 and 2005, and after the dot-com bust, 36 new biotech firms successfully launched IPOs and listed on the KOSDAQ.[51]

Macrogen is one such firm. It listed on the KOSDAQ in 2000, three years after the company was founded by Jun-Seong Seo, a professor at Seoul National University (SNU). Macrogen is considered Korea's first "real" biotech firm to raise funds through an IPO. Macrogen is described by Seo as a "lab venture"—it was not technically spun out of SNU through a formal transfer agreement but rather grew out of Seo's university lab. Seo's research at SNU at the time focused on design and production techniques for micro-arrays and DNA sequencing. Green Cross, a domestic drug firm, was Macrogen's earliest investor. The government's Korean Technology Investment Corporation came on around the same time. Positioned in the market as a research service firm, Macrogen provides DNA sequencing services for pharmaceutical companies as well as upstream labs. As of 2005, about half of Macrogen's revenue stream came from DNA sequencing. Macrogen's initial business model was to gain market share through competitive pricing, providing

49. MOST, *Statistical Indicators.*

50. Joseph Wong, "From Learning to Creating: Biotechnology and the Postindustrial Developmental State in Korea," *Journal of East Asian Studies* 4 (2004); Molly Webb, *South Korea: Mass Innovation Comes of Age* (London: Demos, 2007). MOCIE figures estimated approximately 450 bioventure firms in Korea early in the first decade of the 2000s. The Korean Bioventure Association counted approximately 600 firms.

51. Ministry of Science and Technology (MOST), *Bio-Vision 2016* (Seoul: MOST, 2007), 13.

sequencing services at one-quarter the market price. Once the firm went public in 2000, however, Macrogen refocused its R&D plans to develop new competitive advantages in sequencing speed and accuracy. This prompted the founding of Macrogen USA in Maryland, near the National Institutes of Health and the Washington, D.C., biotech cluster.[52]

Bioneer is another bioventure success case in Korea. The firm was founded by Han-Oh Park, a graduate of the Korean Advanced Institute for Science and Technology (KAIST), one of Korea's technology-intensive public research institutes. Bioneer was among the first firms to be spun out of KAIST and incubated at the Bioventure Center (BVC), which is housed in the adjacent Korean Research Institute of Bioscience and Biotechnology (KRIBB). The firm is based in the Daeduk Science Town in Daejon, Korea's major science park, located near the KAIST, KRIBB, and BVC. Bioneer was founded in 1992. By 2003, it had become the second-fastest-growing biotech firm in the Asia-Pacific region, and in 2005, Bioneer listed on the KOSDAQ. Like Macrogen, Bioneer is a research service firm, specializing in DNA synthesis. But unlike Macrogen, Bioneer is a true start-up: its initial investments were almost solely out-of-pocket. Some venture capital (VC) investment trickled in, though according to Park, Bioneer survived its first decade on bank loans and revenues. Bioneer benefited greatly, though, from its location in Daejon, where it serviced KRIBB and KAIST labs. Because Bioneer is considered a "homegrown" firm, local researchers were willing customers. Bioneer was thus able to generate a modest revenue stream early on, underpricing competitors by 25% with its proprietary synthesis process.[53]

Diffusion and Integration

The Korean state no longer has the capacity or the willingness to "husband" chaebol firms in the life sciences sector. And as I have described so far, it has taken on a more indirect role in facilitating the development of fully integrated biopharmaceutical firms by allocating resources to upstream and midstream R&D and by supporting the growth of technology-intensive, R&D-focused SMEs. The state's efforts are thus aimed at nurturing a supporting cast of actors with which to draw in and help develop Korea's would-be national industrial champions in the commercial biotech sector. This supporting cast can also be seen as the state's indirect role in facilitating

52. Author interviews, Seoul, Korea, July 11, 2003; September 7, 2005; and July 9, 2003.
53. Author interviews, Daejon, Korea, July 7, 2003; May 23, 2003; September 8, 2005; and September 14, 2007.

the diffusion of knowledge. By this I mean the spread of knowledge up and down the technology R&D division of labor, across the public and private sectors, and spanning large integrated chaebol conglomerates as well as small, savvy, and specialized technology firms.

But the diffusion of knowledge alone is not enough; integrating these disparate bases of knowledge is what drives technological innovation and the development of commercial breakthroughs. Molly Webb, in her recent study of Korea's innovation system, finds that nearly two-thirds of R&D productivity among technology-based SMEs during the late 1990s and into the 2000s was generated through interfirm collaboration, not firms working in isolation.[54] She concludes, therefore, that for technological innovation to be facilitated within Korea's leading chaebols, diffuse and disparate bases of knowledge must be integrated in complementary and collaborative ways. The diffusion of knowledge is helpful in the innovation process only if the various bits of knowledge, expertise, and availability of research services can be used by industry.[55] Public and private, upstream and downstream linkages need to be complementary.

How would such complementarities emerge in the biotech sector? The short answer in Korea is that they have not so far. Knowledge diffusion has been thorough, prompted, as I have argued, by both state and industry efforts. However, the consensus among biotech stakeholders in Korea is that the integration of such knowledge has been shallow. The formation of linkages that bring together leading firms and their supposed supporting casts has been slow. When asked about the likelihood of collaboration between biotech SMEs and chaebols invested in the life sciences sector, Bioneer's Han-Oh Park responds simply, "In biotech, there is no interaction at all in Korea."[56] To the extent that any linkages have been formed among firms and labs, they have by and large been based on supplier-buyer relations and not on R&D collaboration.

There are several reasons for such shallow integration. First, there is a weak tradition of interfirm R&D collaboration in Korean industry, especially in comparison with firm behavior in Japan and Taiwan. Korean companies are historically less willing to cooperate with one another, and chaebol firms in particular have tended to eschew premarket R&D consortia involving other

54. Webb, *South Korea: Mass Innovation,* 18.
55. Author interviews, Seoul, September 13, 2007.
56. Author interview, Daejon, Korea, July 7, 2003.

enterprises. They prefer to do their R&D in-house.[57] Second, R&D outputs from both upstream research institutes and smaller bioventures remain too distant from the market, too "raw" for meaningful R&D linkages to be formed with biopharmaceutical firms in Korea. Chaebols such as LGLS recognize that good research is being conducted at Korean universities, public research institutes, and R&D-intensive SMEs. Yet they also find that the R&D is neither far enough along downstream nor a good enough match with their firms' specific needs to be of use to commercially oriented pharmaceutical companies. In other words, the R&D gap between actors remains quite sizable.

Perhaps most important is the fact that the state is simply reluctant to coordinate the formation of such linkages.[58] In the past, the postwar developmental state directly organized collaborative linkages from the top down. Today, however, the state perceives such practices as no longer sustainable in intensely science-based industries. For one, as alluded to in the previous chapter, the multidisciplinary complexity and functional imperatives of biotech innovation have undermined the coordinative capacity and expertise of the state and its economic planners. It is increasingly clear that complementarity and integration in science-based industrial development cannot be engineered from above.[59] But the state also purposely eschews the burdens of managing biotech's myriad uncertainties, meaning that it is not only no longer capable but also no longer willing to target, pick, and gamble on specific subsectors, technological applications, products, or firms in biotech. Put another way, while the Korean state remains willing to indirectly help *make* winners, it has left the business of *picking* winners to industry, or more generally, to chance.

Leveraging the International in Singapore

Unlike in postwar Korea and Taiwan, where FDI represents a very small portion of industrial investment, MNCs and FDI play a significant and historical role in Singapore's economic development. Poor in natural resources though

---

57. Matthews and Cho, *Tiger Technology*; Suh, "Korea's Innovation System"; Mariko Sakakibara and Dong-Sung Cho, "Cooperative R&D in Japan and Korea: A Comparison of Industrial Policy," *Research Policy* 31 (2002). For an overview of weak interfirm collaboration in the Korean biotech sector, see Dong-Sung Cho, Eunjung Hyun, and Soo Hee Lee, "Can Newly Industrializing Economies Catch Up in Science-Based Industries? A Study of the Korean Biotechnology Sector," *Journal of Interdisciplinary Economics* 18 (2007).

58. Author interview, Seoul, Korea, September 13, 2007.

59. Author interviews, Seoul, Korea, September 13, 2007, and July 9, 2003.

abundant in human capital (i.e., cheap skilled labor), Singapore's Economic Development Board set out early on to attract global firms. Multinational firms created jobs and stabilized domestic labor markets, which were especially crucial in the early stages of state consolidation after Singapore separated from Malaysia during the 1960s. Over time, foreign firms also transferred greater value-added industrial activities to Singapore and labor was continually up-skilled to attract more FDI. Global firms are, in this respect, the engines of industrial upgrading in Singapore. But Singapore's historical reliance on foreign direct investment has inhibited the growth of indigenous technology-intensive firms. Patent data reveal how it is global rather than local firms that are the core of technological innovation in Singapore. Not surprisingly, Singapore's current strategy for biomedical industry development continues to center on the inflow of FDI and the location of global life sciences firms there.

Continuities in industrial strategy in Singapore are not for lack of policy creativity on the part of stakeholders. Attracting life sciences MNCs is not solely a function of path dependency; there is a strategic rationale unique to Singapore's circumstances. Global firms, for instance, are expected to create jobs for Singapore's continually up-skilling labor force, especially for newly trained engineers and scientists. Such firms are expected to transfer talent to the tiny city-state, whose scale disadvantages in human capital resources are exposed in the current era of science-based industrialization. Singapore has also become less satisfied with being just the skilled manufacturing hub for multinational firms and is looking to position itself as an R&D hub for world-class biomedical firms. Stakeholders in Singapore anticipate that foreign firms will bring with them potential "winners" in their pipelines, which can be further developed in Singapore. And finally, due to their scale and diversified R&D capacities and portfolios, MNCs are also believed to be better able to absorb the risks and costs associated with biotech's myriad uncertainties. Singapore's strategy of leveraging the international, in other words, shifts industrial leadership and thus the conundrum of managing uncertainty to international firms. Multinational firms, rather than local ones, are expected to shoulder the burdens of commercial biotech's technological and economic uncertainties, while Singapore looks to benefit from the externalities gained from the MNCs' presence.

Singapore's emerging biomedical industry has indeed benefited from this leveraging strategy. Investments by global firms give Singapore international credibility, necessary if the city-state is to become a global biomedical hub.[60]

---

60. Author interview, Singapore, June 17, 2004.

Multinational firms are also attracting world-class R&D talent to Singapore. Over the past several years, Singapore has recruited the "who's who" of the world's leading scientists to serve on company boards, in research institutes, and on government advisory councils. The inflow of biomedical FDI and the location of global firms in Singapore also ensure the state's continued commitment to develop biomedical R&D infrastructure, including government investments in upstream R&D and public research institutes dedicated to life sciences research and commercial biotech.[61]

Singaporean firms have particularly benefited from this leveraging strategy. As was the case for the semiconductor and electronics sectors, the location of global firms in Singapore has prompted the development of supply chain linkages for local SMEs in the biomedical sector. Local firms and start-ups are positioning themselves not as cutting-edge innovators in life sciences industry per se, but as suppliers of materials and research services for multinational firms. Kooprime, for example, is a bio-informatics spin-off from the state-funded Institute for Molecular and Cell Biology (IMCB), specializing in information technologies for managing biological databases. With investments from the state's Bio*One venture capital fund and collaborations with the National University of Singapore (NUS), GlaxoSmithKline (GSK), and locally based Merlion Pharmaceuticals, Kooprime has grown its business operations in Singapore and across the region. BRASS, an NUS spin-off founded during the late 1990s, provides preclinical testing services for medical device firms. A-Bio, a Singapore-based biologics contract manufacturer, entered into an agreement with GSK in 2004 to supply its pharmaceutical ingredients. All these ventures are essentially enabling firms in that they are far from the cutting edge of biomedical innovation yet sufficiently good enough to have earned revenue-generating partnerships and contracts with global clients.[62] Simply put, the recent growth in Singapore's indigenous SMEs in the life sciences sector reflects the inflow of foreign investment from global biomedical firms.[63]

The most important externality, from the perspective of Singapore's economic planners, is the potential relocation of global biomedical firms' R&D operations to Singapore, transforming the existing "made in Singapore" model into a higher value-added "discovered in Singapore" path. Techno-

61. Cynthia Fox, *Cell of Cells: The Global Race to Capture and Control the Stem Cell* (New York: Norton, 2007).

62. Author interview, Singapore, December 11, 2002.

63. Author interviews, Singapore, June 16, 2004; December 1, 2006; December 13, 2003; and June 16, 2004.

logical spillover in R&D is seen as the most important means by which Singaporean researchers and entrepreneurs can eventually climb the value chain in the biomedical sector and build a more robust critical mass of local bioentrepreneurs. To that end, biotech stakeholders in Singapore have geared their efforts toward establishing a competitive industrial and research environment for global, R&D-intensive biomedical firms. Such efforts include strengthening local R&D capabilities, training a new generation of R&D talent, growing R&D-intensive bioventures, and further solidifying Singapore's regulatory regimes.

Singapore's Gamble

Of course, the decision to locate value-added R&D activities to Singapore is ultimately not Singapore's to make, and certainly not its state's. When it comes to technology transfer, global collaboration, and transnational R&D partnerships, such decisions are always made in global corporate boardrooms and not within the government.[64] Singapore's prospects for climbing the bio-industrial commercial value chain thus depend on multinational firms, investors, and individual researchers to deliver new R&D opportunities and value-added commercial activities to the city-state. The long-term development of Singapore's biomedical industry hinges on the strategic decisions of others. This is Singapore's gamble and the basis of its uncertainty in biomedical industry upgrading. Though the Singaporean approach to growing biomedical industries essentially shifts biotech's technological and economic uncertainties to global firms and global actors more generally, the state must first assume the risks inherent in attracting R&D and commercial activities to Singapore. To that (uncertain) end, state policy has been directed at increasing the likelihood that global firms will choose to locate their value-added operations in Singapore.

The first phase of the state's Biomedical Sciences Initiative (2001–2006) mainly focused on strengthening local R&D capacity through the creation of new biomedical research labs and the growth of local life sciences R&D talent. Before the 1990s, R&D infrastructure in the life sciences sector was considerably weaker than in competitors such as Korea and Taiwan. There were few public research institutes dedicated to biomedical research, and

64. Kai-Sun Kwong, "Singapore: Dominance of Multinational Corporations," in *Industrial Development in Singapore, Taiwan and South Korea,* ed. Kwong et al. (Hackensack, N. J.: World Scientific Press, 2001); Poh-Kam Wong, "Singapore's Technology Strategy," in *The Emerging Technological Trajectory in the Pacific Rim,* ed. Denis Fred Simon (Armonk, N.Y.: M. E. Sharpe, 1995).

universities were still primarily training institutions rather than knowledge-creating centers of research excellence. To catch up, the state invested heavily in developing Singapore's science and technology capabilities. In 2005, public funding accounted for nearly two-thirds of total R&D spending in the biomedical field, much more than from the private sector. Singapore's two research universities, National University of Singapore and Nanyang Technological University, received 15% of all biomedical R&D funding. Meanwhile, public research institutes managed by the A★STAR accounted for 35% of biomedical R&D spending, a proportion larger than the private sector's share of total investment in the sector. Indeed, more than half the researchers located in Biopolis, Singapore's world-class commercial biotech R&D hub, are employed in labs overseen by the A★STAR.[65]

Phase 2 of the biomedical industry plan (2006–2011) emphasized translational R&D, or the downward transmission and commercialization of scientific knowledge.[66] The EDB and A★STAR co-administer competitive funding schemes to seed promising venture businesses in life sciences industry. The A★STAR also established international partnerships such as those with Johns Hopkins University and Duke University's medical school to provide opportunities for local researchers to gain experience in applied health technology development and clinical R&D. The Hopkins and Duke campuses in Singapore were heavily supported by state funds. As in Taiwan and Korea, technology transfer centers have also been created to deepen linkages between the academy and industry. The A★STAR established its in-house technology transfer arm, Exploit Technologies, early in the first decade of the 2000s. Exploit's principal role has been to mine publicly funded A★STAR labs to help commercialize promising technologies through formal technology transfer, licenses, or the creation of spin-off firms. Life sciences R&D and commercialization activities are also clustered in or near Biopolis. In sum, the first and second phases of Singapore's biomedical industry plans have been a coordinated effort by the state to increase the probability that foreign MNCs will locate their value-added R&D intensive operations there, a risk proposition that policymakers in Singapore have, thus far, been comfortable with.

But has this strategy paid off? There are two ways to evaluate the situation. On the one hand, efforts to attract biomedical MNCs to Singapore

---

65. The seven A★STAR research institutes are the Bioinformatics Institute, the Bioprocessing Technology Institute, the Genome Institute of Singapore, the Institute of Bioengineering and Nanotechnology, the Institute of Molecular and Cell Biology, the Center for Molecular Medicine, and the Singapore Bioimaging Consortium.

66. Author interview, Singapore, October 31, 2007.

have definitely been rewarded. Virtually all the major global pharmaceuti-cal firms have a significant presence in Singapore. Britain's GSK set up a sales and distribution center in Singapore in the 1980s and subsequently invested in manufacturing plants as well as R&D labs. American firm Eli Lilly established a research lab in Biopolis in 2002 and later expanded it into its Center for Drug Discovery in 2007. Swiss firm Novartis invested in a tableting plant in 2005 and announced two years later its plans to establish a cell culture production facility in Singapore. Meanwhile, Pfizer has invested US$300 million in a plant for pharmaceutical ingredients. In the areas of biologics and biopharmaceuticals, multinational firms Genentech, GSK, and Lonza made commitments in 2007 to invest in new production facilities. In total, Singapore received US$1.5 billion in foreign investment for biologics manufacturing between 2005 and 2007.

A global industry presence in Singapore has definitely translated into jobs, investment capital, the creation of new supply chain opportunities for local firms, and commercial output. But as I argued above, in addition to these im-portant externalities, the attraction of global firms to Singapore is intended to be a stepping-stone for the eventual inflow of more sophisticated, early-stage and higher value-added R&D.[67] The strategic rationale, according to biotech stakeholders in Singapore, is that once global firms are in Singapore, in whatever capacity, they will recognize the benefits of moving their R&D operations to the city-state. Singapore would become a global R&D hub.

As it turns out, attracting biomedical manufacturing is one thing, while bringing in value-added R&D and sparking innovative commercial activity in Singapore is another. Despite coordinated government efforts to encour-age value-added foreign investment in the life sciences, it appears that Sin-gapore's gamble has not paid off, or at least not at the pace once anticipated. According to industry stakeholders in Singapore, value-added investment in the form of R&D has fallen well short of expectations. Of the billions of investment dollars that pharmaceutical and biomedical MNCs have poured into Singapore, much of it has been directed at the manufacturing side of biomedical industries, where value-added gains are most modest. Accord-ing to government data, between 1997 and 2009, manufacturing output in biomedical industries grew from just S$2.6 billion to S$20.7 billion, an impressive eightfold increase. Meanwhile, value-added manufacturing out-put in the biomedical sector, for which business complexity and innovation are key drivers, grew from S$1.9 billion to S$9.1 billion, a fivefold increase

---

67. Author interview, Singapore, November 30, 2006.

over the same period, to be sure, but nonetheless a slower pace of growth than in overall manufacturing in the sector. In 1997, value-added output equaled nearly three-quarters of the value of total biomedical manufacturing output; by 2009, that share was 47%.[68] These data suggest that growth in commercial biomedical output in Singapore is becoming more, not less, concentrated in lower value-added manufacturing activities, despite hopes for the opposite.

The anecdotal evidence reinforces this perception. For example, when Britain's GSK announced in 2007 a US$300 million investment in a biologics manufacturing facility in Singapore, that same year the firm invested just US$13 million in its R&D drug discovery lab. Other big pharmaceutical and biomedical firms have made similarly skewed investment decisions. Multinational firms have also been cautious about integrating local talent into their R&D operations. Most Singaporean scientists are recruited at the junior level, while senior scientists and directors are almost always recruited from abroad.[69] Meanwhile, efforts by the government to establish collaborative partnerships with prominent foreign universities have resulted in, at best, relatively modest outputs. The once lauded partnership between the A★STAR and Johns Hopkins University (JHU) came to an end in 2006. The dissolution was reportedly acrimonious. The government claims that JHU failed to bring to Singapore the high-profile researchers and R&D projects expected by the EDB and the A★STAR. JHU's response was that decisions about research personnel and R&D programming are its to make, and not the Singaporean government's.[70] Beyond the specter of what was a very public breakup, the failed partnership underscores the serious challenge that Singapore faces by relying on foreign investments to prompt its transformation from a predominantly manufacturing center to a world-class life sciences and commercial biotech R&D hub. In the end, Singapore's biomedical future hinges on the decisions of others, whose interests may not align with the city-state's aspirations. Some are becoming wary of this approach; in late 2006, the government's biotech development strategy was criticized for being too ambitious by one of Singapore's leading scientists, Lee Wei Ling, who is also former Prime Minister Lee Kuan Yew's daughter.

---

68. EDB data for 1997 to 2003, cited in Govindan Parayil, "From 'Silicon Island' to 'Biopolis of Asia,'" *California Management Review* 47 (2005), 63. For EDB data for 2009, see Economic Development Board, *Biomedical Sciences: Factsheet 2010,* available at http://www.sedb.com (accessed October 15, 2010).

69. Author interview, Singapore, June 15, 2004. One biomedical MNC executive notes that only 50% of his firm's research staff are local Singaporeans and that most are junior scientists. Senior researchers are by and large foreign expatriates. Author interview, Singapore, October 30, 2007.

70. Ai-Lien Chang and Daryl Loo, "How a Perfect Marriage Fell Apart," *Straits Times,* August 13, 2006.

Singapore's Innovation Deficit

Why have Singapore's apparent advantages in attracting huge amounts of investment in biomedical manufacturing not swiftly translated into other opportunities in higher value-added outputs and innovation-intensive commercial activities? Part of the answer rests with the internal organization of global firms themselves. Manufacturing and R&D operations within a global pharmaceutical firm, for instance, are organizationally distinct. As one MNC executive explains, "there is a wall which separates" manufacturing and sales on one side from R&D on the other, and the "two sides of the firm do not speak to one another." They operate according to different logics. Economic and financial incentives attract manufacturing investment. He adds that manufacturing is "basically a tax game," a viewpoint echoed by other management executives of global biomedical firms with some presence in Singapore. The corporate decision to outsource R&D high-value operations overseas, however, has much more to do with the host country's capabilities in life sciences R&D, its expertise in biomedical industry commercialization, and the pool of viable firms with which to collaborate.[71] Executives of global biomedical and pharmaceutical firms perceive Singapore as lacking a critical mass of R&D talent and bio-industrial entrepreneurs.

Given the sluggish growth in the global biopharmaceutical industry and the paucity of drug candidates in existing pipelines, global biomedical firms are looking to embed themselves within innovation-oriented R&D environments rather than service- or manufacturing-intensive economies. Over the past two decades, the highly competitive global pharmaceutical industry has restructured to manage uncertainty through a new global division of R&D labor, in which innovative venture firms discover drug candidates further upstream while large drug firms focus more on downstream commercialization. What MNCs need, therefore—and why they outsource their R&D operations in the first place—is a robust pool of innovative biomedical firms and research labs that can provide viable leads for commercialization.[72] Cost, the main variable in manufacturing-related decisions, is less relevant when it comes to innovative R&D.

Empirical evidence from Singapore suggests that there has been little collaboration among Singaporean bioventures and multinational firms, and that the skeptical view shared among global firms is a valid one.[73] Though

---

71. Author interview, Singapore, October 30, 2007.
72. Author interview, Singapore, June 17, 2004.
73. Nanyang Technological University and Nanyang Business School, *Collaboration in the Biopharmaceutical Industry: Implications for Singapore SMEs* [summarized main findings], 2007. This view

the Biomedical Sciences Initiative was intended to nurture indigenous bio-industrial growth to complement the eventual expected inflow of R&D investment, the development of Singapore's R&D intensive bio-venture sector has been relatively slow.[74] With the exception of a small handful of firms targeted by the state as potential "stars" in the biomedical sector (discussed in Chapter 4), even government officials in Singapore admit that the performance of the domestic biotech sector has been underwhelming. The lack of innovative firms in Singapore translates into fewer collaborative R&D opportunities domestically and with multinational firms.

Some contend that Singapore's industrial culture is hardwired against creativity-driven entrepreneurship.[75] Unlike in Taiwan, where innovative SMEs have been and continue to be the bases for its industrial dynamism, efforts to develop small and innovative firms in Singapore have historically been subordinated to the MNC sector. According to Mark Goh and Irene Chew, Singapore's is a deeply entrenched "non-entrepreneurial culture."[76] The paternalistic state and an education system that emphasizes rote learning have socialized a conformist, risk-averse ethic among Singaporeans rather than the free-wheeling mindset required of innovation and entrepreneurial creativity.[77] Cutting-edge innovation "implies a readiness of letting go and allow[ing] for chaos," an attitudinal imperative that has failed to resonate in Singapore.[78]

The culturalist take is just one of many for explaining the slow growth of Singapore's bioventure sector, however. Other factors matter as well, and perhaps even more so. With the exception of the government's Bio*One fund, venture capital, particularly from the private sector, has been hesitant to invest in the life sciences sector. Venture capital is generally risk-averse when it comes to the biomedical industry, and it lacks the patience demanded by biotech's technical and market uncertainties. One official describes biotech VC promotion as an "abject failure" in growing local biomedical firms.

---

was echoed in every interview I conducted with senior managers and executives at foreign multinational biomedical firms.

74. Author interviews, Singapore, December 12 and December 14, 2002. See Ernst and Young, *Beyond Borders: Global Biotechnology Report, 2008* (Cleveland: Ernst and Young, 2008), 105.

75. Author interview, Singapore, December 12, 2002.

76. Mark Goh and Irene Chew, "Public Policy and Entrepreneurship Development—Singapore Style," *Journal of Enterprising Culture* 4 (1996), 88.

77. Regarding the issue of creativity in Singaporean research labs, one senior executive at a global pharmaceutical firm recounted to me that "in the U.K., if you ask [for someone's opinion], they tell you what they think. In the U.S., they will tell you even if you don't ask in the first place. In Singapore, you may ask and they still won't tell you." Author interview, Singapore, October 31, 2007.

78. Check-Teck Foo and Check-Tong Foo, "Socialization of Technopreneurism: Towards Symbiosis in Corporate Innovation and Technology Strategy," *Technovation* 20 (2000), 561.

Investors, he adds, have been slow to appreciate the long-term uncertainties of biotechnology innovation.[79] They are, as one entrepreneur put it, "very uncomfortable with illiquidity," and the notion that a "promising biotechnology firm can have little to no revenue is inconceivable."[80] The reality in Singapore is that if an entrepreneur is unable to successfully appeal to government sources of investment in high-risk sectors such as biomedical industries, there are few other options for venture funding.

Singapore is also without the institutional platforms to facilitate the deepening of collaborative linkages among researchers in public labs and industry. The costs for firms to locate at Biopolis, for instance, are described as prohibitive for domestic start-up firms.[81] What is more, the means for technology transfer and midstream R&D have only recently been institutionalized in Singapore.[82] Exploit Technologies, the technology transfer arm of the A★STAR, is criticized for its lack of business development expertise. Though it is noted for its legal and administrative proficiency, Exploit is viewed primarily as a passive repository of intellectual property (IP) rather than a proactive manager of commercially viable IP.[83] Entrepreneurs further criticize the state for neglecting its role in facilitating opportunities for interfirm collaboration, asserting that the state continues to expend resources on attracting multinational firms to Singapore rather than growing local firms alongside MNCs.[84] Critics quietly point out that the state, as in the past, has traded off domestic industry development in favor of securing foreign investment. State officials, meanwhile, explain that the legacies of weak domestic industry development have undermined the organization of industry associations, which has, in turn, fragmented the sector's cohesiveness and constrained opportunities for interfirm collaboration even further.[85]

Singapore has also been unable to compensate for its scale disadvantages. Singapore is tiny, even when compared with Korea and Taiwan, never mind

---

79. Author interview, Singapore, November 1, 2007.

80. Author interview, Singapore, November 1, 2007.

81. Author interview, Singapore, June 23, 2004.

82. Only recently have efforts been made to remedy this midstream gap, notably with the formation of the Experimental Therapeutics Center (ETC) in 2007. Located in Biopolis and headed up by renowned British scientist Sir David Lane, the ETC is expected to bring promising leads and compounds developed in A★STAR labs further downstream for the pharmaceutical sector. Envisioned as being "commercially savvy," the ETC is intended to engage a strategy of "target refinement" for the purposes of partnering local research labs with large pharmaceutical firms. Author interview, Singapore, November 2, 2007.

83. Author interview, Singapore, November 2, 2007.

84. Nanyang Technological University and Nanyang Business School, *Collaboration in the Biopharmaceutical Industry.*

85. Author interview, Singapore, November 1, 2007.

other global competitors such as the United Kingdom, Germany, Japan, and the United States. Because it is so small, Singapore has trouble achieving the scale and critical mass of local firms needed to match technologies with prospective partners.[86] Due to scale constraints, the prospects for "needs-based" collaboration are also weak in Singapore,[87] exacerbating what one executive calls the "translational R&D gap" between researchers and industry.[88] Indeed, investment opportunities in Singapore are scant, meaning that from the perspective of the investor, the risks of investment cannot be diversified across either a portfolio of firms or a range of biotech applications. Put another way, there simply are not enough viable prospects in Singapore for investors to strategically cover their bets.

But perhaps most important is the fact that Singapore's talent pool remains very small, despite government efforts to train locals and entice overseas researchers to return home.[89] Executives of multinational biomedical firms point out that while government initiatives to nurture local life sciences researchers are a step in the right direction, the fact of the matter is that foreign nationals continue to make up a significant proportion of world-class researchers with industry experience working in Singapore. They worry that Singapore is particularly susceptible to talent flight. Therefore, despite the state's commitment to ramping up its local R&D and bio-industrial bases—in short, to make Singapore attractive to global biomedical firms looking to locate their R&D operations there—serious concerns prevail with respect to Singapore's scale-related capacities to help global firms bet on biotech.

The Retreating State

Commercializing biotech is a complex process, involving many moving parts chasing after many moving targets. Given the dearth of blockbuster cases, however, we still know very little about the processes of generating new knowledge, translating this knowledge into something usable by industry, and then transforming these new technologies for the market. We do know, however, that the innovation and commercialization processes involve the diffusion and integration of otherwise disparate groups of actors and stakeholders.

---

86. Author interview, Singapore, October 30, 2007.
87. Author interview, Singapore, October 31, 2007.
88. Author interview, Singapore, November 2, 2007.
89. Winston Koh and Poh-Kam Wong, "The Venture Capital Industry in Singapore," NUS Entrepreneurship Centre, Working Papers, 2005.

We know as well that there needs to be a critical mass of knowledge and expertise for there to be commercially viable outputs in biotech. And we know that narrowing the gaps in the innovation process requires various types of interactions among actors and stakeholders, whether competitive, collaborative, or both. But to reiterate my earlier point, we still know very little about how to actually facilitate these complex processes in ways that ultimately foster technological and economic returns. More specifically, there is no single organizational model that can be emulated to generate, translate, and commercialize new biotechnological knowledge.

In the absence of any such winning model for commercial biotech innovation, it is no surprise that distinctive national styles in the organization of bio-industry have endured in Korea, Taiwan, and Singapore. In Korea, the prospects of commercial biotech innovation continue to rest on potential collaboration among a broadly diversified group of actors, though with the chaebol firms at the core of the strategy. In Taiwan, on the other hand, the organization of bio-industry continues to center on growing technologically savvy SMEs through a hit-and-miss logic and the mobilization of resources around what might emerge as potential winners. Meanwhile, in Singapore, the prospects of biomedical innovation and commercialization depend on the ability of the state and industrial stakeholders to compel global biomedical firms to locate their value-added R&D operations in the city-state.

To a great extent, then, the organizational characteristics of bio-industrial development in Korea, Taiwan, and Singapore reflect past practices in industrial organization among each of the three. Decision makers in both government and industry have reverted to preexisting strategic repertoires. The emphasis on chaebol leadership in Korea, for instance, reveals a logic that is rooted in the presumed advantages of economies of scope and scale, just as the "many sprouts" approach in Taiwan reflects a historical normalization of SME failure and "guerrilla" entrepreneurship. These distinctive approaches make strategic sense to decision makers in each of the three places, even if they might make little strategic sense outside their national contexts. To be sure, Singaporean entrepreneurs are less likely to embrace the notion that failure is the basis of creativity and the norm when it comes to commercializing innovation, just as it would be inconceivable for biotech stakeholders in Korea to expect anything but the chaebol sector to lead the sector's development over the long term.

Distinctions in national styles of organizing bio-industry also reflect stakeholders' technological and economic objectives, which vary among the three. For Korean firms, the principal objective has been and continues to be capturing as much of the commercial biotech value chain as possible; hence the focus on growing fully integrated, lab-to-market, biopharmaceutical firms. In contrast, Taiwan's commercial biotech ambitions are to develop specialized niches and thus generate value in small segments along biotechnology's long and otherwise unintegrated commercial value chain. Meanwhile, Singapore looks to position itself as an R&D hub and is therefore more concerned about attracting value-added R&D activities than about growing local firms into global ones.

Yet, national distinctions aside, this chapter also reveals how the state in all three cases has similarly retreated, no longer playing the role that Robert Wade once referred to as "big leadership." In betting on biotech, the state has refrained from making those risky bets that are "on a large enough scale to make a real difference to investment and production patterns in an industry."[90] In this respect, the relationship between the state and industry more generally has evolved quite considerably *and similarly* in Korea, Taiwan, and Singapore, a departure from the ways in which industry was organized by the postwar developmental state. The state's earlier dominance over the private sector has waned. The policy instruments it can use to steer industry have also weakened over time. And most important, industry, and not the state, has taken the lead in industrial upgrading. The state's coordinative role in organizing industry has diminished. As argued in the previous chapter, the state no longer has the authoritative capacity to coordinate very complex, intermural, and R&D-intensive sectors such as the life sciences. But as I have shown in this chapter, it is not only the erosion of the state's coordinative capacity that is significant; rather, the state has also become *less willing* to coordinate actors in intensely science-based industries such as biotech. The state has opted to facilitate commercial biotech by allowing niches and core competencies to grow from the bottom up, as in Taiwan; through the diffusion and eventual integration of knowledge, as in Korea; or by the decisions of global biomedical firms, as in Singapore. In other words, the state is increasingly less capable *and* less willing to gamble on very high-stakes bets about which there remains tremendous technological, economic, and temporal uncertainty.

---

90. Robert Wade, *Governing the Market: Economic Theory and the Role of Government in East Asian Industrialization* (Princeton, N.J.: Princeton University Press, 1990), 28.

CHAPTER 4

Manufacturing "Progress"

In late 2007, I gave a talk in Taiwan on the development of commercial biotech. By then, Taiwan's drive to upgrade into biotech had been in full gear for nearly two decades, and Taiwan's aspirations in the sector had become a central part of the discourse about the island's economic future. I began my talk by recounting a recent biotech investment deal that had been spearheaded by the government, one that seemed, at least from a technical perspective, to be based on a promising drug candidate. I suggested that it was by all industry-insider accounts a sound, if not spectacular, investment deal. It was also pointed out that the Taiwan government had invested US$20 million into the start-up firm. During Q&A, an audience member asked how many new jobs would result from the creation of this firm. Given its start-up nature, I responded that likely 15–20 employment opportunities would be a reasonable expectation, to which the questioner asked, I assume rhetorically, "And how is this deal a good investment for Taiwan's economy?"

A Waning Appetite

I recount this story because it reveals quite clearly the popular evaluations of Taiwan's ongoing efforts to make it in commercial biotech. The exchange highlighted people's growing impatience and frustration with the slow pace of biotech development in Taiwan. It betrayed a sense that people outside the sector were beginning to feel the extraordinary efforts, investments, and resources committed to commercializing biotech were perhaps not worth it. There was, to be sure, a palpable skepticism among many in the audience. The concern about how these investments would specifically benefit Taiwan's economy in terms of economic returns and new job opportunities also revealed a techno-nationalist impulse. President Chen Shui-Bian himself had described biotech as the "most important industry to Taiwan's future economic development,"[1] also stating, "If we don't do this today then we will regret it tomorrow."[2] Analytically, the challenge from the audience member illuminated how the notion of "progress" is contested: what I saw as a promising commercial lead was to someone else an example of technological largesse from which reasonable returns were unlikely.

What was most significant about the exchange, however, was that it confirmed a growing sense that in Taiwan (and elsewhere) the appetite for the long-term realities of biotech development is beginning to wane, and that the long-range prospects of overcoming the myriad uncertainties inherent in commercializing biotech have become less tolerable, or simply viewed as no longer worth it. People's patience is understandably beginning to run out. Indeed, although billions of dollars have been allocated to commercial biotech from government and industry over the last two decades, growth rates in both inputs (investment) and outputs (commercialization) are leveling off. Economic returns have been underwhelming. Fewer than expected new higher-value jobs have been created. And to the extent that developments in the biotech sector are resulting in any wealth accumulation, such wealth is concentrated among only a few. People in Korea, Taiwan, and Singapore are beginning to question the socioeconomic value of the biotech sector, just as governments there have also begun to wonder about the political value of continuing to bet on biotech. What has become particularly troubling is that private sector investment in the life sciences has slowed considerably in recent years, threatening the long-term imperatives of biotech innovation. In Korea, Taiwan, and Singapore, investors have begun to lose their tolerance for the uncertainties inherent in betting on biotech.

---

1. Cited in Jim Boyce, "Taiwan's Biotech Clock Ticking..." *Topics: The Magazine of International Business in Taiwan* 32 (2002).

2. Cited in Dan Nystedt, "Chen Asks Foreigners to Help in Building Biotech," *Taipei Times,* August 7, 2001.

There are multiple reasons for this, many of which have been covered in this book thus far but are nonetheless worth reviewing. First, as relative newcomers to the life sciences field and science-based industrialization more generally, Korea, Taiwan, and Singapore have had to confront a very long and steep learning curve. As I described in Chapter 3, there is a lack of both investment and bio-industrial experience in the region. It is not as though stakeholders in Korea, Taiwan, and Singapore do not understand the long-term imperatives of biotech innovation, however. Rather, after several years of modest growth, they have only begun to appreciate just how long-term the innovation process can be. That the global commercial biotech sector has more or less underperformed to date, even in places such as the United States, casts further doubt on the viability of bio-industrial growth in recent entrants such as Korea, Taiwan, and Singapore.

Second, many suggest that the prevailing business model for bio-industry development needs to be reconceived. Past practices in growing technology-based firms have to be rethought in light of the challenges of biotech innovation. There is no consensus yet, however, about an optimal business model for biotech firms. From the perspective of venture investors and bio-entrepreneurs, for instance, the long-term realities of biotech innovation have sealed off many of the conventional exit strategies used by risk capital to recoup their investments. In addition, because returns on investment have been much slower in life sciences industries than in other endeavors, standard exit mechanisms such as listing on the stock market or business consolidation (through mergers and acquisitions) have become less and less tenable. Valuing market potential for venture firms has also proven difficult when technologies remain so distant to the market. The cash burn rate for life sciences firms is uniquely rapid. Consequently, venture capitalists, institutional investors, and would-be entrepreneurs have become increasingly less inclined to invest in biotech. It is simply becoming more difficult for risk capital to be patient. One experienced drug industry observer recently pointed out to me that in his opinion the VC-driven model of information technology upgrading is unsuited to the sorts of uncertainties inherent in cutting-edge life sciences innovation. His is a view echoed by many.

Third, investors and entrepreneurs are, understandably, increasingly hedging their bets by continuing to invest heavily in other value-added high-technology sectors. Information technologies and advanced electronics are viewed as much safer investments than the life sciences in terms of timely economic returns and effective exits. They are also high-growth technology sectors in which Korea, Taiwan, and Singapore already enjoy competitive advantages in downstream R&D and manufacturing. Domestic firms in the region command significant global market share in these sectors, and they have continued to grow much more rapidly than the life sciences sector. The underwhelming performance of the global biotech industries and relatively slow growth in the pharmaceutical sector have deterred further investment in the life sciences. The dot-com bust early in the first decade of the 2000s and the subsequent contraction of the VC market, which forced venture investors to reevaluate their risk management strategies and thresholds for high-risk enterprises, have also made it increasingly difficult for the commercial biotech sector to attract and retain investment. Frankly, there are other high value-added investment opportunities that are safer and less uncertain than biotech.

The waning appetite for the long-term realities of commercial biotech innovation presents a host of problems for the state and bio-industry stakeholders in Korea, Taiwan, and Singapore. This chapter examines how the challenges of *temporal uncertainty* are requiring the state and bio-industry stakeholders to take on a new kind of political economic leadership role to stem people's growing impatience regarding the slow pace and unpredictability of commercial biotech development. Biotech stakeholders in Korea, Taiwan, and Singapore have had to reorient expectations about progress in the sector away from what one informant referred to as the prevailing mindset of "short-termism" to a more realistic "long-termism." The challenges of managing commercial biotech's temporal uncertainty require the state to expand the temporal horizon of expectations and to recalibrate the measures of progress in order to essentially buy more time. This chapter examines how commercial biotech stakeholders in Korea, Taiwan, and Singapore have attempted to manufacture progress in the near term in order to sustain an appetite for biotech over the long term.

Stakeholders agree that what is needed is a success case, a compelling story about the development of a "star." The value of such a success would extend beyond just the economic returns from a single firm or the credibility gained by a blockbuster research project. Rather, its demonstration effects would entail much larger implications and positive externalities for stakeholders in government, research labs, industry, and the investment community. A star could be held up as a model from which lessons can be learned, proliferated, and emulated. A star also provides hope that despite long-term uncertainties, some measure of success or progress is possible in uncertain endeavors such as commercial biotech. The development of stars and the strategic portrayal of success stories are expected to reconfigure prevailing expectations about the speed of economic returns and the likelihood of failed initiatives, and to narrow the wide gulf between the lab and the market. Star stories would therefore be a source of inspiration and emulation, as well as a sort of reality check on the high-risk, high-reward realities of the sector. Thus, the emergence of a star—*any* star—is required in the near term to revive and sustain an appetite for the long-term challenges of life sciences innovation; it would portray the prospects of commercial biotech development in a less—albeit slightly less—uncertain light.

Portraying Biotechnology

East Asia's entry into biotech has been a very public venture. Beginning in the 1990s, the state explicitly identified biotechnology as a future "star" industry and a "pillar" of the region's industrial upgrading trajectory. The prospects of biotech have been hyped, and the media and governments themselves have trumpeted their commitment to growing the life sciences sector. New investments by government and industry are regularly reported on the front pages of newspapers, not buried inside the business sections. The construction and development of new research infrastructures are conspicuous. Even the most casual observers of the economy in the region are aware of the supposed importance of biotech to their economic futures. The stakes have become extraordinarily high, and because of this, the development of biotech has become central to public debate and a topic of everyday conversation. In other words, the prospects of success in commercial biotech industries have become political.

The state actively shapes this political conversation. It portrays biotechnology, and this portrayal is politically strategic.[3] For example, because of the newness of bio-industrialization and biotech in Korea, Taiwan, and Singapore, the state has had to play an educative role for the general public. It has launched campaigns to inform and educate people about how life sciences innovation can improve health care and also be a major source of future industrial growth. The biomedical sector is characterized as a critical industry in the knowledge economy. Biotech and applications of the technology have had to be demystified and made more accessible to the general public so that popular support can be built for the push to grow a biotech industry. The state's educative role has also extended to issues of regulation and the public interest more generally. Because clinical R&D is central to the biotech

---

3. I first got a sense of how central the strategy of "portraying" biotechnology is to life sciences development in Asia when I arrived for my initial round of research interviews in Singapore in 2002. After all my scheduled interviews with EDB and A*STAR officials were canceled at the last minute, the EDB sent a binder full of news clippings and government press releases concerning the development of Singapore's biomedical industries. All the news reports cast a positive light on the prospects of biomedical industry growth in Singapore; of the 200 or so pages of reports, not one was pessimistic or critical.

innovation enterprise, particularly as projects move closer to market, the state has had to clarify the regulatory imperatives of safety and patients' rights. It mediates debate surrounding bioethics and arbitrates the normative aspects of life sciences R&D. To varying degrees, Korea, Taiwan, and Singapore have adopted a public stakeholder model of regulatory deliberation, for which the state's portrayal of the biotech innovation process is crucial.

Ironically, the state is therefore responsible for having transformed the distant and uncertain prospects of the biotech sector into the very public spectacle that it now must skillfully manage if it expects to sustain a long-term commitment to innovation. In this respect, the state is also responsible for reporting on development and progress in the sector. Reporting—or, put another way, portraying—progress in the sector is crucial for biotech stakeholders. Gaining and maintaining buy-in into the life sciences field requires that the state be accountable for its efforts in growing the biotech sector. But balancing progress (or the lack of it) against prevailing expectations is not easy to do. On the one hand, the state has to portray developments in the biotech sector as having progressed and continuing to do so, and it has to show that the trajectory remains upward. On the other hand, it also needs to manage popular expectations about the realistic prospects, especially the speed and pace, of such growth, especially in higher value-added commercial activities in biotech. That the postwar developmental state is perceived to have essentially delivered rapid industrialization makes handling this tension between reporting growth and managing expectations even more difficult, as people's expectations of the state are, wrongly or rightly, inflated. As I have argued in previous chapters, prevailing expectations about the ability of the state to deliver industrial success are unrealistic when it comes to science-based industries such as biotech. Nevertheless, the state must strategically portray the sector in ways that deepen rather than undermine long-term commitment to biotech innovation.

Managing Expectations

One obvious strategy for portraying progress in biotech development would be to highlight commercial blockbusters, and in particular those firms that have gained significant market share or are on the cutting edge of biotech. However, the reality is that few such firms have emerged in Korea, Taiwan, and Singapore and the economic impact of innovative value-added development has, thus far, been far smaller than expected. In the absence of star cases to celebrate, the state has had to resort to other strategic portrayals of biotech. One involves the *recalibration and management of expectations* regarding the processes and prospects of biotech industry development.[4] In all three places, the state is attempting to portray commercial biotech innovation as a necessarily long-term endeavor and to downplay expectations for commercial blockbusters in the near term. As Johnsee Lee, president of Taiwan's ITRI during the first decade of the 2000s, aptly puts it, "if the electronics industry is a sprint, then the biotech industry is a marathon relay."[5] His is a message that is continually reported to the general public, industry stakeholders, and investors.

Managing expectations entails a recalibration of popular or lay expectations and the formulation of a new metric that reflects more reasonable, and thus more attainable, indicators of biotech industry development.[6] Put another way, measures of progress and success, short of a blockbuster product or cutting-edge discovery in the lab, have to be recalibrated. Policymakers are introducing intermediate benchmarks that portray the development of biotech with a more positive prognosis. It goes without saying that portraying the sector as fledgling would be disastrous for the heavily invested state and biotech industry stakeholders. In this respect, benchmarking, and more precisely the construction of those benchmarks, has been a strategic exercise.

Intermediate measures of commercial biotech development include, for example, the recruitment of international R&D talent to the region. Overseas Taiwanese with bio-industry experience are lured back to Taiwan to head up firms and public research institutes, notably the Development Center for Biotechnology and Academia Sinica. Singapore, given its dearth of local talent, has been the most aggressive in its efforts to recruit star researchers from industry and star scientists from academia in the United States, Europe, and Japan. The government has overhauled its immigration and tax policies specifically to attract foreign R&D talent.[7] In 2006, Philip Yeo, then head of the A★STAR, boasted about his efforts to lure top scientists to Singapore, saying

4. See Michael Hopkins, Paul Martin, Paul Nightingale, Alison Kraft, and Surya Mahdi, "The Myth of the Biotech Revolution: An Assessment of Technological, Clinical and Organizational Change," *Research Policy* 36 (2007), 586.

5. Cited in Ming-Ling Hsieh, "Taiwan's Biotech Outbreak," *Commonwealth Magazine*, August 15, 2007.

6. Author interview, Singapore, December 1, 2006.

7. Between 2001 and 2006, the number of biomedical personnel in Singapore increased from 100 to 4,600. In addition, the A★STAR has reported that it intends to recruit 1,000 R&D personnel (with doctoral degrees) by 2015, up from just 10 in 2001. In 2004, nearly one-third of state scholarships administered by the A★STAR went to non-Singaporeans studying in the life sciences field. See Alexius Pereira, "Whither the Developmental State? Explaining Singapore's Continued Developmentalism," *Third World Quarterly* 29 (2008), 1196.

that "Once I catch a whale, I know other whales will follow. I have quite a large collection of sirs and Nobel prize winners here now."[8]

Even Korea, thought to be the most insular of the three in terms of foreign talent recruitment, has looked to globalize its universities and public research institutes and to facilitate life sciences research exchanges among local and foreign labs. Indeed, international collaboration is perceived as a source of much-needed global credibility, another measure of biotech development among latecomers in Asia. The selection of Seoul National University (SNU) by the United Nations Development Programme to house the International Vaccine Institute (IVI) has made Korea a magnet for world-class research. As of 2005, the vast majority of biomedical researchers at the IVI were from foreign countries. The decision to put the IVI in Korea is perceived, above all, as a stamp of legitimacy from the international scientific community.

Another strategic portrayal of biotech emphasizes the rapid development of the physical and policy infrastructures supporting life sciences R&D. Singapore's Biopolis complex has captured the public's attention for its design, scale, and the speed with which its construction was completed, signaling the government's unequivocal commitment to promoting cutting-edge biomedical research. Taiwan's National Health Research Institute is located at its own large-scale campus in Miaoli, an hour outside Taipei. Government policies in all three cases are also being revised in line with international standards to facilitate biotech innovation. Intellectual property rights, regulatory compliance, and manufacturing and clinical regulatory standards have been legislated and gradually put into place, not only to ensure domestic protection for patients and firms but also to attract more opportunities for international collaboration. These developments are all intended to reflect progress; they are noteworthy achievements.

Because the distance from lab bench to market is uniquely long in biotech, stakeholders in Korea, Taiwan, and Singapore are highlighting other statistical indicators to demonstrate advances in life sciences R&D and commercial development. Short of a commercial blockbuster, which could most easily be measured in terms of revenue earned or market share, other benchmarks are being reported, such as statistical indicators of publications and patent registrations. Academic publications in international journals and registrations with foreign patent offices are weighted more heavily than domestic ones. That the discoveries published as patents and in academic papers remain a fair distance from becoming marketable technologies and commercial applications is

---

8. Mia Shanley, "Maverick Singapore Bureaucrat Hunts for Scientists," *Reuters News,* February 17, 2006.

beside the point; what is important is that such indicators demonstrate progress. And as I showed in Chapter 2, the trajectory of this measure of progress in Korea, Taiwan, and Singapore has been quite remarkable given their recent efforts in science and technology development. Such measures have allowed stakeholders, notably the state, to recalibrate and thus manage more realistic and achievable expectations in developing commercial biotech.

Reframing Biotechnology

In addition to recalibrating expectations about a more realistic pace for life sciences innovation and commercial biotech development, the state in Korea, Taiwan, and Singapore is *strategically reframing the scope of what is meant by biotechnology* and thus how it measures economic output in the life sciences industry more generally. As the example of the STAG's proposed benchmarks for biotech commercialization among public labs in Taiwan suggests (see Chapter 2), counting is strategic, and how one defines the parameters of what is being counted matters in portraying political-economic realities. In Taiwan, for example, the state has purposely expanded the definition of biotech industry to include a range of non-biotech products (or at least not conventionally counted as biotechnology), such as cosmetics, health foods, traditional Chinese medicines, and mechanical medical devices and other electronics hardware. These are all health-related products, though far from what are typically classified as biotechnologies. But they nonetheless matter in the portrayal of the growth of the biotech industry in Taiwan. The government regularly reports that biotech and pharmaceutical industry revenues are growing by double-digit rates each year, an impressive figure, to be sure. In reality, however, a significant portion of that revenue growth is attributable to the distribution and sales of health foods and the local manufacture of pharmaceutical ingredients and medical diagnostic kits. In fact, according to figures from the National Science Council in Taiwan, biotech R&D conducted in science-based industrial parks (such as Hsinchu and Tainan) represented a mere 0.20% of total sales in 2000, and biotech ranked lowest in terms of productivity when compared with other technology sectors covered in the survey.[9]

The Singaporean government has similarly reframed its biotech program by incorporating a much broader notion of what it calls the "biomedical sciences industry." By doing so, the state counts pharmaceutical manufacturing,

9. Productivity here is measured as the ratio of R&D expenditures to sales revenue. See National Science Council (NSC), *Indicators of Science and Technology 2002* (Taipei: NSC, 2002), 110–117.

marketing, and distribution—all essentially low-tech activities—as part of the total economic output from the biomedical industry sector. Every year the EDB and A★STAR report impressive growth rates in the life sciences, measured in terms of revenue, job creation, and inward investment. Yet it needs to be noted, as I did in the previous chapter, that the fastest growth segment of the biomedical sector reflected in such economic measures is in the manufacturing side of the industry. In the meantime, the proportion of value-added output (as a share of total manufacturing) has actually decreased over the past decade. In other words, by strategically incorporating commercial biotech innovation and firm creation into the broader category of biomedical sciences industry, the state is able to portray the life sciences industries as having rapidly expanded, even if cutting-edge biotech innovation and its share of national economic output are lagging.

Efforts to strategically portray development in biotech are not intended to deceive. In fact, many argue that in the case of Singapore, the state's primary objective is in fact to grow the biomedical sciences industry in the aggregate, and the state is therefore less concerned about the development of cutting-edge firms and labs in the innovation process; that is, sales, jobs, and investment are in fact the intended measures of growth. Nonetheless, the key point is that stakeholders in all three places are reframing the biotech sector—or, put more accurately, are subsuming the objectives of biotech innovation under a broader conceptualization of health technology industries—in order to cast the life sciences industry and its prospects in a more positive light. Portraying the biotech sector in these ways is intended to sustain an appetite for the long-term uncertainties of first-order biotech innovation. It allows stakeholders, particularly the state, to bolster figures for economic and R&D output in the near term. It gives them more of the time needed to translate promising research into marketable products and services. In these respects, managing expectations about the long-term realities of the innovation process and reframing the biotech sector are politically expedient responses to coping with uncertainty. Given the massive amounts of resources that have been invested in the sector, the state cannot politically afford the perception that its efforts to grow biotech in reality teeter on the brink of failure.

Manufacturing Stars

Notwithstanding efforts to portray the development of biotech with an optimistic prognosis, the prevailing consensus among biotech stakeholders in Korea, Taiwan, and Singapore is that a star case or a success story is needed soon to rejuvenate and sustain the appetite for the long-term imperatives of commercial biotech innovation. Such a star, it is argued, would serve as a model for emulation and a source of inspiration. After all, increased returns from manufacturing or from the health-food industry are not the long-term objectives for biotech stakeholders in Asia. They do not endeavor to be the manufacturing plants for the global pharmaceutical industry. Rather, Korea, Taiwan, and Singapore look to climb the commercial value chain and ultimately to become biotech industry leaders and innovators. But people are getting impatient. The growth rate in biotech industry is increasingly viewed as unacceptably slow. There is a growing sense that maybe the challenges of managing commercial biotech's technical, economic, and temporal uncertainties are beyond the capacities, scale, and patience of stakeholders in Korea, Taiwan, and Singapore—that maybe they should no longer bet on biotech.

The state has therefore taken on the more direct role of *manufacturing stars,* to artificially cast the commercial biotech sector and its prospects in a more positive light. In addition to policies aimed at mitigating risk and coping with uncertainty, described in earlier chapters, the state has looked to manufacture, in the nearer term, success stories or star cases. The state has chosen to allocate public resources to very specific high-profile initiatives in industry and upstream research. By subventing and in effect leading the private sector in these initiatives, the state has thus taken on the financial and administrative burdens of manufacturing these success stories. In fact, it would be more accurate to say that the state has *overallocated* resources to these endeavors to, as best it can, ensure their success. In this respect, the state's interventions to manufacture stars go beyond their otherwise facilitative roles discussed in previous chapters to enhance R&D and bio-industrial growth from a more arm's-length distance. The strategy of manufacturing stars is discrete, limited to specific projects, and one that appends the state's other strategies for promoting life sciences industry development. These stars are not intended to anchor the entire biotech industry in Korea, Taiwan, and Singapore. Rather, their anticipated value is in their demonstration effects. The strategy to manufacture stars is therefore understood by the state as a necessary, high-risk, loss-leader intervention intended to revive and sustain an appetite for biotech's long-term uncertainty.

TaiMed

In the fall of 2007, the Taiwan government announced the formation of TaiMed Biologics, a "supra-incubator" start-up firm for developing biopharmaceuticals.[10] Its first licensing deal featured the transfer of the experimental HIV/AIDS drug TNX-355 from U.S. biotech giant Genentech.[11] Phase 2a human clinical trials for TNX-355 were completed in 2006, and TaiMed's plans were to take the candidate through Phase 2b and 3 trials, first in Taiwan though with hopes of mounting global trials. It planned to bring the drug to global markets in three to four years, making it the first pharmaceutical product to be developed and marketed worldwide by a Taiwan-based firm. It was also expected that TNX-355 would be Taiwan's first drug therapy to be approved by the U.S. FDA. What really set this particular deal apart from other licensing agreements between foreign and local life sciences firms was that the government, through its National Development Fund (NDF), invested US$20 million in the start-up of the firm. Before the 2007 TaiMed deal, government investment in biotech firms tended not to exceed an equity ceiling of 20% (which I have argued is a significant departure from past practices in the developmental state).[12] The state claimed a 40% equity share in TaiMed, however, as it intended to use the government's credibility and networks in industry to draw follow-on investors. The size and proportion of the state's investment in TaiMed, a single firm, was unprecedented for Taiwan's biotech sector.

The supra-incubator formulation was envisioned as the private sector's replication of the ITRI model in technology development and commercialization. The parallels between TaiMed and the ITRI are not accidental, as many of the ITRI's leaders were also involved in the organizational design of TaiMed. Indeed, direct references to the Taiwan Semiconductor Manufacturing Corporation (TSMC) experience were made with respect to the TaiMed initiative. Like the ITRI, TaiMed Biologics focuses on midstream biotech development. To compensate for Taiwan's nascent upstream research capacity in the life sciences, TaiMed aims to replicate ITRI's "license-in, license-out" strategy, acquiring promising leads and taking them further downstream closer to market. As the TNX-355 deal demonstrates, the firm's strategy is to

---

10. Author interviews, Hsinchu and Taipei, Taiwan, September 19, 2007.

11. TNX-355 was acquired by Genentech when it absorbed the smaller U.S.-based biotech firm Tanox in February 2007. The connections between Tanox and Taiwan (and thus indirectly with Genentech) run deep. Tanox, before it was acquired by Genentech, was headed by Nancy Chang, a Taiwanese American. She is also the former spouse of Chang Tse-Wen, a renowned biotechnology researcher who was recruited to Taiwan to head up the parastatal Development Center for Biotechnology early in the first decade of the 2000s. Some have suggested that the Tanox-Genentech deal was made possible through such personal connections.

12. Author interview, MOEA, Taipei, Taiwan, September 16, 2007.

capture a lucrative though relatively small segment of the biopharmaceutical commercial value chain.[13]

State leadership in the TaiMed experiment extended beyond its unusually large equity investment in what is technically a private firm. The creation of TaiMed also involved the state's direct role in prospecting and cementing the Genentech deal in the first place, and subsequently in organizing the firm's management operations. The TNX-355 acquisition from Genentech and the founding of TaiMed were brokered by local political and scientific heavyweights, collectively described in the media as Taiwan's biotech "dream team."[14] The Genentech deal involved negotiations between Ho Mei-Yueh, chairwoman of the Council for Economic Planning and Development (CEPD), renowned U.S.-based AIDS researcher and former *Time* magazine "man of the year" David Ho, and senior officials at Genentech. The government's investment came from the NDF, which is overseen by the CEPD. Former premier Tsai Ing-Wen was appointed chairwoman of TaiMed, with Academia Sinica's president, Wong Chi-Huey, and his predecessor, Nobel laureate Lee Yuan-Tseh, serving on the company's board. Morris Chang, the visionary who founded TSMC during the 1980s, agreed to be an external adviser for the firm.

TaiMed's founding also benefited from fortuitous timing. In 2007, as the TaiMed initiative was being formulated, the Taiwan government pushed through significant legislation that not only encouraged the deepening of academic-industry linkages and increased venture investment in the biotech sector, but also reoriented the Executive Yuan Development Fund (EYDF) to become more aggressive in investing in private sector firms. In addition, it was at this time that the EYDF was transformed into the National Development Fund, which committed to investing an additional US$1 billion in the commercial biotech industry.[15] In short, a fortuitous confluence of government elite networks, the buy-in of industrial heavyweights, and state policy initiatives ensured a successful and much publicized take-off for TaiMed.

Despite the public fanfare that accompanied the government's announcement about the founding of TaiMed, there were some, including those who supported the state's leadership role in founding the firm, who expressed concerns about the profitability and long-term commercial viability of the start-up biotech venture. Several accounts from industry observers and state

---

13. Author interview, Hsinchu, Taiwan, September 20, 2007.

14. Ming-Ling Hsieh, "Taiwan's Biotech Dream Team," *Commonwealth Magazine,* September 26, 2007.

15. Hsieh, "Taiwan's Biotech Outbreak."

officials suggest, for instance, that the TNX-355 initiative is not a particularly good business deal. According to one major investor in Taiwan's biotech industry, the TNX-355 drug will likely command a relatively small market share, and some experts forecast that the AIDS drug would gain only a US$200 million market, which in the pharmaceutical industry is considered very small, especially when measured against the costs of running clinical trials. Insiders also pointed to the fact that the TNX-355 lead was inherited by Genentech when it acquired U.S.-based biotech firm Tanox, and that the reason the experimental drug languished after initial Phase 2 trials was because Genentech did not see TNX-355 as central to its own business plans; in other words, the market was simply too small for Genentech. The TNX-355 drug was essentially a throwaway lead that Genentech did not want and, according to some, was all too happy to license out.[16] There was also concern that because the TaiMed-Genentech deal was based on a single drug candidate, the Taiwan start-up firm would be particularly vulnerable.[17]

The TaiMed initiative revealed the government's anxieties about the waning appetite for commercial biotech in Taiwan. According to state officials, the creation of TaiMed was explicitly intended to "speed things up" in terms of developing Taiwan's biotech industries.[18] In short, TaiMed was to be a compelling success story, a star. The strategic rationale behind the TaiMed initiative, according to industry observers and government officials, was not about the firm's future profitability per se, but rather about providing the government with a star and thus the ability to portray Taiwan's emerging biotech sector as a promising industrial venture. TaiMed's demonstration effects for the broader industry were more important than its revenues earned.[19]

To be sure, the TaiMed-Genentech agreement was extremely high-profile, as it was the first Taiwan-based biopharmaceutical deal to be played out on the international stage. It gave Taiwan instant international credibility. The founding of TaiMed was, it was hoped, a "magnetic catalyst" to reinvigorate investment and bio-entrepreneurship. It signaled to investors, industry, and researchers the government's continued commitment to growing a domestic innovation-driven biotech sector.[20] It also provided local bio-industry the much-needed experience in running clinical trials, establishing clinical R&D facilities and drafting protocols, and forging international collaborative

---

16. Author interview, MOEA, Taipei, Taiwan, September 16, 2007.

17. Author interview, Taipei, Taiwan, September 17, 2007.

18. Author interview, MOEA, Taipei, Taiwan, September 16, 2007.

19. Author interviews, MOEA, Taipei, Taiwan, September 16, 2007, and Hsinchu, Taiwan, September 20, 2007.

20. Hsieh, "Taiwan's Biotech Outbreak."

agreements. TaiMed, in this respect, was expected to serve as a model of how a cutting-edge biotech firm is formed and managed, and one that could be emulated by local industry. TaiMed's supra-incubator model represented a firm-level organizational innovation—by which I mean its downstream developmental function—that could be replicated by industry.[21]

Merlion, ES Cell, and S*Bio

Merlion is a Singaporean drug discovery firm that specializes in the development of anti-infective therapies, using natural product compounds as screening candidates. The start-up firm was established in 2002 with the privatization of the government's Center for Natural Product Research (CNPR), which was at the time a lab within the Institute for Molecular and Cell Biology (IMCB). The CNPR was created in 1993 through a partnership between the Economic Development Board and the multinational pharmaceutical company GlaxoSmithKline. Merlion inherited GSK's extensive catalog of natural product compounds. In the initial contribution to the start-up firm, GSK invested 50% and the government provided the remaining 50%, shared between the EDB and the IMCB.[22] Tony Buss, a former senior executive with GSK, was recruited to head up the new firm. Shortly after its founding, Merlion completed its "A" round of financing, led by Avaris, a foreign venture capital fund with connections to the EDB. The EDB's biomedical investment fund was a follow-on investor.[23]

Merlion's initial business plan was to use its natural product catalog, considered the largest in the world, to screen new drug therapies. Drug development was to be carried out in-house, aided through R&D collaborations with local labs and with multinational pharmaceutical firms that had located some of their R&D projects in Singapore. Merlion's business model was revised in 2006, however, when the strategy of in-house drug discovery and development proved too slow and financing was drying up. Without a revenue stream and without an exit option for the near term, local and foreign investors became increasingly cautious about the firm. Merlion thus took on a more aggressive business plan, acquiring in 2006 two biotech firms, Germany's Combinature and Switzerland's Athelas. Both were in financial distress, but each had developed an anti-infective drug candidate through preclinical R&D and was about to enter Phase 1 trials. Merlion acquired their drug

---

21. Author interview, Hsinchu, Taiwan, September 19, 2007.

22. Author interview, Singapore, December 12, 2002.

23. Author interviews, Singapore, June 17, 2004.

candidates and at the same time raised nearly US$30 million in its "B" round of financing. This time the government's Bio★One fund co-led the investment with Avaris.[24] Merlion began Phase 1 trials in late 2007. The firm also set out to recruit new research talent at that time, specifically researchers and management personnel with expertise in clinical R&D.[25] Merlion won the Scripps Award that year for "best company in an emerging market." It is seen as one of Singapore's star firms.

ES Cell International (ESI) was formed in 2000, when scientists from Australia's Monash University and the National University of Singapore (NUS), led by Professor Ariff Bongso, successfully replicated a line of embryonic stem cells, the scientific basis for the development of cutting-edge stem cell therapies. The firm was established in Singapore, in part because of the relatively liberal regulatory regimes governing human stem cell research and also because of the government's commitment to developing biomedical industry, especially in the area of stem cell research. Alan Colman, who had led the Scottish team of researchers that cloned Dolly the sheep in 1997, was recruited to ESI to become its chief science officer in 2002; he was made CEO in 2005. In 2001, ESI was selected by the U.S. National Institutes of Health as one of ten research organizations eligible for U.S. federal government funding for stem cell research. ESI was envisioned as a stem cell therapy development firm, focusing on treatments for diabetes and cancer. The future looked bright for ESI.

As of 2005, the government's Bio★One fund had invested over US$26 million in ESI,[26] which accounted for reportedly just under a 50% stake in the firm.[27] It was expected that ESI would have therapy candidates ready for human trials in 2007 and marketable products by 2010. Because revenues were slow, however, the firm diversified its business model by selling its stem cell lines to labs for research use. While Colman admits that the business of selling lines was not the firm's core objective, the rationale was that it would help raise ESI's profile domestically and internationally.[28] As such, ESI was portrayed by the state as a success case, not so much because of its revenue-generating potential—to be sure, the firm was reorganized in 2007 after it failed to gain a new round of financing—but rather as an example of

---

24. Author interview, Singapore, November 29, 2006.

25. Author interview, Singapore, October 29, 2007.

26. Jessica Cheam, "Biogenesis: Potential Stem Cell Venture," *Straits Times,* August 13, 2005.

27. John Burton, "ES Cell International: In Singapore, a Company with Ambitious Goals Leads a 'Privileged Existence,'" *Scientific American,* June 27, 2005.

28. Author interview, Singapore, November 28, 2006.

how cutting-edge upstream research from within the university lab could be translated into a potentially viable commercial venture.

S★Bio, another one of Singapore's star firms, was formed in 2000, when U.S.-based Chiron Biotechnology (acquired by Novartis in 2005) and the government's EDB formed a partnership to spin out a new biopharmaceutical firm. Focusing on small molecular and genomic technologies, S★Bio is currently developing anticancer drugs, particularly HDAC inhibitors. The firm's initial investment amounted to US$40 million, with Chiron claiming a 19% stake and the EDB investment arm (now Bio★One) fronting the remaining US$32 million (or over 75%). S★Bio was high-profile from the beginning, inheriting Chiron's gene expression technology and gaining access to some of Chiron's anticancer drug leads. The long-term realities of drug discovery quickly set in for the firm, however. S★Bio was reported to have been running out of capital by late 2005. Chiron had in fact divested itself of the enterprise. The management team of S★Bio was subsequently changed, with Jan-Anders Karlsson, a former senior research executive with Bayer, taking over as CEO in 2005. The firm's fortunes took a turn for the better in 2007 when it announced that one of its drug candidates had entered Phase 1 trials and that two other anticancer HDAC inhibitors were far along preclinical stages of development. In 2007, S★Bio began pursuing its "B" round of financing. It eschewed what it saw as risk-averse local VCs, focusing instead on internationalizing the firm in terms of its clinical R&D, investment, and manufacturing. If commercially successful, S★Bio would be Singapore's pioneering anticancer therapies firm in arguably the most high-profile and lucrative drug market of all.[29]

Merlion, ESI, and S★Bio were intended in their conception to be stories of success in biomedical industry development in Singapore. Common across the three was state leadership in manufacturing what it hoped would be eventual bio-industrial stars. The state was a critical source of business investment, given the dearth of local VC investors willing to shoulder the risks of commercial biotech development. State resources were also patient capital, evidenced by long-term investments in ESI and S★Bio. Alan Colman, CEO of ESI, suggests the stem cell firm enjoyed a "privileged existence" in Singapore because of the government's financial commitment. He adds that ESI "would not be alive [as of 2006] if we had been based in either Australia or the U.S."[30] Singapore's star firms also benefited enormously from the networks provided by the government and specifically the EDB. Tony Buss of

29. Author interview, Singapore, October 30, 2007.

30. Author interview, Singapore, November 28, 2006; Burton, "ES Cell International."

Merlion explains that even though Avaris led the first round of investment in the firm in 2002, much of that start-up initiative was owed to the EDB's introductions to local and foreign investors and to the EDB's international credibility.[31]

The state actively selected and targeted Merlion, ESI, and S★Bio to be star firms; adhering to a classic developmental state strategy for infant industry promotion, it provided these firms with advantages and protection from local competition. ESI was Singapore's only dedicated stem cell therapy discovery firm. S★Bio is considered Singapore's flagship anticancer drug development company. They were provided advantages that other firms were denied, whether in terms of investment, R&D resources, collaborative opportunities, talent recruitment, or media attention.[32] The state thus leveraged its comparative institutional advantages, and specifically its international networks, to facilitate local commercial biotech industry growth. In turn, it expected these star firms to have a positive demonstration effect on the rest of the biomedical sector, to spark follow-on investment, and to restore or at least whet a waning appetite for cutting-edge biotech innovation. Merlion, ESI, and S★Bio were intentionally high-profile stories.

Hwang Woo-Suk

In early 2006, the once celebrated Korean researcher Hwang Woo-Suk admitted to committing scientific fraud. He and his team published what were thought to be landmark articles in the prestigious research journal *Science*. His 2004 article claimed that his lab had successfully cloned human embryos. The 2005 piece asserted that he had tailored stem cell lines to match their donors. Both findings, if valid, would have moved the field of stem cell research and the development of stem cell therapies a giant step forward. Hwang's work was considered revolutionary. It turned out, however, that Hwang had fabricated evidence. He had also breached important ethical regulations in the acquisition of donor eggs.

Before these revelations and his own admission of guilt, however, Hwang was Korea's most famous scientist, arguably Korea's most celebrated celebrity.

---

31. Author interview, Singapore, December 12, 2002.

32. One local venture capital investor recounted how he had approached the government's Bio★One fund with an investment proposal for a foreign-based cancer drug development firm. The company had already listed on the prestigious NASDAQ, and its product was near market (i.e., in Phase 3 clinical trials). This was thought to be a safe investment. The response he received from Bio★One was that its "flagship" anticancer firm was S★Bio and it was therefore not interested in investing in its competition. Author interview, Singapore, October 30, 2007.

People imagined he would be Korea's first Nobel Prize laureate in the sciences. Hwang was a star who at the time was single-handedly propelling Korea toward becoming one of a few global leaders in upstream life sciences research. He brought tremendous credibility to Korea's scientific research establishment. A commercial biotech industry could be built, it was reasoned by industry and government, on the achievements and credibility of Hwang and his team at Seoul National University. But just as Hwang manufactured evidence to bolster his research standing, his star status had been manufactured by the government and by Korean society, which wanted to rapidly upgrade its global standing—to "leap ahead"—in the life sciences.[33]

Hwang's star status was critical to Korea's long-term plans for developing its biotech industry. Manufacturing Hwang's star paid off in terms of international stature and the perception of global leadership in basic research in the life sciences. The prestige that was won through Hwang's purported groundbreaking findings led prominent labs elsewhere to either abandon or rework their stem cell research agendas. Hwang's work had that much impact. Had his research been legitimate, not only would Hwang have successfully taken on world leaders in cutting-edge stem cell research; he would have raised the bar for all future developments in the field. The payoff was instant international credibility. Korea emerged as a player in the global biotech scene, hastening the formation of new collaborative R&D opportunities for Korean labs, universities, and firms. Local industry looked to benefit. Investors gained confidence in the sector. The chaebols were expected to move more decisively into life sciences innovation. Simply put, Hwang's international star status was a significant, if indirect, stimulus for Korea's infant life sciences industries.

Hwang's rise to research prominence was more than just facilitated by the state; it was unequivocally a *product* of direct government efforts. Hwang was anointed Korea's "top scientist" by President Roh Moo-Hyun. The MOST funded Hwang upward of US$65 million in research funds, a not insignificant share of Korea's total basic science research budget. Just before the revelations about his suspect research, the MOHW committed an additional US$15 million to create the World Stem Cell Hub for Hwang and his lab. Hwang became part of President Roh's elite inner circle, where he advised the president on science- and technology-related policies.[34] Korea's

33. Norimitsu Onishi, "In a Country That Craved Respect, Stem Cell Scientist Rode a Wave of Korean Pride," *New York Times,* January 22, 2006.

34. Nicholas Wade, "Clone Scientist Relied on Peers and Korean Pride," *New York Times,* December 25, 2005.

regulatory regime for embryonic stem cell research was effectively retro-fitted to support rather than constrain Hwang's ongoing research.[35] And finally, the government turned a blind eye to early suspicions about Hwang's research. As one Korean scientist reported after Hwang's admission of guilt in early 2006, "Many of us didn't trust him. But pressure from the public and the government to support him actually inhibited our criticism. We couldn't say anything."[36] Political economists David Kang and Adam Segal note that Korean efforts to bolster Hwang and his research were driven by a "technonationalist" impulse. In Korea, the imperative to manufacture a star scientist was intense.[37]

Such technonationalist sentiments were not the government's alone. Hwang's story resonated with, and was fanned by, a wave of popular nation-alism, and it penetrated deeply into Korea's national consciousness. His rise was couched in national, not individual, terms. He was, as one analyst put it, "a beacon of light in the dark," and he "triggered Korean sentiments of nationalist pride."[38] People saw Hwang as a deliverer of greatness to Korea. He was treated like a rock star. In a wired society in which citizens see themselves as netizens, Hwang naturally had an online fan club. The government created a postage stamp in his honor. Early responses to the Hwang crisis went so far as to suggest that accusations of fraud were an American conspiracy to humiliate a rising Korea. When Hwang was charged and later indicted, his detractors were seen by some to be antipatriotic.[39]

The Hwang debacle finally came to a head in early 2006, though the effects of his downfall continued to linger. His fraudulent research claims and initial resistance to owning up to the evidence against him undermined Korea's—and, more generally, Asia's—credibility in life sciences research. It lent credence to Francis Fukuyama's assertion that Asians by and large ap-proach biotech development with little ethical grounding, driven solely by financial and status-based motivations.[40] Hwang's downfall also brought up serious concerns about the credibility of the peer review process in academic journals, raising red flags in other parts of Asia, most notably the Chinese academy. Hwang had become an embarrassment to the Korean government,

---

35. Joseph Wong, "Korea's Stem Cell Debacle: How a Nation's Disgrace Can Ultimately Be Its Victory," *Munk Centre Monitor* (2006).

36. Onishi, "Korean Pride."

37. David Kang and Adam Segal, "The Siren Song of Technonationalism," *Far Eastern Economic Review,* March 2006.

38. Quoted in Onishi, "Korean Pride."

39. Wong, "Korea's Stem Cell Debacle."

40. Francis Fukuyama, *Our Posthuman Future: Consequences of the Biotechnology Revolution* (New York: Farrar, Straus and Giroux, 2002).

the nation, and Seoul National University. The story of Hwang clearly illuminates the political economic pathologies of extreme technonationalism
and the strategy of manufacturing stars.

Still, Hwang continues to enjoy a small but dedicated corps of supporters
in Korea. To some he remains the pride of Korean science. Perhaps most important, however, is that despite Hwang's fallen star, many Koreans continue
to believe, as his supporters did when Hwang was first found guilty of having
fabricated evidence, that "biotechnology is our future."[41] In other words, to
the extent that a loss-leader strategy to manufacture Korea's own star scientist
was intended to help sustain an appetite in Korea for biotech's long-term
uncertainties, Hwang's rise and fall achieved just that. Korean stakeholders
did not abandon their biotech ambitions in the wake of the Hwang affair.
Indeed, it is arguable that the Hwang debacle hardened even further Korea's
resolve to succeed.

The Political Economy of Manufacturing Stars

The stories of TaiMed, Merlion, ESI, S*Bio, and Hwang Woo-Suk are exemplary of what I mean by the strategy of manufacturing stars: the creation
of national champions by the state. While the individual experiences differ
in important ways, the various stories recounted here have common features.
All the cases have been high profile, attracting media attention locally and
globally. Each has benefited from the allocation of disproportionately large
amounts of state resources in terms of investment capital, protection from
competition, and political stewardship. It is not unreasonable, in fact, to assert that the state in Korea, Taiwan, and Singapore overallocated resources to
these targeted initiatives.

These specific enterprises were intended to be successes. However, unlike
during the postwar period, their success was not expected to anchor the entire
biotech industry, as we saw with the entry of Samsung into semiconductors
or the creation of TSMC in Taiwan during the 1980s. Though they were
hoped to be national champions in their own right (i.e., earn revenue, gain
market share, and produce path-breaking publications), their achievement
of star status was primarily intended to yield other positive externalities and
demonstration effects for the long-term development of biotech and bio-
industry. They were intended to be exemplars of manufactured "progress."

41. Cited in Nicholas Wade and Sang-Hun Choe, "Researcher Faked Evidence of Human
Cloning, Koreans Report," *New York Times,* January 10, 2006.

In other words, the value-added gains from their respective successes rested in the stars' ability to convey credibility for recent entrants such as Korea, Taiwan, and Singapore; to provide a model for emulation among local firms and labs; and most important, to reinvigorate and sustain an appetite for the long-term uncertainties of commercial biotech innovation.

In some respects, the efforts by the state to manufacture such stars have more or less been successful. They have provided compelling stories and important lessons for would-be entrepreneurs, investors, and scientists involved in the biotech sector. But the processes by which biotech stars have been manufactured in Korea, Taiwan, and Singapore also reveal limitations and tensions in the strategy. This is not to say that the strategy to manufacture stars and national champions is terribly flawed or that it is poor government policy. In fact, there are compelling reasons to view such efforts as necessary, given biotech's temporal uncertainties. Nor is it my intention to suggest that such limitations and tensions are unique to the biotech sector. Rather, my point is that significant political and economic tensions are brought to the analytic fore when the state attempts to take on a direct leadership role in manufacturing stars in biotech, tensions that are rooted in the state's developmental or leadership role, on the one hand, and real commercial imperatives inherent in market forces, on the other.

Overinvestment by the state has, for instance, led to concerns about *firms' market fitness,* drawing critical views on how resource allocation decisions are made. In Taiwan, criticisms have been raised about the commercial viability of the recently formed TaiMed, especially since its management team is made up mainly of high-profile political heavyweights rather than those with biotech industry experience and expertise. Similarly, in Singapore, executives in targeted star firms admit that excessive reliance on state patronage can undermine the perception of firms' market fitness, especially when it comes to attracting nongovernment investment. Fears have emerged that resources from the government's Bio*One inadvertently fuel the perception that investment decisions are a function of state clientelism rather than sound industrial policy or market fitness. In this respect, ESI's "privileged existence," as CEO Alan Colman describes it, entails some negative consequences for the firm. Most notably, ESI was unable to gain subsequent rounds of financing after 2006, a development that some suggest is due to the firm's close ties to the Singaporean government.[42] Industry insiders in Singapore similarly explain how it is often assumed that S*Bio is a state-owned enterprise

---

42. Author interview, Singapore, November 28, 2006.

(which it is not) and that the firm therefore "has nothing to worry about" because it is in the "government's interest to bail S★Bio out." This common if incorrect perception of the firm is shared among investors both inside and outside Singapore. It is a damaging misperception, to be sure, but one that has been difficult to correct given S★Bio's close ties with EDB and the Bio★One fund.[43] Informants in Singapore tell me that smaller firms in Singapore in fact deliberately eschew state financing for fear they might be perceived as market-failing firms, unable to gain private sources of financing and thus in desperate need of state subvention. Such firms, having learned from the examples of ESI and S★Bio, prefer to go it on their own, to "grow their business organically," and to ensure some distance from the state.[44]

The state-led strategy of selectively manufacturing stars also illuminates what are seen as fundamentally conflicting agendas in how states make their resource allocation decisions. Questions surrounding whether the strategy of manufacturing stars is intended to be an instrument for sectoral industry growth more generally (stars as models for emulation and demonstration) or the growth of a specific firm (a viable commercial business) have emerged among biotech stakeholders and industry watchers. The two roles—developmental versus commercial, industry building versus business investing—may appear on the surface to be complementary. In reality, however, they are not. Outputs are evaluated differently. The developmental approach emphasizes positive externalities gained more generally from a specific initiative, while the commercial dimension focuses on the returns derived from specific investments. The original intent of manufacturing stars in Korea, Taiwan, and Singapore was to emphasize the industry-wide developmental role of the state. Over time, however, people have come to evaluate the payoffs or outputs of such stars in much narrower terms, such as commercial returns. In other words, the strategy to manufacture stars has led to conflicting expectations about outcomes and also fundamentally conflicting logics of resource allocation.

For example, the emerging consensus among most industry observers in Taiwan is that the TaiMed enterprise is not likely to be a particularly good business deal in terms of commercial returns. State officials have echoed similar expectations but assert that the state's motivation in forming TaiMed in the first place was more developmentally oriented and thus for the benefit of the biotechnology sector as a whole. This has not, however, assuaged the many— such as the audience to which I spoke in 2007—who regard the TaiMed

43. Author interview, Singapore, October 30, 2007.
44. Author interviews, Singapore, June 16, 2004, and November 28, 2006.

deal strictly as a business investment and one that ought to be evaluated as such, in terms of job creation, wealth accumulation, revenue generation, and market share. Expectations about TaiMed's performance have been confused. There has been a similar dynamic at play in Singapore. The Bio★One venture fund was originally formed by the Singaporean government to play a developmental role for biomedical industry growth; it was a fund to spark bio-industrial development. Bio★One financed ESI, even though the firm (as well as its supporters in the EDB) quickly realized that its intended business plan to translate basic research in stem cell therapies into marketable goods was going to be extremely long term. The Bio★One's investment motives were nonetheless centered on elevating the status of stem cell research in Singapore and on generating collaborative opportunities between ESI, the various institutes at the Biopolis, and of course foreign labs and firms. And it did just that. Nevertheless, many in Singapore expected the Bio★One-invested ESI to be a commercial success, a firm that brings in revenues. As in Taiwan, expectations of such state-led efforts to manufacture stars have been confused and conflicted.

The role of Bio★One illustrates particularly well the tensions between the state as *industry builder* and its perceived role as *business investor*. Bio★One was created to facilitate the growth of Singapore's biomedical industry, and it has invested domestically and abroad to do so. Outbound investments have tended to be conditional on the invested firm locating some of its operations in Singapore. Bio★One also invests in foreign VCs to gain expertise in carrying out its own due diligence and to prospect collaborative projects elsewhere. Local investments, however, are expected to fund market loss leaders, such as ESI, in order to generate positive spillovers for the sector. Reflecting this developmental role, the Bio★One fund has by and large been staffed by government bureaucrats tasked with executing government industrial policy, rather than conventional private sector investors interested more narrowly and conventionally in commercial returns. Yet expectations that Bio★One investments produce commercial returns—that the fund be used as a revenue-generating tool as opposed to a developmental instrument—have emerged in Singapore. Its investment logic has thus been gradually transformed, driven by pressures that the fund adhere to a more commercially oriented logic of resource allocation. Though Bio★One continues to fulfill its broader developmental role, it has also begun to let "failed" investments go, much as a "normal" investment fund would.[45] The most conspicuous example of this

---

45. Author interview, Singapore, November 1, 2007.

came in 2007, when ESI, one of Singapore's most important star firms, was forced to abandon its core business plan in therapeutic drug discovery and was reconstituted into a de facto research lab.[46] The fate of ESI was big news in Singapore, in large part because the government had effectively admitted that the enterprise had failed, at least as a commercial entity.

The story of ESI also demonstrates how this strategy of manufacturing stars shifts the costs of these potential failures to the state, something the state has otherwise looked to avoid, as I argued in Chapters 2 and 3. Stars have been created in Korea, Taiwan, and Singapore to compensate for the dearth of resources coming from the private sector. But how do states mitigate the effects of inevitable failures, especially when the motivation for creating these stars was to sustain enthusiasm for biotechnology in the first place? One way, as I have already suggested, is to recalibrate popular expectations about the prospects of commercial biotech innovation, so that failed initiatives are understood to be inevitable and even positive. The transformation of ESI into a public research lab and its integration into the Biopolis, for instance, demonstrate how an orchestrated "soft landing" can actually be portrayed as an indicator of progress.[47] Expectations can be recalibrated to anticipate the possibility of failure and to stress lessons that can be learned from failed initiatives.[48]

Still, anticipating and portraying failure is difficult to do, particularly when the political stakes of such investments have been so heightened in the political mainstream. By this I mean that the failure of stars is not just about the failure of a firm or a particular university lab, but rather is about the failure of a star initiative intended from the outset to entail much broader externalities for the sector as a whole. If Taiwan's TaiMed, for instance, proves to be a commercial failure over the next few years, its losses to Taiwan's biotech stakeholders would measure far more than the $20 million the government invested in the project. It would signify not only a failed firm but a *failed model* that was expected to be emulated in the sector more generally. Therefore, overinvestment in a single firm in Taiwan or Singapore, or in the case of Korea, Hwang Woo-Suk and his lab, heightens the political and economic stakes of potential failure, the burden of which is absorbed by the state. As the story of Professor Hwang illustrates, a key challenge in the strategy of manufacturing success stories is balancing the potential promise of spectacular stars

46. Author interview, Singapore, November 2, 2007.
47. Author interview, Singapore, October 29, 2007.
48. Author interview, Singapore, October 30, 2007.

against the risk of equally spectacular failures. And in the case of Korea, the state has had to bear the brunt of such failure.

Managing Temporal Uncertainty

Only five years after Samsung boldly announced its entry into the semi-conductor sector in the early 1980s, the firm emerged a global leader in the industry and other Korean firms successfully upgraded into the advanced electronics sector. It was less than a decade after UMC was formed that TSMC launched its pureplay foundry model and quickly integrated Taiwan's IT industry into lucrative global markets. In other words, it was not long after Korea and Taiwan first laid bets on these important industrial sectors that there was sufficient evidence to strongly suggest that the bets had paid off or were on their way to paying off. The same could be said of Singapore's efforts to upgrade into the production of high-technology electronics and computer peripherals. The development of commercial biotech industries, however, has thus far played out quite differently in Korea, Taiwan, and Singapore. Biotech innovation and commercialization has turned out be expensive, fraught with economic and technological uncertainties, and very long term. Investment in the life sciences over the past two decades dwarfs past initiatives in industrial upgrading in Korea, Taiwan, and Singapore, and yet very little in commercial returns has been realized thus far. The uncertainties of biotech innovation have been exacerbated by the fact that the bets are not only expensive but also conspicuously public; everyone is keenly aware of the gambles that have been undertaken.

Biotech's temporal uncertainty, which is a function of the sector's technical and economic uncertainties, thus poses an entirely new set of political economic challenges for the state and its industrial allies. The state finds itself needing to sustain a long-term appetite for commercial biotech innovation among stakeholders, investors, and even the general public. Biotech stakeholders understand the long-term imperatives of commercial life sciences innovation. But they also understand that they must transform prevailing short-term expectations into a much longer temporal horizon. Failing that, betting on biotech may prove to be not only economically costly but politically costly as well.

The evidence presented in this chapter demonstrates how the state in Korea, Taiwan, and Singapore is attempting to strategically portray the development of commercial biotech in ways intended to recast unreasonable short-term expectations as more realistic long-term opportunities.

The state plays an active role in educating the public about the health and economic benefits of biotech innovation. It has also strategically recalibrated popular expectations about biotech, devised new measurements of intermediate "progress" in the life sciences, and even reconceptualized the scope of what counts as biotech in order to portray a positive growth trajectory in the sector. Simply put, the state has strategically portrayed the development of commercial biotech in an attempt to buy time to ride out its bets over the long term.

Perhaps most conspicuous have been efforts by the state to manufacture stars, whether in industry or in the university lab. In one sense, this strategy might appear to mirror past practices of the postwar developmental state in which state leadership created successful firms on which entire industrial sectors could grow. Though I have argued throughout this book that the logic of state leadership in commercial biotech has seen the state retreat from picking and making winners, the selective cases of manufactured stars presented in this chapter certainly point to an enduring heuristic bias that favors such loss-leader strategies. Indeed, one could reasonably explain the decision to manufacture stars as a path-dependent legacy of the postwar developmental state and its successes in growing new industries. But it also needs to be emphasized that these choices to manufacture stars have in fact been rationalized by decision makers in Korea, Taiwan, and Singapore along a different strategic logic. The strategy is less about making market-dominant national champions and more about creating stories and models for emulation, demonstration, and inspiration in the sector as a whole and over the longer term. Thus, the anticipated success of TaiMed or ESI or Professor Hwang was not intended to commercially anchor the biotech industry. Rather, the success of a potential star was its value for other positive externalities. As I have suggested, the upside of this strategic rationale is that a star firm, lab, or scientist can help revive and sustain a long-term appetite for what is an uncertain commercial endeavor. The downside of this strategic bet, of course, is that failure may accelerate the decline of what is already a waning appetite for biotech, and the political and economic costs of such failure will fall on the state.

CHAPTER 5

Regulatory Uncertainty

This chapter focuses on a very specific dimension of commercial biotech development—regulation—and the ways in which the state in Korea, Taiwan, and Singapore has both contributed to and attempted to manage regulatory uncertainty. Regulatory considerations are an important aspect of the biotech innovation process, and the extent to which regulatory certainty, predictability, and clarity are achieved go a long way toward determining commercial returns and health care outcomes. By regulation I mean the enforced standards of appropriateness that govern a broad range of market and premarket activities, including R&D, technology commercialization, and market access. Regulation is simply an inherent aspect of the entire biotech innovation enterprise. And to that end, states matter. Regulatory regimes are ultimately the domain of the state, though as I show in this chapter, they can be intensely contested within and among nonstate actors.

For obvious reasons, regulation, in practice, is a source of temporal uncertainty. Regulation makes the innovation process longer. The very existence of premarket and market regulations poses potential obstacles for transforming an upstream discovery into an applied technology and eventually a commercially viable product or service. However, it is not the fact that regulatory regimes exist which is the problem for bio-industry stakeholders; regulatory standards, as I have suggested, are simply a given. Rather, the *problem of temporal uncertainty is exacerbated by regulatory uncertainty* within the state. Regulatory conflict and interest unalignment, particularly among state actors, can impede the innovation process further, intensifying rather than mitigating biotech's myriad uncertainties. Therefore, the problem for would-be commercial biotech innovators is not the fact of regulation itself, but rather the added obstacles that result from regulatory uncertainty and inconsistency.

The regulatory state can be inconsistent, in both its policy content and the implementation of regulatory regimes. As Cynthia Fox concludes in her study on stem cell R&D, the "world has accumulated knowledge about the "enormous" potential of stem cells with "remarkable speed"...Knowledge may well accumulate faster with time. Ignorance will undoubtedly fester and spread just as rapidly. Regulations established to best utilize this knowledge and temper the ignorance will sometimes be too restrictive, sometimes too loose."[1] The anticipation of inconsistency and uncertainty is not surprising given how regulatory standards in any industry, and especially new industries such as biotech, are continually evolving. Regulation and the regulatory "sciences" are dynamic, constantly ebbing and flowing, shaped by political, social, and economic forces as well as informed by new discoveries in science. For recent entrants into new sectors, such as in Asia, the development of regulatory regimes involves more often than not a process of institutional catch-up, in which various aspects of regulatory regimes are implemented at different times, experimented differently across sectors, and constantly revisited and revised.

The "regulatory state," David Levi-Faur explains, eludes neat categorical state types. It is not simply the case that regulatory regimes are consistently of liberal, mercantilist, pluralist, or transnational types. The regulatory state is not monolithic, and it can at once encompass characteristics of all of these categorical state types, "a complex reality [which] is often overlooked from the extreme positions of the 'state debate.'"[2] Regulatory regimes, rather than being coherent and comprehensive wholes, are a reflection of contending industrial, transnational, domestic political, and economic pressures. Regulation thus entails the *multiple stakeholder state,* in which various interests inside the state apparatus attempt to influence regulatory policy outcomes. The regulatory state is a site for intense political contestation, where the

---

1. Cynthia Fox, *Cell of Cells: The Global Race to Capture and Control the Stem Cell* (New York: W. W. Norton, 2008), 462.

2. David Levi-Faur, "Governing Dutch Telecommunications Reform," *Journal of European Public Policy* 6 (1999), 119.

push-and-pull of contending interests and priorities exacerbates rather than ameliorates regulatory uncertainty.

The state in Korea, Taiwan, and Singapore has experienced both interest alignment and unalignment in the regulation of the biotechnology sector. In some areas of the regulatory process, decision makers in Korea, Taiwan, and Singapore have been able to align various interests relatively easily, providing a fair degree of regulatory clarity and certainty. This is best exemplified, as I show, in the early regulation of clinical R&D. States have also established a relatively coherent stance in bioethics regulation, the second example looked at in this chapter, though only after considerable contestation among state and nonstate actors. The state in all three cases has largely failed, however, to resolve intrastate conflicts about the regulation of health technology markets, conflicts that are between state actors with contending priorities, expertise, and regulatory policy interests. These three regulatory regimes, governing clinical R&D, bioethics and markets, are explored in detail in this chapter.

Regulating for the Market

Regulation can both constrain and facilitate technological innovation. In this respect, then, regulatory policy is an integral part of a state's industrial policy mix. It is generally accepted, for instance, that a state's capacity to enforce intellectual property rights is a key factor in attracting foreign investment and R&D activities, whereas its absence is an obstacle to innovation. Beginning in the 1990s, the states in Korea, Taiwan, and Singapore revamped their existing intellectual property rights regimes, which resulted in significant increases in innovative R&D, most notably in transnational R&D activities. Regulatory reforms in financial markets, especially with respect to the capitalization of venture capital funds, have also encouraged growth in the number of technology venture firms. Changes to regulations governing public-private R&D collaboration, such as those that lifted obstacles to university-industry linkages, have prompted publicly funded researchers (such as university professors) to engage the private sector. Korea's 1997 "special law" (described in Chapter 3), which allowed university professors to form private biotech venture firms and provide consulting services to industry, is a good example of how regulatory policy functions as de facto industrial policy and thus a critical part of a nation's innovation system.

With respect to the health technology sector more specifically, food and drug regulators are credited with both nurturing and stifling the pharmaceutical industry. Regulatory processes matter a great deal when it comes to determining commercial outcomes in drug discovery and development. The

U.S. Food and Drug Administration, for example, is periodically criticized for lax regulatory oversight that has led to the approval of unsafe foods and drugs; such changes to approval processes have been initiated because of pressure from industry, which asserts that regulatory stringency stifles the development of innovative health technologies.[3] Recent corruption scandals involving the Chinese state FDA, which led to the execution of the former agency head in 2008, have stunted investor confidence and commercial interests in the Chinese market and immediately raised concerns about Chinese exports of food and health products.

Both of these examples demonstrate the complex relationship between regulation, innovation, and the market. They show how regulatory policy plays a significant role in shaping the course of commercial health technology and biotech industry development. They also illustrate how regulatory policies are inextricably tied, in complex ways, to both market incentives and nonmarket considerations such as consumer and patient safety. For innovative products and services to be commercially viable, they must satisfy market demands as well as adhere to tough and increasingly globally harmonized regulatory standards. Making and meeting such regulatory standards is thus critical for policy decision makers, firms, and researchers engaged in commercializing R&D.

Again, regulation itself is not the problem. In the life sciences sector, regulation is simply a part of doing biobusiness in global markets. What exacerbates commercial biotech's temporal uncertainty, however, is regulatory inconsistency and unpredictability. The examples of the U.S. FDA and the Chinese state FDA demonstrate how regulatory inconsistency—the waxing and waning of regulatory policy and the politics therein—can have profoundly negative effects on commercializing biotech. On the other hand, regulatory clarity and certainty are important to bio-industrial development. As one health policymaker in Singapore explained, it is not so much the content of regulatory regimes that matters most for facilitating cutting-edge R&D, as actors can adjust and learn to adapt; rather, what is important is that policies be consistently enforced, transparent in their creation, and unequivocally clear. Put simply, *biotech stakeholders demand regulatory certainty*. The evidence from Korea, Taiwan, and Singapore suggests that regulators there have been quite effective in harmonizing regulatory regimes that govern at least one aspect of the life sciences innovation process: clinical R&D.

---

3. Stephen J. Ceccoli, *Pill Politics: Drugs and the FDA* (Boulder, Colo.: Lynne Rienner, 2004).

Regulatory Alignment

One area of commercial promise in biotech, particularly for recent entrants without the capital and expertise to do lab-to-market biotech commercialization, is in premarket clinical R&D. Major efforts are currently under way in Asia to capture some market share in this high value-added biotech niche. Singapore's recent biotechnology plan explicitly focuses on translational R&D, specifically in clinical applications of upstream life sciences research. The example of TaiMed discussed in Chapter 4 highlights Taiwan's strategy to capture value in clinical R&D activities related to the drug development process. Meanwhile, clinical R&D, and notably the lucrative business of clinical trials, has become a significant area of commercial interest among health industry stakeholders in Korea, especially given the size of Korea's domestic health care technology market.

Premarket clinical R&D involves testing new health care interventions on patient populations. Because human subjects are involved, clinical R&D is highly regulated to ensure patient safety. The challenge of regulating clinical R&D is to balance the inherent risks and uncertainties of clinical research on human subjects—in other words, *protection*—against the potential promise of health care technology innovation and possibly commercial returns—or industry *promotion*. As it turns out, when it comes to clinical R&D, nonmarket and market imperatives can be easily aligned, in that there is a market-reinforcing imperative for ensuring patient safety. That is to say, regulation and regulatory credibility are market-supporting.[4] The example of Vioxx and its voluntary recall by Merck and the several cases of tainted food exports from China demonstrate how regulatory blind spots or outright regulatory negligence can have disastrous consequences for both human health and commercial returns. In fact, the 2008 Ernst and Young report on commercial biotech industry identifies regulation and the ability of the state to enforce regulatory policies a source of national advantage, a "competitive differentiator" that can go "a long way to boost investor confidence" and "help foster homegrown companies that are competitive on the global stage."[5]

Regulatory and market alignment in Korea, Taiwan, and Singapore emerged as far back as the 1970s and 1980s, when governments there began to impose stricter regulations on health technology development. There was

---

4. John Lim, head of Singapore's Health Sciences Authority, suggests that one of Singapore's key comparative advantages in attracting clinical R&D opportunities is its "brand" and "credibility" in regulatory matters. Author interview, Singapore, November 29, 2006.

5. Ernst and Young, *Beyond Borders: Global Biotechnology Report, 2008* (Cleveland: Ernst and Young, 2008), 92.

little resistance from industry. Moreover, safety-related regulations initiated by health policymakers also prompted little opposition from more industry-focused stakeholders within the state. Into the 1990s, government efforts in Korea, Taiwan, and Singapore, again led by the health ministries, to devise and enforce national guidelines for Good Clinical Practices (GCP) similarly met little resistance and opposition from industry stakeholders. The enforcement of GCP guidelines and efforts to harmonize the guidelines with global standards aligned with industry's commercial objectives. Regulatory efficacy was important.

Throughout the 1990s and early 2000s, the state in Korea, Taiwan, and Singapore continued to sponsor new regulatory initiatives such as the creation of publicly managed clinical trial centers, international certificate training programs for regulators, and the institutionalization of inspection and oversight procedures.[6] Most notable among these later regulatory initiatives was the establishment of institutional review boards (IRBs). Learned from other advanced industrial economies, IRBs are governance mechanisms that function as gatekeepers overseeing the application of clinical research protocols. Attached to research centers, IRBs are intended to ensure that both ethical and scientific best practices are adhered to by researchers.[7] They therefore operate as an extension of the regulatory state, as de facto subsidiary agents of the state. They allow the government to regulate from a distance, insulated from various interests. Since 1995, national GCP guidelines in Korea have required that all clinical trial protocols be overseen by an IRB as a condition for eventual approval and registration by the Korean FDA.[8] Rather than experience the IRBs as a constraint, however, industry and R&D stakeholders in Asia view such regulation as aligned with market demands. Moreover, the impetus and administrative lobbying for deepening the IRB system in

---

6. For a more detailed overview, see the *Drug Information Journal* 32 (1998) as well as the *Drug Information Journal Supplement* 37 (2003). See also Mary Ellen Rosenberg, "Implementing GCPs in Asia," *Quality Assurance Journal* 4 (2000); In-Jin Jang, "Regulatory Perspectives and Clinical Trial Status in South Korea" (paper presented at the 6th Kitasato University–Harvard School of Public Health Symposium on Advanced and Global Drug Development Techniques, Tokyo, Japan, October 2005).

7. See Bioethics Advisory Committee, "Advancing the Framework of Ethics Governance for Human Research, Annex B," Consultation Paper, Singapore, September 16, 2003; Herng-Der Chern, Ing-Tiau Kuo, Low-tong Ho, Hsin-Nan Lin, and Sheng-Muo Hou, "The Joint Institutional Review Board in Taiwan," *Drug Information Journal* 32 (1998); Ock-Joo Kim, "Current Status of Institutional Review Boards in Korea: Constitution, Operation and Policy for Protection of Human Research Participants," *Journal of Korean Medical Science* 18 (2003).

8. A 2002 study found that most IRBs surveyed in Korea were founded after 1995, when the Korean GCP guidelines were first introduced. The survey was conducted by the Korean Association of Institutional Review Boards. See Kim et al., "Institutional Review Boards in Korea."

Korea, Taiwan, and Singapore came from the medical R&D community and biomedical industry and not from the state.[9]

Regulatory efficacy is critical for gaining market share in the business of clinical R&D. However, regulatory and administrative *efficiency* is equally critical for realizing commercial returns in clinical health technology development. More than half of expenditures for new drug development are accounted for by the costs of clinical R&D (i.e., clinical trials).[10] Thus, increasing regulatory efficiency to reduce expenditures is desired by industry, so long as regulatory efficacy is maintained. Both efficacy and efficiency are a significant competitive advantage. Regulatory inefficiency, on the contrary, is a disadvantage. In the past, redundant administrative structures and the lack of regulatory expertise frustrated efforts to attract more clinical R&D opportunities to Korea, Taiwan, and Singapore. Furthermore, comparatively long approval times for research protocols kept global clinical trial activities and the commercial business of clinical R&D outside the region.[11] Regulatory regimes were effective, but they were also inefficient.

Administrative reorganizations were launched in all three places beginning in the late 1990s to streamline cumbersome bureaucratic processes and eliminate administrative redundancies. The Korean Food and Drug Administration (KFDA) was elevated in status in 1998 to that of an administrative agency. The KFDA subsequently took over the responsibilities for monitoring clinical trials and clinical R&D from the Pharmaceutical Affairs Bureau. Taiwan's ministerial-level Department of Health created the Center for Drug Evaluation (CDE) in 1998 to review and screen all clinical R&D protocols submitted to the Department's Bureau of Pharmaceutical Affairs (BPA). As a result of these efforts to streamline administrative processes, approval times for clinical trial protocols were reduced dramatically. In Korea, approval times dropped from around 110 days in 2000 to an average of 30 days in 2004.[12] In Taiwan, approval times similarly decreased after the establishment of the CDE, from 90 days to between 30 and 45 days.[13]

---

9. Faiz Keramnia and Rory Gallagher, "The Promise of Korea," *Applied Clinical Trials* (2005); see also Bioethics Advisory Committee, "Ethics Governance for Human Research."

10. See *Drug Information Journal Supplement,* 2003.

11. Piero Olliaro, Ramani Vijayan, K. Inbasegaran, Chim Choy Lang, and Sornchai Looareesuwan, "Drug Studies in Developing Countries," *Bulletin of the World Health Organization* 79 (2001).

12. Jang, "Regulatory Perspectives."

13. Sandra Ho-Lin Jao, Herng-Der Chern, and Mong-Ling Chu, "Reinventing Drug Regulation in the Asia Pacific Region: Taiwan's Experience and Vision for the Region," *Drug Information Journal Supplement* 37 (2003); Hui-Po Wang and Sue Shu-Yi Chen, "Clinical Trials in Taiwan: Regulatory Achievements and Current Status," *Drug Information Journal Supplement* 37 (2003).

A similar process of institutional streamlining occurred in Singapore during the early 2000s. In 2001, the Ministry of Health combined five departments to form the Health Sciences Authority (HSA), the sole body tasked with regulating clinical R&D activities. Later, in 2004, the Center for Drug Evaluation and the Center for Pharmaceutical Administration were merged to become the Center for Drug Administration. In both instances, as was also the case in Korea and Taiwan, institutional reorganization was intended to streamline administrative processes, to limit regulatory redundancies, and ultimately to ameliorate interagency conflict by centralizing existing regulatory bodies. According to industry watchers, administrative reorganization resulted in more efficient regulatory practices, which have become a key advantage for Singapore. When compared with regional competitors in Southeast Asia, Singapore has the quickest approval times, just three weeks, for regulatory approval of clinical trial protocols, and it has maintained positive perceptions of its regulatory rigor.[14]

Regulatory efficiency, provided that efficacy is not compromised, is a competitive advantage in an increasingly crowded market in clinical R&D activities.[15] And in these Asian cases, institutional streamlining (efficiency), combined with the implementation of IRBs and the enforcement of GCP guidelines (efficacy), is paying off in terms of increasing activity in their respective clinical R&D sectors. This is especially pronounced in the business of clinical trials. In all three places, multinational or international clinical trial activities increased markedly after these efforts in regulatory reform. And Korea, Taiwan, and Singapore are attracting more R&D opportunities in early-stage clinical trials and clinical R&D, where value-added gains and the complexity of the work are both higher and more lucrative.[16] The number of

---

14. According to Ellick Wong, this figure does not include the IRB approval process, which is not a parallel process and accounts for over 55 days on average, equaling a total approval time of over 75 days, as of 2003. Ellick Wong, "The Regulatory Environment and Clinical Trials in Southeast Asia," *Drug Information Journal Supplement* 37 (2003).

15. Industry observers note that Japan's relatively fledgling biotech sector is due in part to "a stifling regulatory system" and a "drug reimbursement pricing system that provides relatively insufficient commercial incentives to drug companies." See Ernst and Young, *Beyond Borders,* 92.

16. Between 1978 and 1997, only 465 clinical trial certificates were issued in Singapore. From 1998, the year that GCP standards were imposed, to 2004, the number of clinical trials increased to 1,090. Likewise, in Taiwan, after the introduction of national GCP standards in 1996, clinical trial protocol reviews grew from just 33 in 1993 to 102 in 1997, with half the reviews conducted in 1996–1997. In 2002, when Taiwan upgraded its GCP to International Conference on Harmonisation (ICH) standards, multinational clinical trials accounted for nearly half of all protocols reviewed that year. After the Korean government harmonized its GCP regulations to ICH standards in 2000, the number of clinical trial cases increased dramatically, totaling 464 projects between 2003 and 2005, which equaled more than four times the activity recorded between 2000 and 2002. Furthermore, the number of multinational trials hosted in Korea in 2001 tripled from the year before, and by 2004

clinical trials in Asia remains comparatively small by global market standards, to be sure, but what is nonetheless significant is that the scope and amount of clinical R&D activities have expanded quite considerably, and that governments in Korea, Taiwan, and Singapore are putting into place the necessary regulatory frameworks in anticipation of and in preparation for growing their domestic biotech and life sciences industries.

The development of clinical R&D regulations in Korea, Taiwan, and Singapore shows that when interests are aligned, particularly with respect to balancing market and nonmarket priorities, regulatory certainty, enforceability, and consistency can be achieved, and that such alignment, as I have called it, can bolster biotech industry success. Patient protection and industry promotion, at least in terms of clinical R&D, are mutually reinforcing and market-supporting priorities.

The Multiple Stakeholder State

Regulatory regimes are a critical part of the industrial policy mix in the life sciences sector. The state and its ability to make regulatory policies that balance potentially contending pressures and interests are important variables in regulatory certainty. The development of clinical R&D regulations and oversight institutions, for example, illustrates how the balance between market imperatives of industry promotion and nonmarket considerations of patient safety can be reconciled in productive ways. However, achieving such a balance is far from certain; conflict or the unalignment between regulatory and market imperatives can just as likely emerge. The state, as both the regulator and promoter of biotech industry, is, in practice, a *multiple stakeholder state* wherein the prospects of regulatory unalignment are very probable.

Balancing protection and promotion is difficult to do because of the inherent uncertainties of life sciences innovation and the tolerance thresholds for what is unknown. For instance, both industry and regulators concede that there can be no guarantees of patient safety, regardless of how stringent regulatory policies are; there is always uncertainty. They also recognize that clinical R&D involves a delicate though uncertain balance between risk and reward in terms of what is a tolerable trade-off. Gerd Gigerenzer and

---

multinational trials outnumbered local ones. Tan Shook Fong, "Development of Clinical Trials in Singapore," *Drug Information Journal* 32 (1998); Health Sciences Authority, "Creating Value," *Annual Report of the Health Sciences Authority* (Government of Singapore, 2005); Jen-Pei Liu, "The Integrated Clinical and Statistical Report for Registration in Taiwan," *Drug Information Journal* 32 (1998); Wang and Chen, "Clinical Trials in Taiwan"; Korean Food and Drug Administration, *KFDA Database, 2006,* available at http://www.kfda.go.kr (accessed March 2008).

colleagues explain that "much of medicine, is in fact, about evaluating risk and making effective decisions in the face of uncertainty and when it comes to settling on a decision, one must understand that there is no certainty and no zero-risk but only risks that are either more or less acceptable."[17] With respect to regulatory policy, then, decision makers strive to keep the swing of the protection-promotion "pendulum" in an acceptable balance. But stakeholders also understand that this is difficult to achieve. As one health policy official in Singapore explains, regulators are always anxious about the swing of the protection-promotion pendulum, knowing that if regulatory constraints are perceived as too stringent, then industry will press for more lax oversight, but that if patient safety is threatened, then accusations of regulatory negligence will be voiced and the credibility of the regulatory authorities will be tarnished. And of course, patient safety will be in jeopardy. The lessons of the Vioxx experience and other regulatory scandals have not fallen on deaf ears among regulators and industry in Asia.[18]

The tensions between protecting and promoting, and the uncertainty of achieving a balance between them, has recently begun to be played out in the regulatory state in Korea, Taiwan, and Singapore, particularly as bioindustrial growth has been much slower than hoped. Some argue that commercial biotech growth is hampered by overly stringent regulations, that the pendulum swings too far in favor of *over*regulation and constraint, and that regulation is stifling commercial innovation. For example, senior officials in Taiwan's Bureau of Pharmaceutical Affairs were dismissed by the Department of Health when a simmering conflict between the BPA and the Center for Drug Evaluation came to a head. The CDE was created during the late 1990s to make approval processes for clinical R&D activities (i.e., clinical trials and product registration) more efficient while ensuring continued regulatory efficacy. The BPA, on the other hand, insisted that approval barriers remain high and that patient safety be the primary, if not the sole, concern of health regulators. The BPA worried that the pendulum was beginning to swing dangerously toward the interests of industrial efficiency at the expense of patient safety and regulatory efficacy. The CDE, meanwhile, felt that an obstructionist BPA was imposing too many regulatory gatekeepers, and that the CDE's approach to "regulatory science" more optimally balanced the

17. Gerd Gigerenzer, Wolfgang Gaissmaier, Elke Kurz-Milcke, Lisa M. Schwartz, and Steven Woloshin, "Helping Doctors and Patients Make Sense of Health Statistics," *Psychological Science* 8 (2008).

18. Author interview, Singapore, November 29, 2006.

tensions between promotion and protection.[19] Reportedly under pressure from the economic ministry, the BPA leadership inside the health ministry was forced out. From the perspective of industry, firms were unsure of the direction of the state's regulatory practices. They watched events unfold with great uncertainty.

The story of the BPA and CDE in Taiwan illustrates how regulatory policymaking can be uncertain and how the implementation of such regulations is not automatic. Regulation and the regulatory state are shaped by conflicts of interests, stakes, and priorities. As one Taiwan health policy official succinctly described it, "the Ministry of Economic Affairs is supposed to do the *promoting* while the Department of Health is supposed to do the *protecting*."[20] When conceived of in this way, it is clear how the regulatory state is in practice a multiple stakeholder state.

The tension between protecting and promoting is captured in an important 2000 OECD report by Stephane Jacobzone on the global pharmaceutical sector. Focusing on the state's multiple stakeholder roles, Jacobzone contends that "ideally, instruments of policy should be specific to each goal, while not distorting the achievement of other goals," though, as he points out, the reality is that governments actually play a "double role." And these roles are not necessarily complementary, nor are they mutually reinforcing. Regulatory policies that both promote and protect, for instance, are pushed by different sets of actors, usually the economy ministry for the former and the health ministry for the latter. At times, promoting and protecting can be aligned, but as Jacobzone points out, more often than not, they work against each other.[21]

Regulatory policies are contested among different actors, representing various ministerial interests as well as civil society. Actors also have an array of expertise, making it even more difficult to arrive at some sort of regulatory consensus. Regulators know the science of clinical regulation whereas industrial planners are experts in designing incentives to promote cutting-edge R&D. Meanwhile, health economists have the expertise to determine the economics of health care accessibility. As expert communities, actors also hold different worldviews and priorities. Indeed, bio-ethicists in all likelihood contemplate the desirability of stem cell research differently than, say,

---

19. Author interviews with informants in Taipei, Taiwan, during 2004 and 2005.

20. Author interview, DOH, Taipei, Taiwan, December 14, 2004.

21. Stephane Jacobzone, "Pharmaceutical Policies in OECD Countries: Reconciling Social and Industrial Goals," *Labour Market and Social Policy Occasional Papers,* No. 40 (2000), 9.

R&D policymakers, just as health policy officials probably understand the risks of clinical R&D differently than industrial policy planners.

Actors' varied expertise, interests, priorities, worldviews, and thus regulatory policy positions increase the complexity of coordinating regulatory policymaking. As we saw in Chapter 2, the decentralization of expertise and the absence of any overarching leadership in regulatory policymaking within the state apparatus make it difficult to achieve any sort of regulatory consensus. And as the story of the BPA and the CDE in Taiwan illustrates, striking an agreeable balance between the imperatives of protecting and promoting, among actors that understand the priorities of clinical regulation in fundamentally different ways, can be elusive. Regulating biotech innovation is a multidisciplinary endeavor, and it invariably invites intermural conflict inside and outside the state apparatus. The regulatory state, as described by Jacobzone, is a state with conflicting roles.

Arbitrating Bioethics

A flashpoint in current regulatory debates in biotech centers on the controversies surrounding stem cell research, a debate that emphasizes the broad range of actors and interests involved in regulatory policymaking as well as the intense conflicts inside and outside the state. The ethical implications of life sciences research and innovation, especially with respect to embryonic stem (ES) cell R&D, are hotly contested. Debates are not limited to questions of the societal desirability of ES cell research, but also concern the ethical appropriateness of the acquisition of stem cells and, of course, the potential abuses of cloning. There is also considerable debate about the use of patented discoveries that result from ES cell R&D. The state's mediation of these debates and ultimately the state's regulation of biotech are essentially nonmarket considerations of not only what can be commercialized but, even before that, what is considered ethically appropriate research. In other words, the state functions as both a market and premarket regulatory gatekeeper, a role that influences the course of commercial biotech industry development, as current debates in the United States demonstrate.

The Conventional Wisdom

The conventional wisdom, especially among conservative Western pundits, about bioethics and Asia is that most Asian states have opted for relatively liberal and lax regulatory regimes. Rightly or wrongly, it is commonly understood that, for example, Alan Colman, the team leader who helped successfully clone Dolly the sheep, moved to Singapore in part because of its less stringent regulatory regimes for ES cell research. Lax regimes, it is suggested, entail a competitive if unethical advantage for countries looking to enter the cutting-edge areas of stem cell research. That the global leader in biotech, the United States, has imposed relatively strict constraints on ES cell research strengthens the competitive edge for those states with less strict regulatory regimes. The conventional wisdom suggests that late entrants in the life sciences sector such as Korea, Taiwan, and Singapore are deliberately shaping their ES cell policies in ways that privilege economic benefits and corporate profits over ethics, and that industry has enjoyed overwhelming influence over the state's ability to otherwise regulate and constrain stem cell research. Regulatory policies, it is said, have been crafted to promote industrial growth with little regard for the ethical consequences of life sciences research. Arguments from this camp furthermore suggest that shallow democratic institutions, such as in Singapore, permit unilateral decisions by the state to open up opportunities in ES cell research, with less pressure to fully engage contentious ethical positions that might emerge from the bottom up. The absence of deep religiosity and the undermobilization of religious groups also contribute to the perception that places such as Korea, Taiwan, and Singapore are legislating from the top down what are relatively liberal regulatory regimes in the area of stem cell R&D.[22]

This conventional wisdom is, in my view, gleaned as much from comparisons with conservative U.S. stem cell policy as it is from surface impressions of Asian late developers in the life sciences field. For one, the reality is that there is considerable variation among the Korean, Taiwanese, and Singaporean cases with respect to ES cell regulation, and specifically the acquisition of embryonic stem cells, the most controversial aspect of bioethics. For example, in Korea and Taiwan, the use of embryos developed from in vitro fertilization for research purposes is prohibited.[23] Singapore, on the other hand, permits

22. Bruce Einhorn, Jennifer Veale, and Manjeet Kripalani, "Asia Is Stem Cell Central," *Businessweek,* January 10, 2005; Francis Fukuyama, *Our Posthuman Future: Consequences of the Biotechnology Revolution* (New York: Farrar, Straus and Giroux, 2002); Lisa Krieger, "As the US Hesitates, Other Countries Move Ahead with Embryo Research," available at http://www.siliconvalley.com/mld/siliconvalley/news/3210920.htm (accessed July 2006).

23. Taiwan's Department of Health stipulates that stem cells for research be acquired solely from "fetal tissue from miscarriage...from abortion...and 14 days-fertilized-egg leftover from human assisted reproduction." See UK Stem Cell Initiative, "Global Positions in Stem Cell Research: Taiwan," available at http://www.advisorybodies.doh.gov.uk/uksci/global/taiwan.htm (accessed November 2006).

such R&D activity.[24] Also contrary to the conventional wisdom, regulatory regimes in Korea, Taiwan, and Singapore have been derived, in part, from ethical principles, as opposed to pure profit motivations. In fact, they are relatively constraining in terms of ES cell research, in line with most other advanced industrial countries. Human (reproductive) cloning, for instance, is explicitly prohibited, as it is elsewhere, and the use of any incentives for the procurement of ES cells is illegal in Korea, Taiwan, and Singapore.[25] They are not liberal outliers. Most important, the emergence of national regulatory guidelines for stem cell research in all three places was the result of continual deliberation, contestation, and conflict, and only over time was some resolution achieved. The extent to which there is currently some regulatory clarity and certainty in the area of ES cell research is a consequence of an intensely political process of consensus building. In short, regulatory uncertainty has had to be overcome, and the outcomes of these political processes were not givens.

The Politics of Consensus

The conventional wisdom described above glosses over the political debates regarding the appropriateness of ES cell research in East Asia. Due to the ethical conundrums presented by biotech, various groups—grassroots religious, human rights and democracy, consumer, and patient activist—mobilized and shaped the processes of regulatory reform. In Taiwan, human rights activists forced the National Science Council to abandon its plan for a national genetic database, citing the need for stronger parallel legislation in privacy protection, informed consent protocols, and patenting.[26] Similarly, in Korea, civic group coalitions were formed in 2005 to oppose the government's Bioethics and Biosafety Act, arguing that the proposed bill failed to include sufficient protections for patients. Civic groups asserted that the act was unconstitutional and reckless with respect to the protection of human life.[27] Even in nondemocratic Singapore, nongovernmental organizations (NGOs) mobilized in 2001 to pressure the state's Bioethics Advisory Committee (BAC) to address concerns about patenting activity in ES cell research and the need

---

24. Dennis Normile and Charles Mann, "Asia Jockeys for Stem Cell Lead," *Science* 307 (2005).

25. "DOH Announces Regulations on Stem Cell Research," *United Daily News* (Taiwan), February 20, 2002.

26. Chueh-An Yen, "Full Public Discussion Needed on DNA Bank," *Taipei Times,* February 6, 2006, 8.

27. Keun-Min Bae, "Bioethics Law May Face Court Review," *Korea Times,* January 6, 2005.

for consistent enforcement of ethical regulations among private and public researchers.[28] Bioethics "watchdog" organizations have also emerged in all three places to monitor biotech R&D and regulatory policies. In 2004, for instance, the Korean Bioethics Association publicly pushed the government to investigate Professor Hwang Woo-Suk and in particular the questionable means by which he acquired human eggs used in his research. We now know that Professor Hwang's disgrace was hastened by Korean civic groups.[29]

Bottom-up civic activism and the increasingly prominent role of societal stakeholders in biotech development are forcing the state in Korea, Taiwan, and Singapore to create new institutional channels to facilitate the flow of information between state and society. The state has had to become more responsive, recognizing that ES cell regulatory policies cannot be legislated unilaterally from the top down, contrary to the conventional wisdom. The National Bioethics Committee, created in Korea after the passage of the Bioethics and Biosafety Act, includes members representing nonstate actors, such as academics, religious organizations, and other social movement groups. In Taiwan, the ministerial-level Department of Health similarly sanctioned the founding of the Taiwanese Society for Reproductive Medicine in order to facilitate debate about government policy in ES cell research. In both Korea and Taiwan, the state fosters rather than constrains deliberation and contestation among a broad range of state and nonstate stakeholders.[30]

The absence or presence of democracy does not seem to have affected the extent to which states engage in policy consultation and welcome politically charged ethical debates. In Singapore, the cabinet established the Bioethics Advisory Committee, a group of academics, NGO leaders, and foreign advisers.[31] In all three cases, the development of ES cell regulatory policy has involved processes of contestation and consultation. Actors approach the regulatory debate with different interests, reflective of different values and

28. Bioethics Advisory Committee, "Ethical, Legal and Social Issues in Stem Cell Research, Reproductive and Therapeutic Cloning," *A Report from the Bioethics Advisory Committee* (Government of Singapore, June 2002).

29. David Cyranowski, "Korea's Stem Cell Stars Dogged by Suspicion of Ethical Breach," *Nature,* May 6, 2004.

30. In light of the Woo-Suk Hwang debacle, the Korean government has planned to base further funding for stem cell research on stricter review and protocol review processes. This is intended to encourage competition among researchers, to develop expertise for scientists to monitor and assess one another's work, to reduce undue pressures to produce outcomes in the near term, and to institutionalize ethical practices in scientific activities. See Dennis Normile, "South Korea Picks Up the Pieces," *Science,* June 2, 2006; Herbert Gottweis and Robert Triendl, "South Korean Policy Failure and the Hwang Debacle," *Nature Biotechnology* 24 (2006); Mildred Cho, Glenn McGee, and David Magnus, "Lessons of the Stem Cell Scandal," *Science,* February 3, 2006.

31. Author interview, Singapore, November 28, 2006.

worldviews about the ethical place of ES cell research. The state, in turn, has been forced to broker, rather than impose, regulatory clarity and certainty. This process has unfolded over a period of time. And indeed, the consensus building process has not always been smooth.

Korea's comprehensive Bioethics and Biosafety Act was passed in 2005, though it took twelve attempts between 1997 and 2003 to align a policy consensus within the multiple stakeholder state. Internal politics within the state frustrated the processes of consensus building. Civic groups also mobilized to ensure that their voices were heard in policy deliberation. Coordinating policy responses was also complicated by the political dynamics internal to the multiple stakeholder state. The Ministry of Science and Technology and the legislative committee in charge of science and technology policy in the National Assembly pushed for more lax regulatory oversight by the state. Excessively stringent rules, they reasoned, hindered upstream life sciences R&D and ultimately commercial bio-industry development. The Ministry of Health and Welfare opposed this policy direction, arguing instead for a stronger government role in overseeing and constraining certain types of controversial research, including ES cell R&D.[32] Interministerial conflict stymied bioethics legislation for several years, during which time ES cell R&D was conducted, in effect, in a regulatory vacuum. This period of regulatory uncertainty is thought to be one of the principal factors that contributed to the serious ethical breaches and research misconduct revealed recently in Korea's stem cell R&D activities.[33] In this case, conflict, and thus the absence of policy clarity and certainty, set back Korea's efforts to emerge on the cutting edge of ES cell R&D.

Recounting the development of bioethics regulation in Korea, Taiwan, and Singapore demonstrates how the processes of regulatory policymaking are intensely contested among various stakeholders. The lines of conflict reflect broader clashes of interests, priorities, and professional expertise over regulatory policy and biotech innovation. As the example of Korea demonstrates, conflict is endemic in regulatory policymaking, in which consensus and regulatory certainty are achieved only through a process of considerable contestation among stakeholders over time. Contrary to the received wisdom, then, interest alignment in bioethical debates has had to be politically constructed in Asia, mediated by and within the multiple stakeholder state.

32. Sung-Goo Han, Young Je You, and Wha-Joon Rho, "New Cloning Technologies and Bioethics Issues: The Legislative Process in Korea," *Journal of Asian and International Bioethics* 13 (2003).

33. Edison Liu, "Can It Happen in Singapore?" *Straits Times,* December 30, 2005.

Regulating and Making Markets

The challenges of resolving regulatory uncertainty are further revealed when we consider how the multiple stakeholder state shapes markets. Regulation policy is inextricably tied to the market, as either a facilitator or a constraint on commercial biotech innovation. In some instances, such as with clinical R&D, market incentives and nonmarket imperatives for patient safety can be aligned. The same can be said of ES cell regulation, although the alignment process in this case, as I have described it, was considerably more contested inside the state. In other instances, however, the state's multiple roles and interests can become unaligned and remain so. The impact of the unaligned regulatory state is most pronounced in those regulatory policies that are intended to explicitly *make markets*.

Making Markets

The long-term prospects of the commercial biotech industry in Asia will depend on not only the supply of technologies but also the market or demand for such technologies. Markets in highly regulated sectors such as biotech are not constituted solely by consumer demand and industry supply, however. Rather, markets are shaped by the regulatory functions of the state that shape market access for biotechnological innovations. Put simply, markets hinge on the regulatory state's gatekeeper role of determining what technologies can in fact be allowed into the market.

Biomedical firms in Korea, Taiwan, and Singapore aspire to supply to global markets in the West and Japan and to the potentially large consumer markets in China and India. Yet domestic markets matter too, for several reasons. For one, supplying local demand enhances firms' credibility, making it easier to jump regulatory hurdles elsewhere and thus gain access to global markets. Furthermore, domestic markets in these rich though otherwise small Asian economies are in fact quite sizable, due to their wealth and unusually large demand for high-quality, cutting-edge health care technologies. Singapore's efforts to become the regional hub for high-technology health care services (i.e., health care tourism), for instance, have increased demand for innovative health technologies. The Korean and Taiwanese pharmaceutical markets were ranked the nineteenth and twentieth largest in the world, respectively, during the 1990s, each accounting for US$2–3 billion in sales. Upward of one-quarter of total health care spending in Korea and Taiwan is for the purchase of drugs.[34]

---

34. Soonman Kwon, "Technology and Health Policy: Rapid Technology Diffusion and Policy Options in Korea" (paper presented at Canada-Korea Social Policy Symposium, Toronto,

Pharmaceutical and health technology markets more generally are determined by regulatory policies. Due to persistent market failure and the high risks involved in clinical applications of new life sciences technologies, state intervention, or more accurately the construction of markets, is the norm. Take, for example, Singapore, understood to be among the freest economies in the world, which is also technically the case in the medical care market. In Singapore, there are no set prices for innovative drugs. There are also few regulatory obstacles, and as I described earlier, approval processes for new innovative drugs have been streamlined and made more efficient than in the past. However, the government subsidizes the cost of medicines prescribed in Singapore's public health care clinics and hospital wards. The state thus indirectly encourages the use of lower-priced generic medicines in public facilities in order to contain overall health care spending. The market effect of this policy has been to push down prices on innovative, R&D-based drugs. Multinational drug companies have complained to Singaporean health policy officials about the government's indirect cost-containment policy, asserting that public subsidies that favor the use of generics have a negative effect on the drug industry's ability to produce and market innovative therapies.[35] My point is that even in tiny free-market Singapore, the health care market is constructed to some extent by government regulatory interventions.

The Singaporean market is small; potential markets in Korea and Taiwan are not, however, and thus the impact of regulatory policies on market formation is magnified. Both Korea and Taiwan introduced publicly managed national health insurance systems during the late 1980s and 1990s, and the take-up rates for medical care and the purchase of health care products and services increased across the board.[36] Total health care spending has also grown in both places. What is most significant, however, is that in these state-run insurance systems it is the state that is the monopsonistic buyer (on behalf of insured patients) of health care and health technologies such as pharmaceuticals, diagnostics, health data, and other medical care interventions. As the sole purchaser of health care, the state enjoys tremendous leverage in constructing health care technology markets.

The state has two key regulatory policy instruments with which to shape the health care market. First, the state has an impact on *market access,*

January 27–28, 2005); Hui-Po Wang, "Pharmaceutical Regulatory Affairs of Chinese Taipei" (presentation at the APEC LSIF Readiness Assessment Pilot Project, September 7, 2004).

35. Author interview, Singapore, November 27, 2006.

36. See Joseph Wong, *Healthy Democracies: Welfare Politics in Taiwan and South Korea* (Ithaca: Cornell University Press, 2004).

especially in determining which products and services are to be included on the list of interventions reimbursable by the health insurance system. Making it onto the reimbursable list is critical for suppliers, as over 75% of all market-approved drugs (and other health care products and services) qualify for reimbursement by the government-managed insurance carrier. In other words, those products or services not on the list are effectively out of the market. The upshot is that government regulatory policy, and not pure market forces per se, determines which products and services can enter the market in Korea and Taiwan. Second, the state, as the monopsonistic purchaser of care, also affects the *price* of all health care products and services on the reimbursable list. It is not simply the supply of innovative technologies that drives costs in the health care system, which is often assumed to be the case for patent-protected innovative technologies; rather, it is the interaction of supply and demand, and the latter is shaped by government regulations, as opposed to the market. One could therefore argue the case that health care policy is in effect industrial policy.

But we also know that government policies in health care are motivated by different and potentially conflicting concerns and priorities. On the one hand, state officials might be motivated by the imperatives of providing affordable health care, in which case cost containment would be the main regulatory policy priority. Yet the multiple stakeholder state might, on the other hand, use health care policy to facilitate, through demand-side manipulation, the growth of the health care technology industry by pushing prices upward and thus fueling investment and returning profit back to industry. In the multiple stakeholder state, these motivations are not necessarily complementary. In fact, they can be intensely zero-sum. And when they are in conflict with each other, they are a tremendous source of regulatory uncertainty for biotech stakeholders.

Market Access

Before the late 1990s, health care regulatory regimes in Korea and Taiwan actively proscribed the introduction of imported innovative and R&D-intensive drugs. In Korea, such high-cost products were effectively left off the insurance system's reimbursable list. The regulatory regime in Taiwan similarly imposed high barriers of entry for new imported products, requiring, for instance, that drug makers produce clinical validation data from other global markets, the effect of which was essentially a regulatory market barrier. In other words, regulatory policies were used to restrict market access. This inevitably drew tremendous opposition from foreign governments and pressure from industry, and such pressure eventually came to bear on the government in Korea and Taiwan.

In the first decade of the 2000s, faced with pressure from foreign and by then a nascent but growing domestic biomedical industry, regulators in Korea and Taiwan began to amend their gatekeeping standards, accepting, most notably, foreign clinical trial data for domestic market approval and product registration. Approvals for new and innovative products were quicker and easier. Consequently, the number of health care products registered and marketed (and thus reimbursable through insurance) in Korea and Taiwan increased dramatically. By the early 2000s, Korea's reimbursable list included over 21,000 items, far outnumbering other countries with national health care systems, including the United Kingdom (12,000) and Sweden (3,000).[37]

Concerns about the size of the reimbursable list and thus the cost-effectiveness of having introduced so many products and services into the domestic market quickly emerged in Korea and Taiwan. Health policy officials worried that there were too many products in the market, resulting in product redundancy. They were also concerned about the increasing cost burden on their national health insurance systems, particularly as health care providers (physicians and pharmacists) tended to overprescribe. Thus, health policy decision makers in Korea and Taiwan began to adopt health technology assessment schemes, learned from other industrialized nations, for the purposes of cost rationalization.[38] Policymakers began to employ, for instance, pharmaco-economic analysis in order to evaluate the cost-effectiveness of individual treatments, to determine which items ought to be included on the health insurance reimbursable list and which could potentially be delisted.

The creation in 1998 of the Center for Drug Evaluation in Taiwan was intended to involve more pharmaco-economic evaluation of reimbursable health benefits, but it was the Korean health care system that more rapidly adopted the technology assessment approach. In 2002, the Ministry of Health and Welfare established the Health Insurance Review Agency (HIRA), an independent office attached to the administration of Korea's national health insurance system. While the Korean FDA is tasked with evaluating and reporting on the clinical efficacy of new drugs and other medical care products, the HIRA was intended to evaluate the cost-effectiveness of such interventions,

---

37. Bong-Min Yang, "Health Care Reform in South Korea: Any Lessons from Canada?" (paper presented at the Canada-Korea Social Policy Symposium, Toronto, January 27–28, 2005).

38. David Banta, "The Development of Health Technology Assessment," *Health Policy* 63 (2003); Jo Hsieh, Lillian Wang, and Jason Heng-Shu Chen, "The Future of Pharmacoeconomics and Outcomes Research in Asia," *Drug Information Journal Supplement* 37 (2003).

balancing economic value (i.e., costs) with clinical effectiveness. The HIRA makes recommendations to the MOHW's benefits advisory committee.

Participation in the HIRA review process was voluntary, though firms were encouraged to participate. To induce participation, regulatory policy decision makers in Korea concerned with rationalizing the costs of health care signaled that they would be more inclined to facilitate market entry for those products that measured cost-effective, an evaluation made possible only for those firms that voluntarily complied with HIRA regulations.[39] Health technology assessment has therefore allowed the state to more directly mediate market access. Not surprisingly, industry, both foreign and local, and especially those firms looking to introduce new, innovative, and R&D-intensive technologies, have opposed the state's role in these matters.[40] Conflicts along these lines have emerged in Korea and Taiwan. From the perspective of industry, this enduring and yet unresolved conflict poses great uncertainty with respect to future markets.

Market Pricing

The regulatory reach of the state is not limited to mediating access to the market. As the administrator of national health insurance systems and as the monopsonistic buyer of health care products and services, the regulatory state also effectively determines market prices for health care products and services. Tensions between industry and the state, and ultimately among different interests within the multiple stakeholder state, are even more significant in this respect. While sales volume and market share are a function of market access for the innovative firm and obviously are important to the firm's overall returns, a technologically cutting-edge firm's profitability is ultimately determined by price. Innovative biomedical firms need high (or market) prices; they cannot rely solely on volume sales. Thus, strategic health care pricing policy in relatively large markets such as in Korea and Taiwan can have an indirect but very significant effect on biomedical industry outcomes.

In both Korea and Taiwan, health care pricing policy has created an unusually narrow gap between the reimbursable prices for generic medicines and novel drugs. Price regulators there have imposed a strict price ceiling

---

39. Author interview, Seoul, Korea, September 7, 2005.

40. According to Bong-Min Yang, the chair of the MOHW Benefits Advisory Committee, the use of health technology assessments and the broader issue of pharmaceutical regulation are key points of conflict between the United States and Korea in bilateral free trade negotiations. Author interview, Seoul, Korea, January 17, 2006.

on R&D-intensive and innovative technologies, estimated to be 15% to 30% below international market prices.[41] Meanwhile, health care policy decision makers have maintained very high price floors on generics, such that generic pharmaceuticals are priced at 80% to 90% of equivalent novel drugs.[42] According to industry stakeholders there, these pricing policies effectively squeeze both sales and profitability of innovative and R&D-focused drug companies. On the flip side, however, high price floors for generics serve as a protectionist mechanism for generic drug manufacturers and specifically for local firms. Despite efforts to grow their novel drug development capacities, the vast majority of commercial activity in Korea and Taiwan remains in low-end manufacturing and distribution of generics.

Inflated prices on generics furthermore allow firms to provide discounts to medical care providers, resulting in a significant gap between the actual (i.e., discounted) transaction price and the reimbursement price that health care providers claim against the health insurance system. Both parties—the generic drug firm and the physician-provider—thus benefit under such an arrangement. The firm sells more products, which is critical for generics manufacturing, as volume and not price is what determines firms' profitability (unlike for innovative firms). In the meantime, health care providers pocket the difference (between the actual price they pay and the price for which they are reimbursed) as a kickback. This shady discounting practice is so prevalent that the American Chamber of Commerce in Taipei estimates that during the first years of the 2000s over US$600 million was lost in this pricing "black hole."[43] Health economists point out that the price gap has contributed to the overprescription and thus redundant dispensing of pharmaceuticals and other medical care services, leading to tremendous waste in Taiwan's national health insurance system.[44] Korea's medical care profession has also tended to overprescribe pharmaceutical therapies, for

41. Asia-Pacific Biotech News, "Taiwan Asked to Revise Pharmaceutical Pricing Policy," *APBN Newsletter* 1, 30 (1998); Pacific Bridge Medical (PBM), *1999 Regulatory Update: South Korea's Medical Device and Pharmaceutical Markets* (July 1, 1999).

42. See Soonman Kwon, "Technology and Health Policy"; USTR (United States Trade Representative), "Taiwan," USTR Report, 2005, available at http://www.ustr.gov/assets/Document_Library/Reports_Publications/2005/2005_NTE_Report/asset_upload_file101_7501.pdf (accessed June 2006).

43. American Chamber of Commerce in Taiwan, *AmCham 2003 Taiwan White Paper: Pharmaceuticals* (Taipei: American Chamber of Commerce, 2003).

44. A 2002 Taiwan Department of Health report stated that almost 50% of physicians prescribe four to five drugs per patient visit for upper respiratory infections, and 10% of physicians prescribe more than eight medications per visit; only 14 cases out of more than 100,000 visits showed that no drugs were prescribed. Cited in Tsung-Mei Cheng, "Taiwan's New National Health Insurance Program: Genesis and Experience So Far," *Health Affairs* 22 (2003), 68.

similar reasons and with similar consequences. In response, the government in Korea and Taiwan has attempted to legislate policies to ensure that suppliers and medical care providers align the actual transaction price of drugs and other medical care products with that of the reimbursable price. However, monitoring such transactions has proven very difficult, and outside observers remain skeptical about the government's ability to mitigate this problem.

Pricing policy in Korea and Taiwan (and also in Singapore) for drugs and other health care products has been motivated not only by protectionism for the local generics industry but also by the imperatives of cost control in total health spending. This is most evident in how the government has handled the registration and distribution of expensive novel drugs. To rein in health care spending, the government in both places implemented demand-side and supply-side cost-containment schemes after the introduction of national health insurance. With respect to demand-side measures, the Bureau of National Health Insurance in Taiwan increased out-of-pocket co-pay rates at the point of delivery to curb excessive abuse of the health care system. For the same reasons, the Korean medical insurance authorities maintained high co-pay levies when the insurance system there was first devised. In terms of supply-side cost containment, Taiwan's health insurance system phased in global budgeting schemes to cap provider spending. Meanwhile, in Korea, the government imitated Taiwan's lead by separating the responsibilities of drug prescribing and dispensing among physicians and pharmacists to reduce excessive drug use. In other words, supply-side cost-containment schemes have been implemented to reduce the overall purchasing capacity of the health care system in Korea and Taiwan.

Success in actually lowering total medical care spending, however, has been lukewarm at best.[45] Health care costs continued to spiral upward in the first decade of the 2000s, threatening the fiscal sustainability of Korea's and Taiwan's medical insurance systems. In response, health policymakers turned to price controls on drugs and other health care products. In 2001, the Korean Ministry of Health and Welfare slashed reimbursable prices by 7.63% for one-quarter of all drugs listed on the insurance formulary.[46] Between 2000 and 2002, Taiwan's Bureau of National Health Insurance cut prices on nearly 20,000 items on its reimbursable list.[47] These initiatives resulted,

45. See Y. J. Chou, Winnie C. Yip, Cheng-Hua Lee, Nicole Huang, Ying-Pei Sun, and Hong-Jen Chang, "Impact of Separating Drug Prescribing and Dispensing on Provider Behavior: Taiwan's Experience," *Health Policy and Planning* 18 (2003); see also Wong, *Healthy Democracies;* Cheng, "Taiwan's New National Health Insurance Program."

46. Pacific Bridge Medical (PBM), *Asian Medical Newsletter* 2 (2002).

47. See Cheng, "Taiwan's New National Health Insurance Program."

not surprisingly, in tremendous criticism from foreign and local medical technology firms, especially innovation-driven firms that need high levels of profitability to reinvest in R&D. Cost-containment policies, they contend, stifle firms' innovative capacity. This tension between the imperatives of cost containment and industry promotion is not unique to Asia. Indeed, the most recent Ernst and Young global biotechnology report put it succinctly: "Governments around the world are looking for means of reducing the cost of health care, and drug companies are frequently becoming convenient scapegoats."[48]

Regulation poses obstacles along the way of commercializing biotech innovation. In this respect, regulatory hurdles lengthen the distance to market in the innovation process, exacerbating the problems of temporal uncertainty. But as I have suggested in this chapter, regulation is in and of itself not a problem. It is an expected—and indeed, critical—aspect of life sciences innovation and R&D, and actors adapt to regulatory regimes. Indeed, regulatory policies, as I have shown here, can facilitate commercial biotech innovation. However, regulation becomes a source of greater temporal uncertainty (in what is already a terribly uncertain process) when regulatory regimes are inconsistent, incoherent, contested, and uncertain. As I indicated at the beginning of this chapter, what matters most to biotech stakeholders is not so much the content of regulatory policy, since actors can learn and adapt, as its clarity and predictability.

When interests align, such as in the imperatives of promoting industry and protecting patients, we can expect a greater degree of regulatory certainty. The early development and enforcement of clinical R&D regulations, for instance, proceeded relatively smoothly in Korea, Taiwan, and Singapore, in part because of the pull of global harmonization but also because the imperatives of promoting and protecting, at least in this particular regulatory policy area, were regarded as complementary and mutually reinforcing. In clinical R&D, the first example in this chapter, market and nonmarket pressures have been more or less aligned in that patient safety and regulations to ensure such protections are seen as market-supporting competitive advantages. This chapter also explored a second example of regulation policy, the development of bioethics regulations in Korea, Taiwan, and Singapore—specifically, how contested agendas and interests can be reconciled and balanced over time and how the state is central to this mediation process. Potentially contentious interests and priorities in the multiple stakeholder state were aligned,

48. Ernst and Young, *Beyond Borders,* 5–7.

and this has promoted greater regulatory certainty for biotech stakeholders. But it needs to be emphasized that the arrival of such a consensus involved a political process of aligning various interests, priorities, and expertise within the multiple stakeholder state.

When interests and priorities in regulatory debates become or stay un-aligned, such as in the making of health care markets, regulatory uncertainty ensues. In the example of health care market access and pricing, the multiple stakeholder state in Korea, Taiwan, and Singapore is the site of contestation and conflict among different state interests and priorities, such as the varied proponents of health care cost containment, health technology access, and health industry promotion. The state, due to its many cross-cutting priorities in the development of new health technologies, has been unable to coordinate and align these various interests. And this is significant for two reasons in the larger context of this book. First, regulatory uncertainty exacerbates biotech industry's temporal uncertainty, thus putting even greater pressure on already waning appetites for the even longer-term realities of biotech innovation and commercialization. Second, the persistence of such regulatory uncertainty reveals the cross-cutting interests entrenched within the multiple stakeholder state, a new political economic reality that contrasts with the administrative coherence associated with the developmental state.

Conclusion

Beyond the Developmental State

> The stage has been set, in the labs and government halls of several nations, many researchers say. In the future, no matter which group of scientists, states, or nations pulls into the lead or falls behind in the area of regenerative medicine, there will probably always be another group just behind it, to pick up the slack and carry on. Too many people, from too many different walks of life, have become besotted with the notion that the secret to curing the body has essentially been hiding within the body, all along.
>
> —Cynthia Fox, *Cell of Cells: The Global Race to Capture and Control the Stem Cell*

The race is on. Ever since the rediscovery in the 1970s of the biological heuristic, which prompted the faint and distant hope for a new generation of cutting-edge health technologies, the world has focused tremendous attention on the promise of commercial biotech. And this preoccupation with biotech, broadly defined, has been truly global in scope. Rich countries expect innovative life sciences to be the next foundational pillar of the knowledge economy. Poor countries see biotechnology as the technological harbinger of low-cost medical miracles, alleviating their dependencies on expensive first-world drugs.[1] It was initially believed, naively, that all it would take to realize the biotech revolution was some serious smarts in the lab, some investment savvy, a whole lot of government support, some patience, and a receptive public. Turns out, however, as we now know, that commercial biotech was a long-shot bet from the start, and that the current skepticism surrounding the sector and its underwhelming impact in terms of economic returns and health outcomes is not unwarranted. In a way, this book serves as a cautionary tale, a realistic wake-up call at the least, about the

---

1. Halla Thorsteinsdottir, Uyen Quach, Abdallah Daar, and Peter Singer, "Conclusion: Promoting Biotechnology Innovation in Developing Countries," *Nature Biotechnology* 22 (2004).

tremendous uncertainties of biotech innovation and the commercialization of cutting-edge life sciences technologies.

Korea, Taiwan, and Singapore, three of the world's most dynamic postwar economies, have bet large on the promise of commercial biotech. They were, in one sense, compelled to do so, as their earlier competitive and comparative industrial advantages had begun to erode during the 1990s in the face of competition in industrial manufacturing from other, later developers in the region and beyond. Their economies were gradually being hollowed out. In addition, the global economic crisis of 2008 emphatically underscored just how dependent Asia's postwar export-led strategy had been on a buoyant American economy, which for the previous several decades had acted as the de facto purchaser of last resort. Absent a healthy American core of the global economy, the margins in price competition in industrial manufacturing sectors become even smaller. Industrial Asia's dependence on cost-competitive manufacturing exports has proved to be its Achilles' heel. As the *Economist* recently put it, "Asia's sails have become anchors."[2] Korea, Taiwan, and Singapore thus had to become science and technology innovators, a direction echoed by the World Bank in 2003.[3] Because they had already demonstrated their success as astute and creative technology absorbers and technology imitators, by the 1990s these dynamic industrial economies were positioned to climb the global technology value chain as creators and cutting-edge innovators. Biotechnology thus became a high priority for industrial planners in all three places.

Notwithstanding the fact that Korea, Taiwan, and Singapore had little previous industry and R&D experience in the life sciences field, several factors seemed to suggest at the time that these economies would have a good shot at making it in biotech. They were not industrial technology laggards. They were plugged into the global economy and transnational R&D networks. Governments were committed to facilitating the growth of the industry. The private sector and industry were hungry for new investment opportunities in higher value-added sectors. And all three economies enjoyed what they saw as significant locational advantages as "hubs" and "gateways" for Asian markets and prospective bio-industry partnerships. Besides, the whole world—the rich and poor, the big and small—was getting into the business of commercial biotech. Korea, Taiwan, and Singapore would not be outliers in this regard, and they were most certainly not going to be left behind.

2. "The Export Trap," *Economist,* March 25, 2009.

3. Shahid Yusuf, *Innovative East Asia: The Future of Growth* (New York: Oxford University Press; Washington, D.C.: World Bank, 2003).

Uncertain Bets

But making it in biotech has proven to be very far from a sure thing, even for these three otherwise dynamic industrial economies. Betting in biotech has been very costly. Korea, Taiwan, and Singapore have invested billions of dollars in the sector, spending at levels on a par with other advanced industrial economies. They have reoriented their science and technology regimes to increasingly focus on basic science research, at the same time deepening domestic capacities to translate upstream discoveries into commercializable products and services. They have struggled to reconfigure their regulatory regimes to align and balance industry's needs with the nonmarket imperatives of patient safety, bioethics, and health care accessibility. And they have all had to confront the difficult political challenge of sustaining an appetite among stakeholders for the long-term realities of commercial biotech innovation. Biotech innovation has therefore been not only economically costly but politically costly as well. Simply put, Korea, Taiwan, and Singapore have expended a great deal of political capital on the prospects and processes of commercial biotech development, an extremely high-stakes gamble.

This book examines the biotech bets that have been made by decision makers in Korea, Taiwan, and Singapore, and how these bets have been strategically rationalized. In this respect, this book is about the processes of major political economic change and adaptation to a new paradigm of science-based industrial upgrading. It is a book about choices. It looks to clarify what Richard Doner and his colleagues have identified as a major gap in the innovation studies literature: some sense of the "institutional origins" of industrial technology development systems, the choices made, and their political economic rationales.[4] It seeks to shed light on what Philip Cerny understands as the adaptive political economic imperatives of the current knowledge-intensive "third industrial revolution."[5] It takes seriously Dani Rodrik's notion that innovation systems cannot simply be copied from abroad and replicated elsewhere, and that the institutional origins of any such system are shaped by local adaptations and continual experimentation.[6] It is inspired by Dan Breznitz's assertion that "states and societies still have real choices with regard to developing their own rapid innovation-based

---

4. Richard Doner, Allen Hicken, and Bryan Ritchie, "Political Challenges of Innovation in the Developing World," *Review of Research Policy* 26 (2009), 152.

5. Philip Cerny, "Globalization and the Changing Logic of Collective Action," *International Organization* 49 (1995).

6. Dani Rodrik, *One Economics, Many Recipes: Globalization, Institutions, and Economic Growth* (Princeton, N.J.: Princeton University Press, 2007), 164.

industries."[7] The accounts presented in this book reveal adaptive processes that have evolved in fits and starts, sometimes bearing the appearance of organizational and strategic anarchy. Change and adaptation have been animated by a nonlinear process of continual learning by doing. Mistakes have been made, gambles have been lost, and lessons have been learned. Indeed, at times it has even appeared that betting on biotech in Korea, Taiwan, and Singapore has proceeded in the absence of, rather than according to, some coherent strategic plan, an impression that runs counter to our stylized views of the well-planned and "smart" postwar developmental state.

The postwar developmental state in Asia was indeed well planned and smart. Decision makers made, on the whole, good choices. They bet well. Strategic state interventions facilitated the processes of industrial upgrading in Korea, Taiwan, and Singapore. They made winners, and even more impressive, they more often than not strategically picked winners in what were key industrial sectors. In other words, the postwar developmental state was both able and willing to provide "big leadership."[8] But as I asserted early on in this book, developmental states also benefited enormously from the advantages of late development. They were the beneficiaries of second-mover advantages, whereby the uncertainties of first-order technological innovations had been managed elsewhere. They were spared the uncertainty and the heavy lifting of creating, reaping at the other end the benefits of creatively copying. Upgrading into the informatics sector, for instance, was driven by the state's capacity and willingness to broker technology imports, fund technology R&D, and invest directly in sectors and even promising firms to commercialize such technologies. In other words, the developmentally oriented states in Korea, Taiwan, and Singapore strategically *mitigated the risks* of industrial technology upgrading. They turned risky bets into surer bets.

Primary Uncertainty

Current prospects in first-order innovation in commercial health biotech and science-based industrialization more generally, however, are considerably more elusive than what the postwar developmental state confronted in mitigating the risks of industrial upgrading. Biotech innovation and commercialization

---

7. Dan Breznitz, *Innovation and the State: Political Choice and Strategies for Growth in Israel, Taiwan and Ireland* (New Haven, Conn.: Yale University Press, 2007), 207.

8. Robert Wade, *Governing the Market: Economic Theory and the Role of Government in East Asian Industrialization* (Princeton, N.J.: Princeton University Press, 1990).

more closely approximate what Frank Knight long ago described as "primary uncertainty," which he saw as conceptually and empirically distinct from conventional risk scenarios. Whereas risk can be expressed as a probability distribution of known outcomes, primary uncertainty is characterized by those conditions under which there is so little information, data, and knowledge that the calculability of probability is nearly impossible. According to Knight, making strategic choices amid uncertainty amounts essentially to "pure guesswork."[9] The prospects and processes of managing uncertainty are qualitatively different from those of mitigating risk. In this respect, picking winners to make in biotech appears to be a less and less viable strategic option for even the smartest, boldest, and most decisive of developmentally oriented states and bio-industrial stakeholders.

It is not as though we know *nothing*, however, about biotech and the commercial prospects and processes of life sciences innovation. Rather, it is that even after three decades since the launch of the supposed biotech revolution, we still know *so little* about the prospects and processes of the commercialization of biotech. The existing stock of knowledge about the sector does not permit the sort of risk calculations once relied on by the developmental state in making industrial policy choices. There simply are not enough success cases globally, never mind in Asia, to draw definitive lessons about the sector. Biotechnology remains a far from mature technology, after all. We still know so little about how to translate upstream knowledge about genetics into applied technologies. We also know very little about the market for biotech products and services, a problem that is compounded by regulatory hurdles. There is much still to be learned about structuring biotech industry and effective business models inside firms. And after more than thirty years since the promise of biotech was first identified, after trillions of dollars invested in the sector and so many of the world's best minds working in the life sciences field, we still have scant information about when we might expect to see the commercial life sciences revolution really flourish. The prospective development of commercial biotech and the translation of upstream discoveries into commercially viable outputs remain obscured by technological, economic, and temporal uncertainty.

Yet the reality is that in the face of such extraordinary uncertainties, decision makers nonetheless have to make choices. But what choices? And how are such decisions arrived at when so little is known about the prospects and processes of commercial biotech innovation? Economists tell us that scale can

---

9. Frank Knight, *Risk, Uncertainty and Profit* (New York: Houghton Mifflin, 1921).

help. That is to say, if many people work at it long enough and bet widely enough under conditions of uncertainty, then one can, over time, infer some sense of what works and what does not. But this is not an option for most economies, save the United States and perhaps late-developing giants such as China and maybe India. Most economies, of which Korea, Taiwan, and Singapore are typical, are without the scale to bet indiscriminately and indefinitely. Rather, decision makers in Korea, Taiwan, and Singapore have had to bet discriminately. They must make strategic choices when it comes to resource commitments, the allocation of such resources, the aims of industrial policy more generally, and the design of specific regulatory policies.

The theoretical literatures on global, national, and local systems of innovation, varieties of capitalism, and different kinds of production regimes provide analytical leverage with which we can examine how decision makers make strategic choices.[10] We know, for instance, that the innovation process involves the development of multiple bases of expertise, which on their own bring little value but when integrated (whether in the form of competition or collaboration) can entail new technological and economic value. We know that person-to-person contact and the density of networks are important for innovation.[11] We also know that these processes are mediated through variable institutional configurations. The challenge is in narrowing the gaps between institutionally disparate and multidisciplinary sources of expertise, encompassing the worlds of life science, engineering, finance, management, and the regulatory sciences. But there remains, still, little consensus about what sorts of institutional configurations, organizational forms, or policy strategies are required to narrow these gaps, to promote cutting-edge innovation and the commercialization of biotechnologies. Theory thus provides few clues as to what *specific choices* decision makers in Korea, Taiwan, and Singapore ought to make to promote the commercialization of biotech.

Choices Made

Uncertainty about the prospects and processes of biotech industry development notwithstanding, decision makers in Korea, Taiwan, and Singapore have had to make important choices with respect to the allocation of public and private resources for biotech. Among the three, the choices, as well as the

---

10. See Dan Breznitz, "National Institutions and the Globalized Political Economy of Technological Change: An Introduction," *Review of Research Policy* 26 (2009).

11. Steven Casper, *Creating Silicon Valley in Europe: Public Policy towards New Technology Industries* (New York: Oxford University Press, 2007).

rationales for such choices, have differed markedly. Despite common challenges in managing uncertainty, they have followed different pathways in the allocation of public and private resources and the organization of both the state and bio-industry. Simply put, they have bet on biotech from different strategic points of view.

In Korea, the allocation of public and private resources to commercial biotech over the past two decades has led to a more discernible division of labor among actors involved in the sector. Within the state apparatus, the disbursement of R&D resources dedicated to the life sciences, which amounts to hundreds of millions of dollars each year, has been spread across the entire spectrum of R&D activities, from upstream basic science research to new, publicly funded biotech transfer mechanisms in the downstream. This vertically expansive division of R&D labor among state actors has been mirrored in the organization of Korea's emerging bio-industries. It is generally assumed that the future of commercial biotech and life sciences innovation rests with the chaebols, especially in the field of new drug development in biopharmaceuticals. Only the chaebols, along with a handful of local drug manufacturing firms, are thought to have the scale and internal R&D and manufacturing capability to make it in the drug development business. However, while chaebol leadership in growing the sector continues to figure centrally in Korea's approach to biotech industry development, the evidence presented in Chapters 2 and 3 demonstrates how decision makers there also recognize the imperatives of surrounding the chaebols, such as LG Life Sciences, with a significant supporting cast of dedicated life sciences public research institutes, R&D-intensive small and medium-sized enterprises, and an abundance of venture capital. The logic of the Korean approach to growing commercial biotech has been to broadly diffuse relevant knowledge in the life sciences and biotech industry, but with the expectation that productive linkages will be formed among such knowledge bases over time.

Taiwan's approach to commercializing biotech is significantly different. Unlike in Korea, the allocation of public and private resources in Taiwan tends to emphasize the midstream and downstream aspects of biotech innovation and commercialization. Within the state, for instance, the majority of public resources dedicated to biotechnology—which accounts for almost one-third of all public R&D spending—is allocated to midstream R&D (i.e., applied technology) and the decentralized development of multiple downstream technology transfer mechanisms for industry. In fact, as I showed in Chapter 2, the allocation of public R&D resources within the state has intentionally fostered a competitive dynamic among state actors, measured explicitly in terms of commercial outputs. I describe this as a "hit-and-miss" logic of resource allocation, a logic that is also reflected in the organization of bio-industry in Taiwan. Bets have been spread. Building on existing strengths in SME development, Taiwan's emerging biotech industries continue to hinge on the growth of small specialized firms, or what one entrepreneur calls Taiwan's "many sprouts." The state has, to some extent, seeded these sprouts. For instance, firms have benefited from, among other things, the state's efforts to develop transferable technologies in public research institutes such as the Industrial Technology Research Institute, the Development Center for Biotechnology, and the National Health Research Institute. But firms are also expected to generate near-term revenues and attract private sector investment. Many bio-venture firms will of course fail. However, there is also an expectation that some will survive, and those will in turn help identify specific areas or niches in the commercial biotech value chain where more investment resources can be allocated by public and private bio-industrial stakeholders.

Singapore's approach to biomedical industry development could not be more different from Taiwan's and Korea's. Given Singapore's small size and small talent pool in the life sciences sector, decision makers there have focused their efforts on attracting global biomedical firms to the city-state. Singapore's postwar industrialization strategy rested on the ability of the developmental state to foster the locational advantages with which to attract global capital, such as a disciplined and skilled labor force, tremendous government commitment to infrastructure development, and the use of economic inducements. The Singaporean state allocates public resources for the biotech sector in precisely these ways, in an effort to transform Singapore into a biomedical R&D hub for global firms. The Singaporean strategy is to leverage the international. As I described in Chapter 2, the concentration and centralization of administrative authority within the Economic Development Board and the Agency for Science, Technology and Research during the late 1990s allowed the state to centrally coordinate the allocation of public resources to training and skills development, university research, public research institutes, and bio-industry-oriented R&D programs. Investing in these sorts of locational advantages has paid off somewhat, in that large global biomedical firms are a significant source of industry investment in Singapore's emerging life sciences industries sector. However, as I pointed out in Chapter 3, most of these investments have been in biomedical manufacturing and therefore have not, as yet, translated into the sorts of high value-added spillovers or externalities expected by the state. Most notably, global biomedical firms have not located their R&D operations in Singapore at the pace and scope originally envisioned by biotech stakeholders there.

Payoff?

The potential payoffs of each of these unique strategic approaches to commercial biotech development are not the focus of this book. Still, we can make some reasoned speculations about them, though with a few caveats at the outset. First, the promise of commercial biotech is uncertain. In this respect, the prospects of a major blockbuster drug or a cutting-edge technological innovation coming out of one of these three Asian economies are similarly uncertain and unlikely any time soon. Second, success depends as much on actual innovative products as it does on the metric used to determine and measure "success." Indicators from Korea, Taiwan, and Singapore have indeed demonstrated continual success and an upward trajectory in biomedical (broadly defined, I should add) industries measured in terms of revenues earned, employment, and life sciences R&D credibility. If we look at investment-to-earnings ratios in the sector, however, then things do not look as good. And if we are to measure success solely in terms of commercialized cutting-edge biotechnological breakthroughs, then we can definitively say that anticipated and hoped-for payoffs have not yet materialized.

Still, looking into the future, one could reasonably conclude that given the existing structures of these economies and their past successes in industrial upgrading, the strategic bets made and the approaches adopted in Korea, Taiwan, and Singapore make good sense. Although all three are relatively recent entrants in the life sciences field, they have built on existing industrial strengths, and their strategic choices complement their political economies: Taiwan's continued experimentation with SME development, Korea's expectations of chaebol leadership, and Singapore's efforts to attract global biomedical firms. We have also seen an extraordinary commitment on the part of the state in all three cases to allocate important inputs to the commercial biotech innovation process. Indeed, both public and private bio-industry stakeholders are beginning to put into place the various pieces of the innovation process, to generate and diffuse new knowledge.

One can reasonably imagine, for instance, that biotech SMEs in Taiwan will eventually capture value from exploiting "low-hanging fruit" in the bio-industry value chain, likely not cutting-edge blockbusters but certainly revenue-generating niches. Taiwan is expected, for instance, to do quite well in the design and manufacture of medical devices and other such engineering-based products. Singapore's attempts to attract global biomedical firms and, most important, their R&D operations might very well succeed in the long run, even if, as I showed in Chapter 3, the pace will be slower than initially hoped. To its credit, in its continued efforts to develop the biomedical and biotech fields there, Singapore has created tremendous buzz for the tiny city-state. And while it will likely take much longer for Korea's large firms to gain a significant foothold in the global biopharmaceutical market, increasing interest among the chaebols in the life sciences field as well as continued growth in the number of biotech venture firms bode well for the future of Korea's life sciences industries. One could reasonably assert that of the three economies examined in this book, Korea's is most likely to succeed in the field of new drug development, even if such prospects, as I have suggested, remain distant and uncertain.

There are, however, several mitigating factors that could derail ongoing efforts to grow commercial biotech industries in Korea, Taiwan, and Singapore. As I have stressed throughout this book, there remains tremendous technological and economic uncertainty about the sector. Commercial biotech is still very much underdeveloped, not only in Asia but globally. Much of current life sciences research continues to be in the upstream, with the translation of future discoveries into applied and commercializable biotechnologies a still very distant promise. In addition to technological and economic uncertainty, there remains extraordinary temporal uncertainty.

As I showed in Chapter 4, Korea, Taiwan, and Singapore have had to confront the prospects of waning national appetites for the long-term realities of developing commercially viable biotech. The sector's underwhelming performance has exacerbated this feeling of temporal uncertainty. People there are becoming frustrated with the slow pace of commercial growth and some are beginning to reason, understandably, that biotechnology is not worth the patience and investment, especially given other, less uncertain technology industries in which to invest. To stem this growing impatience and to essentially buy more time for the sector, the state has attempted to strategically portray the appearance of progress in commercial biotech development, using important benchmarks to suggest that if not in the short term, then at least in the longer term there are returns that can be realized. Most important, the state in Korea, Taiwan, and Singapore has attempted to portray success in the biotech sector by manufacturing "stars." Not unlike in the past, the state has selectively *over*invested in certain endeavors—whether a firm, a lab, or even an individual researcher—to ensure, as best it can, its eventual, and more important, *conspicuous* success. Conspicuousness is critical, in that this strategy is intended above all to revive and then maintain an appetite for the long-term realities of commercial biotech innovation. It remains to be seen how effective this strategy will be and if it can be sustained. Its failure, however, will be politically costly for the state and will likely close the window of opportunity for these economies to make it in commercial biotech over the longer term. Temporal uncertainty illuminates the potential perils of nurturing a sector that in the near term necessarily teeters on the brink of spectacular failure.

Regulatory uncertainty may also derail or slow the development of commercial biotech in Korea, Taiwan, and Singapore. As I explained in Chapter 5, regulatory policy is an integral aspect of the biotech innovation process. It can both facilitate and constrain bio-industry development. In this way, it functions as de facto industrial policy.[12] The evidence presented in this book suggests that the regulatory state in Korea, Taiwan, and Singapore has been, on some critical regulatory issues, relatively conflicted among contending interests, priorities, and bases of expertise, despite efforts by state-level decision makers to coordinate regulatory policies. Therefore, rather than a source of regulatory predictability, consistency, and certainty, the emerging regulatory regimes in all three places have demonstrated the opposite qualities. Even in areas of regulation where there has been considerable alignment between market (promoting bio-industry) and nonmarket (protecting patients) imperatives, there remains considerable skepticism about how capable these multiple stakeholder states will be in implementing and enforcing such regulatory policies into the future. The creation of institutional review boards—a critical instrument in the state's regulatory capacity to oversee clinical R&D—has not, for instance, quieted frustrations among regulators, who point to the inconsistent and uneven implementation and enforcement of the IRB mechanism in Korea and Taiwan. Indeed, efforts thus far to create greater regulatory certainty have been made *in anticipation* of the growth of bio-industry. In other words, at the moment, some regulatory policies might appear to be consistent, coherent, and certain. However, skeptics point out that only when commercial bio-industry has taken off can we really judge whether these regulatory policies can in fact balance and align contending interests inside the multiple stakeholder state; observers have reason, they believe, to be skeptical.

Anatomy of Choices

Decision makers in Korea, Taiwan, and Singapore have had to make difficult strategic choices in the face of biotech's extraordinary uncertainties. In some

---

regards, most notably in the allocation of public and private resources for biotech, strategic actors in Korea, Taiwan, and Singapore have chosen varied pathways and approaches to commercial biotech development. Choices thus reflect distinctive logics and strategic rationales. Korea has chosen to "go big," Taiwan has decided to "go small," and Singapore has chosen to "go global."

Imprints of the Past

What explains the variation in strategic choices? First, *path dependency* and the legacies of the postwar developmental state era have clearly mattered in determining actors' choices in the current era of science-based industrialization and biotech innovation specifically. Stakeholders in Korea, Taiwan, and Singapore have had to bet on the prospects and processes of commercial biotech innovation with the "hands" they were dealt. Existing strengths in R&D and structures of industrial organization, financial markets, education institutions, and the organization of the state apparatus have constrained what decision makers are able to do. The processes of political economic adaptation have been shaped by the tug between those decisions for the future and the effects of decisions inherited from the past. Choices have been circumscribed by past choices.

It is no wonder, then, that Korea has staked its bio-industrial prospects on the leadership of the chaebol sector. Likewise, in Taiwan it is not surprising that the existing SME industrial landscape, which is best suited for transferring technology between midstream public and venture firms, has remained the core of the Taiwanese strategy in biotech development. The strategic decision in Singapore to continue to pursue multinational collaboration in technology development has been similarly shaped by earlier strategic decisions. The presence of multinational pharmaceutical firms in Singapore, beginning during the 1980s, virtually locked in this particular approach to commercial biotech development. Divergence in strategic choices among the three, therefore, is a function of the structural and organizational legacies of their unique postwar developmental state experiences.

Second, decision makers in Korea, Taiwan, and Singapore also differ in terms of how they envision their respective bio-industries fitting in the global bio-industry value chain. In other words, they differ markedly in how they strategically see their eventual integration into the global knowledge economy. *Their objectives are different.* In many ways, this variation reflects each nation's political economic worldview and more specifically how it has attempted to manage economic globalization—a worldview that has also been shaped by each place's postwar experiences in industrialization.

According to stakeholders in Taiwan, there are no illusions that local firms will ever compete in the global biotech scene as serious lab-to-market drug discovery firms. Rather, decision makers in Taiwan understand that the growth of the biotech industry there will depend on finding niches. They recognize that because the commercial biotech value chain is long and segmented, specialization can be an asset, as well as a sector in which Taiwanese firms can capture high value-added returns at key links in the chain. Taiwan's narrow but potentially lucrative industry objectives in commercial biotech are thus reminiscent of its approach to growing the IT and electronics sectors a few decades back. Korea, on the other hand, aspires to compete globally with other brand suppliers of cutting-edge health technologies, most notably in the area of blockbuster drugs. Though Korean life sciences industries have benefited from the growth of small and increasingly technologically savvy ventures, the primary objective is for these SMEs to support what stakeholders hope will be fully integrated lab-to-market drug firms. Unlike Taiwan, Korean decision makers have bet on capturing much larger segments of the global value chain in commercial biotech, an aspiration for which relative scale and brand recognition are Korea's competitive advantages. Singapore has chosen to position itself as Asia's biotech R&D and manufacturing hub by attracting global biomedical firms to the city-state. Recognizing how unrealistic it would be to develop homegrown biotech firms in an economy as small as Singapore's, stakeholders there have chosen, as in Taiwan, to capture high value-added sections of the global biotech value chain. However, rather than grow domestic firms, as in Taiwan, Singaporean decision makers envision the city-state as eventually becoming an R&D platform for global biomedical firms. In all three places, commercial biotech objectives differ and have in turn shaped differently the development of commercial biotech among them.

Third, the varied approaches to commercial biotech development in Korea, Taiwan, and Singapore are shaped by each nation's *heuristic biases in managing uncertainty* and in dealing with what they know very little about. Under conditions of primary uncertainty—where there is no information or so little that rational decision makers have essentially nothing to base their decisions on—people will nonetheless make choices as though they can in fact reasonably cope with such uncertainty. To do this, they draw on heuristic devices—values, beliefs, cognitive cues, and mental scripts—to help make, and more important to help rationalize, their choices. Generated from within societies, these heuristic devices are normative frames derived from national experiences and repertoires of proven decisions internalized from the past. They are not essentialist cultural predispositions per se (i.e., Asians are less risky, Asians are good savers), but rather they illuminate what is valued and what is shunned in a given society, what people believe they are good at, and what they are comfortable with. They make up belief systems that inform how strategic decision makers manage uncertainty. Of course, these heuristic devices lead to systematic biases and differences in decision making under conditions of uncertainty.[13]

Informants in Taiwan, when explaining to me the rationale of the hit-and-miss strategy, repeatedly stress the expectation that the vast majority of initiatives in biotech innovation (firms, research programs, labs) will fail. And that, they emphasize, is okay. In fact, it is encouraged. Decision makers there have come to understand widespread failure and high risk taking to be the bases of industrial upgrading, and thus the best approach to technological innovation. The Taiwanese hit-and-miss and "many sprouts" strategies are predicated on the historical normalization of industrial failure and the absorption and spreading of the costs of commercial failure. This inherited heuristic ensures that the social and economic costs of failed initiatives do not discourage future attempts to eventually succeed. Failure is something that Taiwanese "guerrilla" entrepreneurs have learned to be comfortable with, and to even value.

This particular mindset in Taiwan contrasts starkly with prevailing norms and values in Singapore's political economy. Informants in Singapore, from state officials to local entrepreneurs, all emphasize Singaporeans' deep-rooted aversion to failure as a barrier to innovative technological entrepreneurialism. Singapore's postindependence notion of "survivalism" and an enduring discourse of national crisis and vulnerability, combined with a culturally resonant norm of *kiasu* (saving face, or the fear of losing), have made decision makers there tremendously risk-averse when it comes to strategic choices. The strategy to shift biotech's uncertainties to foreign firms and to leverage the international reflects this particular belief system.

Korea's distinctive approach to managing biotech's myriad uncertainties stems from a different heuristic bias, one that is informed by a different set of historical experiences in industrialization. Korea's political economy in the postwar period was fiercely nationalistic. In contrast to Taiwan, where local firms continue to exploit narrow segments of global value chains, Korea's developmental state nurtured its leading firms to become giant, globally branded competitors. Unlike Singapore, which struggled with a profound sense of national vulnerability beginning in the 1960s, Korea's economic

---

13. See David Moss, *When All Else Fails: Government as the Ultimate Risk Manager* (Cambridge, Mass.: Harvard University Press, 2002), 42–45.

rise was fueled by a technonationalist confidence that sought to emerge and challenge industrial leaders in the West and most notably Japan. Thus, when confronted with the technological and economic uncertainties of commercial biotech development, decision makers in Korea have, not surprisingly, chosen to center their efforts on supporting the continued growth of national champions so they can compete with global leaders in new drug discovery, development, manufacturing, and global marketing. The notion "big is beautiful," once the mantra of Korea's postwar chaebols, continues to resonate. To be sure, of the three cases featured in this book, Korea is the only one to have boldly proclaimed its lofty goal of becoming a top global producer of biotechnology by 2010. The Korean script has always been one that privileges the logic of betting big to win big.

Looking to the (Uncertain) Future

We have looked to the past to get a sense of why we see important distinctions among the Korean, Taiwanese, and Singaporean approaches to biotech development. In the face of extraordinary uncertainty, decision makers' choices are informed—scripted—by the institutional legacies of the postwar developmental state, the current expectations of bio-industrial development, and prevailing heuristic biases and worldviews. In short, when confronted with uncertainty, decision makers tend to choose what they know best and what makes sense to them.

The analysis of biotech innovation in Asia and the processes of managing uncertainty in Korea, Taiwan, and Singapore could easily end right there with the conclusion that path dependency—institutionally, organizationally, and cognitively—has informed their distinctive strategic choices and left its imprint on varied national approaches to commercial biotech development. And yet the evidence presented in this book suggests that something deeper is going on, that a more fundamental transformation has been under way in terms of the choices made to support the *future* prospects and processes of commercial biotech innovation in industrial Asia. There is an even deeper story to be told here, but one that has only begun to be articulated by strategic decision makers in Korea, Taiwan, and Singapore. It is also one that is common to all three cases. The unfolding story is about the *retreat of the state* and, in effect, the end of the developmental state era.

To be sure, the broader political economic context in Asia has hastened the ongoing decline of the developmental state over the past decade and a half. The liberalization pressures of the 1980s and 1990s, mounted primarily by the United States, blunted many of the industrial policy instruments once employed by the developmental state, especially in the areas of finance and banking, strategic trade protectionism and foreign exchange manipulation. Meredith Woo-Cumings writes that "by 1997, Korea was a country bereft of industrial policy."[14] While she overstates her case a bit, Woo-Cumings's more general observation could also be made of Taiwan during the economic liberalization period of the 1990s. Furthermore, the democratization of Korea and Taiwan during the 1990s supposedly undermined the bureaucratic autonomy of the state, leaving it vulnerable to both political and partisan interference from within the state and from mobilized civil societies and voters. This came into sharp relief when the 1997 financial crisis exposed the postwar developmental states' weaknesses in managing the new realities of financial globalization and, much worse, the inherently corrosive effects of close and unchecked state-business alliances. The financial crisis illuminated the very fine line between productive cooperation, on the one hand, and unproductive collusion, on the other. The model was delegitimated in the wake of the 1997 financial crisis.[15] What is more, the technoglobalist imperatives of the knowledge-intensive economy, especially among those aspiring to be at the cutting edge of innovation, are in opposition to the technonationalist impulses, self-reliance myths, and neomercantilist policies that had legitimated the postwar developmental state. In other words, the developmental state, as we once knew it, was already in decline. What this book suggests is that the challenges of managing uncertainty in science-based industrialization, the next stage in industrial Asia's economic trajectory, have put the final nail in the developmental state's proverbial coffin.

The slow death of the developmental state described above has, in many ways, been of a structural nature; that is to say, it is the institutional bases of the state—its bureaucratic autonomy, internal coherence, interventionist instruments, and economic nationalist orientation—that have eroded over time. The evidence presented in this comparative study supports this structuralist take on the decline of the developmental state model. As I described in Chapter 2, both the functionalist imperatives and the multidisciplinary nature of biotech have forced the decentralization of expertise and the diffusion, rather than concentration, of resources. The resource allocation process has also become increasingly flattened, particularly as the private sector has taken on a larger

---

14. Meredith Woo-Cumings, "The State, Democracy and the Reform of the Corporate Sector in Korea," in *The Politics of the Asian Economic Crisis,* ed. T. J. Pempel (Ithaca: Cornell University Press, 1999), 117.

15. T. J. Pempel, ed., *The Politics of the Asian Economic Crisis* (Ithaca: Cornell University Press, 1999).

role in science-based industries such as commercial biotech. Even in terms of regulatory policy, the state apparatus has experienced the challenges of balancing various contending interests, priorities, and bases of expertise among actors. Biotechnology has proven too complex and too difficult to coordinate from above. The state no longer enjoys the sort of structural top-down authority it did during the postwar period. It no longer has the corporate coherence and structural capacity to effectively coordinate the allocation of resources and stakeholders' activities, to lead and provide authoritative guidance from above. And the state no longer has the ability to effectively pick industrial technology winners in the life sciences field, a specific mode of industrial policy that was, I contend, the key strategic dimension of the developmental state model. In these respects, then, the retreat of the state is a function of both its internal structural transformation and its more arm's-length interactions with critical stakeholders in the commercial biotech enterprise.

The erosion of the developmental state is not, however, merely a reflection of this structural transformation and thus its incapacity to coordinate; it is also a consequence of the state's strategic choices. The developmental state has *chosen to be less developmental.* Here I am less concerned with the structural dimensions of the state-led industrialization model than with the strategic logic of the developmental state. The literature on the Asian postwar experience tells us that the common logic of the developmental state in places such as Korea, Taiwan, and Singapore was based on choices explicitly intended to mitigate the risks of industrial and technology upgrading. Choices were purposive and strategic. But as I have argued throughout this book, the prospects and processes of commercial biotech innovation have precluded this particular strategy of mitigating risk. Rather, biotech innovation and commercialization is characterized by technological, economic, and temporal primary uncertainties, which, I have asserted, can at best be managed or coped with, but not purposively mitigated.

The state has attempted to off-load these sources of uncertainty. The state still controls extraordinary amounts of resources, to be sure, and decision makers in Korea, Taiwan, and Singapore do not hesitate to employ such resources to help facilitate the growth of the sector. But it is also clear, as Breznitz notes, that the "state's role is no longer to make the decisions and compel private companies to follow them, but rather to motivate private companies to make long-term commitments to operate in rapid innovation-based industries and activities."[16] At the core of this logic is the state's investment in

---

16. Breznitz, *Innovation and the State,* 29.

the long-term and uncertain processes of *discovering* rather than picking winners. The gamble in commercial biotech innovation is thus different than it was in earlier experiences of industrial upgrading. The present gamble is on a process, rather than a particular product, technological application, or firm. Put another way, strategic policy choices have increasingly been based on the tenuous, unpredictable, and uncertain *potentialities* of biotech innovation, or precisely those processes and prospects of innovation over which the state and its smartest decision makers have little control. The state thus refrains from picking winners. It has dealt with the long-term realities and temporal uncertainty of commercial biotech development by retreating.

The retreat of the developmental state is a function of the state's *political* decision to no longer play its postwar leadership role. Having invested billions of dollars in biotech, and with lackluster economic returns so far, the state is under tremendous political pressure to rationalize and justify its efforts to grow the commercial biotech sector. This is even the case in nondemocratic Singapore, where the political legitimacy of the ruling PAP government is heavily vested in the city-state's economic performance. Politically, refraining from picking winners thus prevents having picked colossal (and expensive) losers. And given biotech's technological, economic, and regulatory uncertainties, the prospects of picking winners are so distant and frankly unpredictable that any attempts by the state to lead the way are likely to be politically costly. The retreat of the state, therefore, is intended to mitigate its political risks. The retreating state has strategically hedged its bets.

Betting or Folding?

The metaphor of betting is particularly apt for capturing the political economy of science-based industrialization. The initial decision in Korea, Taiwan, and Singapore to enter the commercial biotech sector was essentially an economic bet. For a host of reasons and rationalizations, life sciences industry was seen as economically viable. The political dimensions of this bet were subsumed under this more narrowly conceived though reasonable economic logic. Political capital for local elites, credibility, and international prestige were bonuses, provided these economies did well in the sector. In other words, betting on commercial biotech made political sense largely because it made economic sense.

As I have intimated in this concluding chapter, these bets might still pay off in Korea, Taiwan, and Singapore. Decision makers have adapted their strategic choices in significant ways. They have made decisions that make sense given what decision makers know, what they inherited in terms of political economic structures, and what they view as their primary objectives in the commercial biotech sector. Therefore, one should not be surprised, for example, if Taiwanese firms eventually carve out commercially viable niches in the life sciences sector, especially in the area of medical devices and clinical R&D, just as one could reasonably expect Korea's chaebols to move more forcefully into the business of new drug development and manufacturing. But these advancements can come only over time, and arguably over the very long term. Temporal uncertainty, as I have suggested here, will continue to mitigate both the prospects and processes of biotech innovation in all three places for the foreseeable future.

The big question decision makers are currently deliberating in Korea, Taiwan, and Singapore is whether these economies should continue to bet on the prospects and processes of commercial biotech innovation or should simply "fold" and move on. Should they start looking for an exit strategy or continue to invest in a sector that so far has delivered less than expected in terms of economic returns? And moreover, how might they rationalize and manage these decisions? These are, in my mind, inherently political questions, which I elaborated on in Chapters 4 and 5. But whereas the decision to enter the life sciences innovation race was rationalized initially as an economic bet, the choice to continue the gamble or fold is a political bet, and must therefore be rationalized and managed in distinctly political terms.

One scenario, for instance, might see decision makers and stakeholders in Korea, Taiwan, and Singapore fold and essentially drop the commercial biotech sector altogether. These economies would simply absorb investment losses, rationalizing and understanding the prospects of biotech innovation as having been loss-leader investments all along. They would be satisfied with some productivity in the sector, even if returns are the result of lower value-added bio-industrial activities. They would merely plod along in the sector, with the hopes that initial investments and institutional developments might spark some innovative outputs. Stakeholders would nonetheless claw back their investments in biotech. They would invest nothing new. They would therefore also forgo whatever political capital they might have gained by taking credit for success in the sector. From what I have learned from informants in Korea, Taiwan, and Singapore, however, this is the least likely scenario. It would be politically tantamount to admitting a colossal industrial policy failure and thus would foment even greater uncertainty about their economic futures. Such a move would be politically disastrous in large part because of already disproportionately huge sunk investments, both economic and political, in the sector.

Still, if decision makers did choose to exit the sector in this way, it would be more likely to happen in democratic Korea and Taiwan, where electoral turnover can provide exit opportunities for incoming administrations to avoid political blame. Democratic institutions can diffuse the political costs of failure by shifting blame to previous governments. But in Singapore, where the dominant ruling party's legitimacy is rooted in the city-state's economic performance, the absence of such electoral possibilities would concentrate political blame on the incumbent regime, thus making this option to fold much less likely to occur. Either way—to exit or not—the decision would be based on a political calculation.

Another plausible though still unlikely scenario is one in which stakeholders and decision makers in Korea, Taiwan, and Singapore would refine their technonationalist aspirations to accommodate the more technoglobalist realities of life sciences innovation and the commercial biotech industry. Knowledge generation, diffusion, and integration in cutting-edge biotech are increasingly transnational enterprises. As I have demonstrated in this book, it is precisely the spatial, along with technical and economic, open-endedness of these processes that has eluded the postwar developmental state's economic logic. Yet, as I have also described, a technonationalist impulse continues to shape how decision makers, especially those inside the state, understand the prospects and processes of commercial biotech innovation and in particular the political consequences of their decisions.[17] The projected payoff in commercial biotech innovation for the state and its bio-industrial allies is expected to be both economic and political. To accommodate a more technoglobalist posture would thus involve important political considerations, a calculation of political gains and losses for the heavily invested state and biotech industry stakeholders.

To be sure, notwithstanding the rhetorical appeal of technoglobalist notions such as technological "gateways," "springboards," and "hubs," the fact of the matter is that bio-industry stakeholders and state-level decision makers in Korea, Taiwan, and Singapore remain terribly unclear as to what they mean by these concepts, precisely because of the uncertain political costs associated with them. Cross-strait tensions, for instance, continue to obfuscate political

---

17. Data on health biotechnology publications between 1991 and 2002 show that the rate of international collaboration among Korean researchers (i.e., coauthors from countries other than Korea) actually decreased, reflecting a general unwillingness to engage in more technoglobalist interaction. Moreover, to the extent that Korean researchers did collaborate with foreign colleagues, most of this effort (over 85%) was concentrated in the United States and Japan. Halla Thorsteinsdottir, Abdallah Daar, and Peter Singer, "Health Biotechnology Publishing Takes-off in Developing Countries," *International Journal of Biotechnology* 8 (2006), 34–35.

discussions inside Taiwan about how it ought to manage its economic and technological interactions with China, and more specifically about how Taiwan can be a technological springboard without sacrificing its political and economic autonomy to the mainland. It would be politically inconceivable in Korea to suggest that its national industrial champions, the chaebols, follow others rather than lead in the area of new drug development. And while Singapore is probably the most comfortable among the three with the idea of being a hub for global firms and capital, even there state-level decision makers express considerable concern about being the manufacturing center for global biomedical firms, especially given how much of the state's performance legitimacy is predicated on Singapore's aspirations to move up the technological value chain. A strategic shift from more technonationalist to more technoglobalist expectations of commercial biotech is plausible (and even desirable), though still unlikely due to the political costs associated with such a change.

The most plausible scenario, in my mind, would see Korea, Taiwan, and Singapore continue to bet on the long-term processes and uncertain prospects of commercial biotech innovation. They have already invested far too much to simply fold, and while decision makers there may or may not recast their technonationalist aspirations to fit with the sector's technoglobalist imperatives, it is most likely that these three economies will continue to be emergent players in the sector. However, it is also likely that they will bury the hype surrounding the biotech sector by forcing it into the background. There will be less attention paid to the inconsistent ebb and flow of the sector's performance. Successes will be downplayed and failures softened in anticipation of unrealistic expectations. As I argued in Chapter 4, the state will have to continue to recalibrate general expectations about the speed and scope of success in the sector. In fact, all this is already happening in Korea, Taiwan, and Singapore. Hopes are still pinned on biotechnology to be a significant contributor to these economies as they move forward, but the sector is no longer thought to be the future foundational pillar of the new knowledge economy. While life sciences R&D remains very much a priority in Korea, Taiwan, and Singapore, it is also no longer the central priority. At best, the prospects of commercial biotech have come to share the economic stage with other high-technology sectors; at worst, biotech has been relegated to the sidelines, at least in terms of visibility and, most important, the scrutiny surrounding progress in the sector. The state and industrial stakeholders have attempted to moderate the stakes in betting on biotech—to retreat—if only to continue, for the time being, their gamble on the sector. Indeed, over the seven years during which I conducted research in Korea, Taiwan, and

Singapore for this book, I saw the star that was supposed to be biotechnology dim quite considerably—though ironically, it appears to have dimmed precisely to save it from being extinguished entirely, at least for now.

Beyond the Developmental State

The retreat of the developmental state, which I have examined in this book, is significant not only for the study of contemporary political economy in Asia, but also for broader comparative analyses of dynamic political economic transformations at the dawning of the commercial biotech revolution and science-based industrialization more generally. Much of the analysis of the postwar developmental state has focused on the distinctiveness of the Asian experience. Most obvious is the fact that the Asian miracle economies, particularly when compared with other late developers, were extremely successful in achieving rapid economic growth and continual industrial transformation. These are not one-shot economic dynamos, but economies that seemed capable of continually adapting to new political economic challenges. The "Asian" economic miracle was thus explained in regional terms, as though it was a regionally bounded phenomenon.

Some argue that deeply entrenched cultural norms that center on family and hierarchy supported the highly interventionist state in Asia. Others have posited that authoritarian political institutions afforded the state both the autonomy and the capacity to implement effective strategic policies. It has also been pointed out that unlike their Latin American comparators, the Asian economies made a decisive turn to export-oriented industrialization during the 1960s and 1970s, which allowed global market forces to pull the processes of industrial upgrading and the development of international competitiveness, instead of relying on inward policies geared to promote secondary import substitution industrialization. Scholars of international relations have furthermore suggested that the economic rise of Asia rested not only on plugging into global markets but also on regionally hierarchical interdependencies and Japanese leadership, reflecting a "flying geese" pattern of regional industrial upgrading. Actual differences among Asian economies were glossed over to propagate an extraordinary and distinctly regional pattern of economic modernization. In so many ways, the Asian developmental state was constructed to be the antithesis of normal.

That was then, but what about now? The evidence from contemporary Korea, Taiwan, and Singapore suggests that perhaps these increasingly knowledge-intensive political economies are trending toward becoming more "normal" economies. By "normal," I do not mean to say that these Asian cases are converging on some global business model for science-based industrialization and commercial biotech innovation specifically. Indeed, comparative research shows that there remains a variety of capitalisms, that production regimes vary widely, that national economies plug into transnational networks differently, that national distinctiveness remains critical, and that innovation systems are institutionally adapted to local circumstances. Normal is variation. Therefore, by "trending to the normal," I instead mean that Korea, Taiwan, and Singapore are beginning to lose some of their Asian or regionally bounded distinctiveness. Despite once being the paragons of a uniquely Asian variant of postwar capitalism, Korea, Taiwan, and Singapore are evolving in ways that allow them to join a broader universe of comparable political economies; their categorical distinctiveness, derived from a specific regional experience, is being blurred somewhat; and the developmental state is becoming obsolete.

The fact of state intervention into the economy itself and the mobilization of public resources for the purposes of industrial upgrading cannot alone sustain an Asian distinctiveness. All governments routinely intervene in the economy with the allocation of resources to offset the inherent market failures of technological innovation, even among the "freest" of neoliberal political economies.[18] Ever since the publication of *Science: The Endless Frontier* in 1945, state involvement in science and technology development has been the norm.[19] The U.S. government funds upward of US$30 billion per year for upstream basic research in the life sciences, by far and away the largest government outlay in the world for biotech-related R&D; this despite the fact that the United States is conventionally considered a lean liberal market economy. All governments, regardless of size and political economic orientation, inject hundreds of millions of dollars into biotech R&D. On this measure, Korea, Taiwan, and Singapore are not at all distinctive. Therefore, if the uniqueness of the postwar developmental state was its willingness to allocate resources to address market-failing endeavors and to offset the risks of innovation for private sector entrepreneurs, then it is quite clear that most, if not all, states are "developmental." The distinction, if formulated in this way, is pedestrian.

---

18. Joseph Wong, "Biotechnology in Hong Kong: Prospects and Challenges," in *Innovation Policy and the Limits of Laissez-Faire: Hong Kong's Policy in Comparative Perspective,* ed. Douglas Fuller (Basingstoke, U.K.: Palgrave Macmillan, 2010).

19. See David Guston, *Between Politics and Science: Assuring the Integrity and Productivity of Research* (New York: Cambridge University Press, 2000); Donald Stokes, *Pasteur's Quadrant: Basic Science and Technological Innovation* (Washington, D.C.: Brookings Institution, 1997).

The more meaningful distinction between the experiences of the postwar Asian developmental state and more conventional models of political economic organization was the developmental state's strategies of deliberately picking and making winners, and industry's willingness to abide by such state directives. The evidence from Korea, Taiwan, and Singapore suggests, however, that biotech development stakeholders have retreated from choosing winners to make. The state has continued to support the development of biotech and bio-industry in significant ways, though its facilitative support increasingly centers on the uncertain and unpredictable *processes of discovery* as opposed to actively targeting winners. Stakeholders have rationalized this significant transformation in terms of strategy and capacity, a reflection of the state's unwillingness and inability to confidently pick winners. Korea, Taiwan, and Singapore, in their efforts to adapt to the uncertainties of science-based industrialization, have thus shifted their approaches to be closer in line with their global competitors. By refraining from picking and making winners, they increasingly appear more normal.

The fact that Korea, Taiwan, and Singapore have thus far enjoyed very little commercial success in biotechnology also suggests that their experiences are not unlike those of most of the advanced industrial world. This may seem a rather trivial point, but it is important to reemphasize that one of the hallmarks of the postwar developmental state was its unquestionably rapid industrial success in strategically chosen sectors. They were extraordinarily fast followers. It was only less than a decade before Korean firms gained significant global market share in the integrated circuit industry, a pattern similar to Taiwan's quick entry into the semiconductor manufacturing industry and Singapore's rapid growth in the computer sector during the 1980s. They were, after all, economies that had gained the moniker "miracles." However, Korea, Taiwan, and Singapore have invested billions of dollars in biotech development since the 1990s with little or no commercial blockbuster success, much like the rest of the advanced industrial world. They are all in the biotech race, but it is not at all clear that they are poised to win, or even seriously contend, for that matter. Like other industrial countries, Korea, Taiwan, and Singapore are struggling to translate upstream research into commercial biotech products and services. They experienced along with the rest of the advanced industrial world a major setback during the early 2000s when risk capital suddenly became more cautious after the dot-com bust. They are struggling to manage expectations about the biotech revolution and to sustain a long-term appetite for the temporal uncertainties of the sector. Simply put, the extraordinary uncertainties of biotech innovation and commercialization are proving to be normal in Korea, Taiwan, and Singapore, as inescapable for these Asian economies as for other national economies.

It also seems that industrial Asia's distinctiveness in what were once broadly similar patterns of industrial upgrading during the postwar period has given way to significantly divergent choices with respect to managing technological and economic uncertainty. This book has shown how Korea, Taiwan, and Singapore are addressing the challenges of commercial biotech development in many different ways, shaped by path-dependent forces as well as prevailing beliefs about how each economy can best cope with biotech's uncertainties. Quite simply, they increasingly look different from one another. In fact, the specific cases of Korea, Taiwan, and Singapore and their efforts to adapt to meet the challenges of biotech innovation bear closer resemblance to other non-Asian experiences than to one another. The Korean strategy to grow its lab-to-market biopharmaceutical industry appears more similar to the German and Japanese experiences, drawing on big government spending and leveraging the brand recognition of existing (drug) firms. Singapore's efforts to grow its biomedical industries by positioning the tiny city-state as a global R&D hub make it look a lot like Iceland and the small Nordic countries. Taiwan's SME approach to commercializing biotech is similar to that of Canada and parts of Europe. The experiences of Korea, Taiwan, and Singapore in biotech innovation are increasingly less distinctly Asian.

It is clear that the biotech revolution and the global race to translate and commercialize the technology will continue in fits and starts, driven more by a process of learning by doing than a reliance on some sort of master plan. The reality is that a global model for biotech innovation has yet to emerge. The relatively poor performance of the sector worldwide has prohibited a consensus on a winning formulation or industry model. The sector is being continually transformed, and all national political economies—including Korea, Taiwan, and Singapore—have experienced and will continue to experience this messy transformative moment. They have experimented with new modes of industrial organization and biotech business models, as well as new strategies in financing, commercialization, R&D, and the allocation of resources. And they have all periodically stumbled in their efforts to achieve some success in life sciences innovation—and more important, they will continue to experiment and stumble. The processes of adapting to the uncertainties of science-based industrialization and specifically biotechnology have been felt similarly across all national political economies. The experiences of Korea, Taiwan, and Singapore as they try to manage uncertainty in the postdevelopmental state era are normal; they are not at all distinctive.

INDEX

Note: Italic page numbers refer to tables.

www.ingramcontent.com/pod-product-compliance
Ingram Content Group UK Ltd.
Pitfield, Milton Keynes, MK11 3LW, UK
UKHW022123090225
454782UK00006B/19/J

9 780801 450327